Faulkner and the Natural World
FAULKNER AND YOKNAPATAWPHA
1996

Faulkner and the Natural World

FAULKNER AND YOKNAPATAWPHA, 1996

EDITED BY
DONALD M. KARTIGANER
AND
ANN J. ABADIE

UNIVERSITY PRESS OF MISSISSIPPI
JACKSON

http://www.upress.state.ms.us

02 01 00 99   4 3 2 1

The paper in this book meets the guidelines for permanence and durability
of the Committee on Production Guidelines for Book Longevity of the Council
on Library Resources.

Library of Congress Cataloging-in-Publication Data

Faulkner and Yoknapatawpha Conference (23rd : 1996 : University of
Mississippi)
    Faulkner and the natural world / Faulkner and Yoknapatawpha, 1996;
edited by Donald M. Kartiganer and Ann J. Abadie.
        p.   cm.
    Papers from the 23rd Annual Faulkner and Yoknapatawpha Conference
held July 28–Aug. 2, 1996, sponsored by the University of
Mississippi in Oxford.
    Includes bibliographical references and index.
    ISBN 1-57806-120-2 (cloth : alk. paper).—ISBN 1-57806-121-0
(pbk. : alk. paper)
    1. Faulkner, William, 1897–1962—Knowledge—Natural history—
Congresses.   2. Yoknapatawpha County (Imaginary place)—Congresses.
3. Human ecology in literature—Congresses.   4. Nature in
literature—Congresses.   I. Kartiganer, Donald M., 1937-   .
II. Abadie, Ann J.   III. Title.
PS3511.A86Z78321166   1999
813'.52—dc21
                                                                98-29568
                                                                    CIP

British Library Cataloguing-in-Publication Data available

Contents

Introduction

The first paragraph of one of the more memorable essays written on Faulkner opens this way:

> *Light in August* begins unforgettably with a pregnant young woman from Alabama sitting beside a road in Mississippi, her feet in a ditch, her shoes in her hand, watching a wagon that is mounting the hill toward her with a noise that carries for a half mile "across the hot still pinewiney silence of the August afternoon."[1]

Exquisitely registering the power of Faulkner's evocative portrait of Lena Grove, Alfred Kazin sums up both her and the world she represents: "And it is this world of Lena Grove from Doane's Mill . . . that becomes in the book not merely a world that Faulkner celebrates but a mythic source of strength." Contrasting Lena with Christmas in terms of "the natural and the urban," and building toward the larger conflict between "life and anti-life, between the spirit of birth and the murderous abstractions and obsessions which drive most of the characters," Kazin asserts that "Lena's world, Lena's patience . . . set the ideal behind the book—that world of the permanent and the natural." "Natural" for Kazin refers less to rivers and soil and trees than to a deeper, less fragile realm, one that indeed speaks to a mythic rather than to a merely naturalist awareness.

When we begin to read Faulkner with some of the more common features of the natural world in mind, a rather startling shift in perspective arises, a good example of which occurred at the 1996 Faulkner Conference during the first moments of Lawrence Buell's opening lecture. Turning, like Kazin, to the first chapter of *Light in August*, Buell quoted and commented on a passage that does not mention Lena Grove at all, but focuses instead on the little town of Doane's Mill. The passage begins, "The brother worked in the mill. All the men in the village worked in the mill or for it. It was cutting pine. It had been there seven years and in seven years more it would destroy all the timber within its reach."

With this reference to another aspect of the "world of Lena Grove," a set of fresh concerns begins to claim our attention: the complication of the "permanent and the natural" with the evidence of the wholesale human destruction of nature: "all the timber within [the mill's] reach" is gone. The potential scope of this brief passage is remarkable, since the fate of the mill (and the surrounding woods) affects Lena's brother and Lucas Burch, whose fortunes are obviously intertwined with Lena's, as well as those such as Joe Christmas and "Joe Brown" who seek work at the mill in Jefferson. Encountering this large and difficult novel exploring race and community, sexuality and violence, in America, we find ourselves shocked, perhaps even irked, by the news from Professor Buell that a number of major characters in *Light in August* "are what they are not just because of who they are but because of where they fit in the history of Mississippi lumbering."

Exploration of "the environmental imagination"—to use the title of Lawrence Buell's most recent book—in Faulkner or any American writer is an approach which much of modern literature and modern literary study would not find congenial. The sources of high modernism are, of course, extremely diverse, yet certainly one of them lies in the late nineteenth-century movement, especially among the French Symbolist poets and their British enthusiasts, "against nature": the attempt to raise art above the merely given, to break the bonds of "exteriority" and move beyond realism and that material world—natural or constructed—that was its stock in trade. The task of art is not to record and report a merely visible reality, but to discover a reality normally inaccessible to us: one we can reach, presumably, only by freeing ourselves from what is palpably before us.

An extremely influential book for the early modernists—very likely including Faulkner—was Arthur Symons's *The Symbolist Movement in Literature*.[2] In his sympathetic account of the French symbolist poets, Symons claims that the nineteenth-century novel was a product, now outmoded, of the "age of Science, the age of material things." As such a product, it performed admirably, in fact "did miracles in the exact representation of everything that visibly existed, exactly as it existed."[3] Now, however (writing in 1899), Symons argues that something else is needed beyond that visible existence, something both more beautiful and truer. The crucial figure for Symons is Mallarmé: "Remember his principle: that to name is to destroy, to suggest is to create. Note further, that he condemns the inclusion in verse of anything but, 'for example, the horror of the forest, or the silent thunder afloat in the leaves; not the intrinsic, dense wood of the trees' (195–96).[4] Symons is convinced that in escaping the real woods the poet approaches their authentic ground. In "disdaining to catalogue the trees of the forest," we are actually "coming closer to nature"; "as we brush aside the accidents of daily life . . . we come closer to humanity, to everything in humanity that may have begun before the world and may outlast it" (8–9).[5]

Clearly, much of high modernism was driven by comparable notions, involving the need for art to conduct a revolution against referentiality itself. Language, instead of functioning as the transparent, passive sign of the object, faithfully reflecting what is already "out there," takes on a greater solidity, a substantiality of its own, enabling it to recover, or invent, a more essential Reality. As Mallarmé put it, the poet must try to articulate not what he sees but what is beyond sight: "the one flower absent from all bouquets" (199).

One of the more extreme versions of this aesthetic attitude in English comes, not surprisingly, from Oscar Wilde. In "The Decay of Lying," in the Dialogue called "The Priority of Art," Vivian speaks:

> Enjoy Nature! I am glad to say that I have entirely lost that faculty. People tell us that Art makes us love Nature more than we loved her before; that it reveals her secrets to us; and that after a careful study of Carot and Constable we see things in her that had escaped our observation. My own experience is that the more we study Art, the less we care for Nature. What Art really reveals to us is Nature's lack

of design, her curious crudities, her extraordinary monotony, her absolutely unfinished condition. . . . Art is our spirited protest, our gallant
attempt to teach Nature her proper place.[6]

New Criticism played a major role in spreading the symbolist
influence on modernism by encouraging the notion of the poetic
image as what Frank Kermode has called "a radiant truth out of
space and time" (2). And as Buell points out in *The Environmental
Imagination,* literary theory succeeding New Criticism has come
no closer to recognition of the plainly real. "All major strains of
contemporary literary theory," he writes, "have marginalized literature's referential dimension by privileging structure, text(uality),
ideology, or some other conceptual matrix that defines the space
discourse occupies apart from factical 'reality.' "[7] In other words,
regardless of its different, often opposed aims, current criticism is
consistent in its tendency to deflect readers from the "natural"
content of literature, and even perhaps writers from attempting to
grant some autonomy to the natural world, whether that world is
one of "rocks and stones and trees" or Emerson's more compre-
hensive "Not-me." For a criticism preoccupied with the contex-
tual production not only of meaning but being, any naturalist attempt to entertain an "essentialist" reality is little less than high
treason.

There exists, nevertheless, an abundance of American writing
that has taken as its goal the move into the terrain of the unbuilt
world. With Thoreau's *Walden* as his model text, Buell describes
the attempt of the "western sensibility working with and through
the constraints of Eurocentric, androcentric, homocentric culture
to arrive at an environmentally responsive vision" (23). That any
writer, regardless of the goal, must work "with and through" a
European cultural base or that of some other culture, goes without
saying. As several of the essays in this collection point out, every
imaginative conception of nature is just that, an *imagined* perspective that cannot help but reflect the culturally informed mind that
is its source.

Still—and this is the argument for the very existence of an environmental imagination—there is the possibility of mind relin-

quishing some of the force of its own sovereignty, giving itself up, as it were, to that which is *not itself,* while still remaining, as it must, an imagining presence. Again, using *Walden* as the model text, Buell insists that such a possibility has in fact been realized at times in our literature, especially so by this "epic of the autonomous self imagining with fascination yet hesitancy the possibility of relinquishing that autonomy to nature" (171).

Faulkner's identity as a writer of the natural world is, as in most things, a complex one. The influence on him of such modernist giants as Conrad, Joyce, and Eliot is clear, as is the appeal of the French symbolist poets and their encouragement to fly by the nets of mundane reality for more ethereal regions. As late as a 1955 interview in Nagano, at least thirty-five years after he probably read Symons's *Symbolist Movement,* when asked to describe his "ideal woman," he borrowed Mallarmé's "principle": "Well, I couldn't describe her by color of hair, color of eyes, because once she is described, then somehow she vanishes. That the ideal woman which is in every man's mind is evoked by a word or phrase or the shape of her wrist, her hand. . . . And every man has a different idea of what's beautiful. And it's best to take the gesture, the shadow of the branch, and let the mind [that is the reader's mind] create the tree."[8]

Of course, the modernism Faulkner read and practiced had to be transformed to a Mississippi context that seemed to share little with the great cosmopolitan centers of modernism in Europe. And yet, as Thomas McHaney points out in his essay in this collection, Faulkner's Oxford did not exactly provide him with a Wordsworthian, Lake District kind of wilderness world. Nevertheless there is a clear sensitivity to nature in Faulkner, including not only the big woods, but the body, animals—especially horses—the life of farming people, that invites us to examine his work with the natural world paramount in mind.

That we find compromises of imaginative relinquishment and possession should not surprise us. One of the most famous scenes in Faulkner provides a superb example of just such compromise. In "The Bear," from *Go Down, Moses,* the young Ike McCaslin

puts aside his gun, compass, and watch in order to make himself
fit, as it were, to see Old Ben. Having renounced his cultural instruments, which apparently enable him to navigate the woods but
not really encounter their presiding spirit, figured in Old Ben,
Ike gets hopelessly lost. None of the woodsman's stratagems, as
"coached and drilled" into him by Sam Fathers, works; in the heart
of the wilderness, it appears, no cultural device is sufficient, not
even that of the human who seems most at home with that wilderness.

Instead of Ike's finding Old Ben, Old Ben, as if invoked by Ike's
ritual of relinquishment, finds *him*. A trail of footprints magically
materializes: "they appeared before him as though they were
being shaped out of thin air just one constant pace short of where
he would lose them forever and be lost forever himself."[9] Old Ben
restores Ike to his abandoned instruments and to the woods as
they are made familiar by them. He then disappears: "It didn't
walk into the woods. It faded, sank back into the wilderness without motion as he had watched a fish, a huge old bass, sink back
into the dark depths of its pool and vanish without even any movement of its fins" (200–201).

The quality of the bear's rescue of Ike demonstrates Faulkner's
compromise, for if the boy's abandonment of his "human" equipment in the face of nature invokes Old Ben's appearance, the manner of that appearance seems miraculous. It suggests less a natural
phenomenon than the product of a human mythic or religious
imagination: a distinctly human conception of how what Words-
worth's "Nutting" calls "a Spirit in the woods" might manifest itself.

Such compromises between nature and the human stances of
Faulkner's fiction—social, economic, racial, the various myths of
Western culture—exist throughout his work. In the great concluding scene of his late novel, *The Mansion,* however, describing the
death of Mink Snopes, we find an indication that Faulkner's sense
of ultimate human destiny might well be a return to nature, a relinquishment of the need to assert human integrity at the expense of
the natural. Following his killing of Flem Snopes, Mink—

"Because he was free now"—begins walking west. Partly as a measure of his new freedom, he decides to lie down, although in doing so he knows he runs the risk of being absorbed by the earth: "Because a man had to spend not just all his life but all the time of Man too guarding against it: even back when they said man lived in caves, he would raise up a bank of dirt to at least keep him that far off the ground while he slept."[10]

And yet that very possibility of absorption quickly becomes for Mink a sign of relief, an end to all "the unnecessary bother and trouble" which a man gives up when he resigns himself to the earth. Death, the sovereignty of the natural world, the human relinquishment of human criteria, human values, human distinction—they become the harmonious voices of Mink's final vision:

> the ground already full of the folks that had the trouble but were free now, so that it was just the ground and the dirt that had to bother and worry and anguish with the passions and hopes and skeers, the justice and the injustice and the griefs, leaving the folks themselves easy now, all mixed and jumbled up comfortable and easy so wouldn't nobody even know or even care who was which any more, himself among them, equal to any, good as any, brave as any . . .

* * *

The essential argument of Lawrence Buell's "Faulkner and the Claims of the Natural World" is that our knowledge of "environmental history can illuminate Faulkner's fiction." That history pertains to natural phenomena such as the great Mississippi flood of 1927, which generates the action of the "Old Man" story in *The Wild Palms,* as well as to cultural/environmental episodes such as the "cut-and-get-out phase" of the timber industry in the Deep South, which plays a significant, if generally ignored, role in *Light in August.* Of course, the two events are not so easily distinguished, given the possible human role in the flood, through what Buell refers to as "unwise manipulations of the river and its tributaries," and the simple natural fact that there were pine forests in Mississippi to enable a planing mill to exit in Jefferson, providing work for Byron Bunch and Lucas Burch, alias Joe Brown. But

Buell's primary focus is on Faulkner's sensitivity to nature in its purer manifestations, overpowering as in "Old Man" or endangered as in *Go Down, Moses*. In the latter, "a serious and sustained work of environmental reflection," Faulkner came to grips not only with the decline of the wilderness but with the complexity of the fact that those who most revere it become complicit in its destruction.

As a result of his upbringing in a town that, despite its small size, had significant links to an increasingly modern world, and the influences of various modernist literary and philosophical traditions, Faulkner tends to present nature in a manner that is "stylized, condensed, extremely limited in naturalistic vocabulary, and bent to comic and dramatic purposes." So argues Thomas L. McHaney in his "Oversexing the Natural World: *Mosquitoes* and *If I forget Thee, Jerusalem*," coming down on the "literary" side of the tension between the homocentric and the naturalist encounter with the natural world. Particularly striking in Faulkner's rendering of that world is his sexual imagery, using nature as a means of presenting the "sexual moods" of his characters, at times their sexual confusion and powerlessness. Covering a fifteen-year span in Faulkner's career, McHaney describes his development from early work such as *Mosquitoes*, in which Faulkner tends to "abstract" us from nature rather than draw us into greater intimacy with it, toward the mature work of *If I Forget Thee, Jerusalem* and *Go Down, Moses*, in which the human and the natural tend to inform each other with their particular force and implicit values. *If I Forget Thee, Jerusalem* is especially important in comparison with *Mosquitoes* because of its similar emphasis on sexuality, like the earlier novel employing the natural world to dramatize libidinal conflict, yet doing so in such a way as to grant both the human and the natural a respective power and significance.

According to Theresa M. Towner's "Unsurprised Flesh: Color, Race, and Identity in Faulkner's Fiction," the most crucial "natural" phenomenon for Faulkner is the body. All else comes under the general heading of "writing," namely, the multiple ways in which we construct the body, making it serve our purposes and

prejudices, making it conform to cultural assumptions so powerfully held as to seem themselves "natural." Throughout his work
Faulkner attends to "the ways that humans try to invent, and reinvent, themselves and their neighbors according to willful and carefully tended conceptions of 'the natural.'" Towner is particularly
concerned with "race" as Faulkner's most striking example of the
cultural manipulations of the body, race that is—as opposed to the
biological fact of color—as what Henry Louis Gates refers to as "a
dangerous trope." Taking examples from a large number of texts,
including *Sanctuary, Absalom, Absalom!, Light in August,* and *Go
Down, Moses,* Towner explores not only instances of people reading "race" so as to satisfy the demands of their cultural fictions,
but characters such as Temple Drake who borrow the cultural
meanings of race in order to exert a modicum of control in a situation where the biological element of "color" is not even present.

In "Writing Blood: The Art of the Literal in *Light in August*,"
Jay Watson continues the focus on the body, literally breaking
through not only the cultural myths and codes that surround it but
the very contours of the body itself to the blood that flows within.
Concentrating on blood and race in *Light in August,* and its multiple incidents of "cutting" and wounding, Watson demonstrates
how blood divests itself of its metaphoric value as the chief index
to race in the South and regains a powerful literal value: becomes
blood that is *only* blood, thus subverting the cultural weight of
"the South's defining social fiction." Even as the novel contains
numerous instances of race identified in terms of certain kinds of
behavior, blood breaks constantly through the surface in order to
explode those cultural assumptions: perhaps the most powerful
example in Faulkner of the "natural world" at least momentarily
freed from human figuration.

Unlike Watson, who reads *Light in August* as a demonstration of
the power of the body to make "noise" that undermines cultural
constructions, Mary Joanne Dondlinger argues that the only way
to "get around" those constructions is through parody: an apparent
fulfillment of social convention that is actually a revision of it. In
"Getting Around the Body: The Matter of Race and Gender in

Faulkner's *Light in August*," Dondlinger distinguishes between
Joe Christmas and Lena Grove by claiming that Joe, despite his
violations of conventional behavior, never alters the values society
imposes on his body, the hierarchy of "white supremacy, patriarchy, and compulsory heterosexuality," while Lena, who seems to
adhere to the values dictating the behavior of women, is in fact
subverting them through parody: she fulfills her assigned role with
"significant differences." Even when claiming he is black, Joe affirms the superiority of whiteness, while Lena, appearing to pursue her proper place as wife and mother, moves outside domestic
containment, threatening the patriarchal power she pretends to
confirm.

In "Thomas Sutpen's Marriage to the Dark Body of the Land"
Louise Westling comes to grips with Faulkner's characteristically
American tendency to describe the relationship between people
(principally men) and nature in terms of a "gendered antagonism
to the natural world." Writing in a tradition at least as old as *The
Epic of Gilgamesh,* Faulkner generally sees nature as female, renders women and people of color in his fiction as animalistic, and
regards miscegenation as a kind of "undifferentiated merging with
nature" that must be avoided in order to maintain male supremacy. *Absalom, Absalom!* becomes a kind of watershed novel in
Faulkner's career, in which he depicts Thomas Sutpen as a man
whose deep ties to the landscape of Haiti and Mississippi are the
true sources of his strength, and whose attempt to reject those ties,
by dismissing his first wife and refusing to recognize his part-black
son, Charles Bon, is the cause of his downfall. The determined and
partially successful efforts of Quentin and Shreve to contain the
Sutpen story in a "Platonic marriage of words" is evidence of
Faulkner's own ambivalence toward the lesson of Sutpen's failure,
an ambivalence he comes much closer to resolving in *Go Down,
Moses.*

In "Faulkner and the Unnatural" Myra Jehlen examines in rich
and evocative detail a single sequence of events in *The Hamlet*:
the love affair between the idiot Ike Snopes and the cow belonging
to Jack Houston. "Nature" in this sequence is portrayed by Faulk-

ner as myth and fact, an occasion of "heavenly revelation" and "thudding autochthony." Jehlen traces the development of the sequence through its alternating accounts of absolute earthiness and divinely inspired gentleness, degenerate and idealized love, to its gradual arrival at "pure myth," in which man and cow maintain their membership in factual reality even as they "float off into a universe of gorgeous lyric." Yet the outcome of the episode, the exhibition of Ike and the cow as a freak attraction for the men of Frenchman's Bend, signifies in Faulkner a dark theme of the failure of nature and ultimately of writing itself. The idealization of Ike and the cow lifts the imagination beyond life itself, while the subsequent exploitation of them suggests a life so base as to be hopelessly beneath the powers of imagination. "Nature, in fact and fiction, has and is lost."

Diane Roberts is concerned not so much with the "unnatural" in Faulkner as his gradual departure from a nearly career-long tendency to characterize his women primarily in terms of natural forces: the land, animals, organic processes, sexuality. Part of this tendency is also the habit of allowing his male characters exclusive rights to control both the destiny and the interpretation of women, usually according to conventional Southern stereotypes. In "Eula, Linda, and the Death of Nature," Roberts examines the Snopes trilogy in terms of this development, beginning with Eula in *The Hamlet,* identified with land, food, livestock—part of "the mock-heroic tradition of the libidinous peasantry"—and culminating with her daughter, Linda Snopes Kohl, in *The Mansion.* By the end of the trilogy Linda has moved beyond "the inscribed feminine" of Faulkner's previous fiction, and become "a *political* person," who overturns virtually all of Jefferson's thinking about women and challenges much of earlier Faulkner's.

In "Taking the Place of Nature: 'The Bear' and the Incarnation of America," David Evans examines, in terms of its cultural burden, what is generally regarded as Faulkner's most detailed fictional account of the natural world. He argues that "The Bear" is very much about the process by which Ike McCaslin invests his hunting experience in the woods with a set of cultural preconceptions that originates with the Puritans. These preconceptions, which locate in nature redemptive qualities specifically designed for a "chosen people," lead Ike into a specific reading of American history, one which borrows the Puritan literary tradition of the jeremiad in order to demonstrate "the essential providential assumptions of epistemological privilege and special election that have subtended that history from the beginning." Ike's act of relinquishment becomes, in fact, an act of invention which appropriates nature for both individual and national purposes.

In "Return of the Big Woods: Hunting and Habitat in Yoknapatawpha," Wiley Prewitt Jr. offers a glimpse of what the wilderness situation in Mississippi actually was during the period when Faulkner wrote his hunting stories. The context of the stories of the 1930s and early 1940s is one of a radically diminished wilderness, disappearing large game, and the substitution of small game as the hunter's only option. In contrast to the fiction of a number of other writers at the time, however, Faulkner's stories continue to focus on the pursuit of large game, even to the point of linking small game—which had adapted to the conditions of small-field agriculture—to civilization and its oppositional relationship to the wilderness. But also unlike other writers, Faulkner introduces in his stories a cycle of destruction and renewal, an imagery of reincarnation similar to that found in Native American belief.

*   *   *

For a number of years it has been customary at the Faulkner Conference to invite a creative writer to participate in the program—not necessarily to talk about Faulkner but to read from his or her work and perhaps comment on it. In the conference "Faulkner and the Natural World," our visiting writer was William Kennedy, the author most recently of *The Flaming Corsage*, one of a group of novels called the Albany Cycle, which revolves around a number of families who dwell and participate in the long history of the city of Albany. Kennedy's creation of a fictional place grounded in a real one—"I have tried to make my city real in ways that it actually was, and fictional in ways it never was"—has inspired readers to link him with Faulkner, a connection which he examines in the concluding essay of this volume. Along the way he also summarizes the story of his own struggles as a writer—a story not unlike Faulkner's, and reflecting a comparable dedication, comparable concerns, and the occasional comparable pride of success. These are links, I should add, that Kennedy describes as part of the general equipment of being a writer, rather than as indicative of any close similarity between himself and Faulkner. His modesty insists—and so I imagine does his pride—that "like unhappy families, writers are also unhappy in their own way."

Donald M. Kartiganer
The University of Mississippi
Oxford, Mississippi

NOTES

1. Alfred Kazin, "The Stillness of *Light in August*," *William Faulkner: Three Decades of Criticism*, ed. Frederick J. Hoffman and Olga Vickery (New York: Harcourt, Brace & World, Inc., 1963), 247.

2. Martin Kreiswirth, "Faulkner as Translator: His Versions of Verlaine," *Mississippi Quarterly* 30 (1977): 429–32, convincingly demonstrates through examination of Faulkner's translations that he had consulted the 1919 edition of Symons's Book (originally published in 1899), which included a selection of symbolist poems. I have quoted from this edition since it is the one Faulkner himself probably read.

3. *The Symbolist Movement in Literature* (New York: E. P. Dutton & Co., 1919), 4.

4. Symons's quotations are from Mallarmé's *"Sur l 'Evolution litteraire,"* an 1891 interview, and *"Crise de vers,"* written 1886–1896. They can be found in *Oeuvres Completes*, ed. Henry Mondor and G. Jean-Aubry (Paris: Gallimard, 1945), and in *Selected Prose Poems, Essays, and Letters*, trans. Bradford Cook (Baltimore: Johns Hopkins University Press, 1956).

5. See Frank Kermode, *Romantic Image* (New York: Vintage Books, 1964) for an excellent discussion of Symons's book and its influence on modern poetry.

6. "The Decay of Lying" [1889], *The Writings of Oscar Wilde*, ed. Isobel Murray (Oxford: Oxford University Press, 1989), 215.

7. *The Environmental Imagination: Thoreau, Nature Writing, and the Formation of American Culture* (Cambridge: Harvard University Press, 1995), 86.

8. *The Lion in the Garden: Interviews with William Faulkner, 1926–1962*, ed. James B. Meriwether and Michael Millgate (New York: Random House, 1968), 127–28. See David Minter's comment on this quote, *William Faulkner: His Life and Work* (Baltimore: Johns Hopkins University Press, 1980), 283, n. 21.

9. *Go Down, Moses* (New York: Vintage International, 1990), 200.

10. *The Mansion: A Novel of the Snopes Family* (New York: Random House, 1959), 435.

A Note on the Conference

The Twenty-third Annual Faulkner and Yoknapatawpha Conference sponsored by the University of Mississippi in Oxford took place July 28–August 2, 1996, with over two hundred of the author's admirers from around the world in attendance. The eleven lectures presented at the conference are collected in this volume. Brief mention is made here of other activities that took place during the week.

The conference opened with a reception hosted by the University Museums and an exhibition entitled *Tom Rankin Photographs*, including a lecture by the photographer. At the opening session Provost Gerald W. Walton welcomed participants, and William Ferris, Director of the Center for the Study of Southern Culture, presented the 1996 Eudora Welty awards in Creative Writing to Will Renick of Ashland and Jessica Mitchell of Cleveland. The awards are selected annually through a competition held in high schools throughout Mississippi.

Following the presentation was the announcement of the winner of the seventh annual Faux Faulkner write-alike contest, sponsored by Jack Daniels Distillery, the University of Mississippi, and Yoknapatawpha Press and its *Faulkner Newsletter*. Authors John Berendt, Tom Wicker, George Plimpton, and Arthur Schlesinger Jr. selected Lance P. Martin, a New Orleans attorney, for his entry entitled "Absaloon, Absaloon!" A special program of "Dramatizations from Faulkner's Fiction," directed by Cindy Gold, of the Department of Theatre Arts at the University of Mississippi, concluded the afternoon program. After a buffet supper, held on the lawn of Dr. and Mrs. M. B. Howorth Jr, and sponsored by Jack Daniels Distillery, Lawrence Buell delivered the opening lecture of the conference.

Monday's program consisted of four lectures and the presentation "Knowing William Faulkner," during which J. M. Faulkner presented slides and stories of his famous uncle. Other highlights of the conference included a panel discussion by present and former Oxford residents—Howard Duvall, Robert Ashford Little, and Patricia Young—moderated by M. C. Falkner, another of the writer's nephews; "Teaching Faulkner" sessions conducted by visiting scholars James B. Carothers, Robert W. Hamblin, Arlie E. Herron, and Charles A. Peek; a lecture (printed in this volume) and reading by writer William Kennedy; and bus tours of North Mississippi and the Delta. Social highlights were a party at Tyler Place hosted by Chuck Noyes, Sarah and Allie Smith, and Colby Kullman; a walk through Bailey's Woods and a picnic at Rowan Oak; and the closing party at the home of Dr. and Mrs. Ernest B. Lowe Jr.

The conference planners are grateful to all the individuals and organizations who support the Faulkner and Yoknapatawpha Conference annually. In addition to those mentioned above, we wish to thank Mrs. Jack Coldfield, Dr. William Strickland, Mr. Richard Howorth of Square Books, Mr. James Rice of Holiday Inn/Oxford, the City of Oxford, and the Oxford Tourism Council.

Faulkner and the Natural World
FAULKNER AND YOKNAPATAWPHA
1996

Faulkner and the Claims of the Natural World

LAWRENCE BUELL

Just as I began work on this project, I was challenged by a reporter who called me about the new so-called ecocritical movement to give a specific example of what difference it makes when you read a literary text with special attention to how it deals with environmental issues. I want to start with the first example that sprang to mind. Since I didn't really have time to unpack it for her, I want to make sure to inflict it on you. It's from the opening chapter of *Light in August*. For years, the initial phase of this novel had organized itself in my mind overwhelmingly around the figure of Lena Grove moving quietly across a more or less undifferentiated landscape in all her innocent serenity: a figure synthesized from several stereotypes (earth mother, Madonna, Southern poor white) into what felt like a luminous and memorable symbolic image with a soft romantic glow.

Reading the novel again in the '90s, however, after a long hiatus, I found myself seeing Lena in relation to a very different sort of ground, much more precisely etched: the world of Doane's Mill, from which she has come, and where she got pregnant by Lucas Burch—that no-good deadbeat she pursues for the rest of the novel. Concerning Doane's Mill, we are told

> All the men in the village worked in the mill or for it. It was cutting pine. It had been there seven years and in seven years more it would destroy all the timber within its reach. Then some of the machinery and most of the men who ran it and existed because of and for it would be loaded onto freight cars and moved away. But some of the machinery would be left, since new pieces could always be bought on the installment plan—gaunt, staring, motionless wheels rising from

mounds of brick rubble and ragged weeds with a quality profoundly astonishing, and gutted boilers lifting their rusting and unsmoking stacks with an air stubborn, baffled and bemused upon a stumppocked scene of profound and peaceful desolation, unplowed, untilled, gutting slowly into red and choked ravines beneath the long quiet rains of autumn and the galloping fury of vernal equinoxes.[1]

Here in one paragraph, Faulkner provides a concise history of the cut-and-get-out phase of the timber industry in the Deep South: a half-century of intensive exploitation and chronic wastefulness (of forest, soil, people, and equipment), starting in the 1880s, that Faulkner probably was well aware was nearly played out. In fact, Southern forest historians identify the early 1930s, the very moment of *Light in August*'s publication, as the point when the large tracks of timber in Mississippi's first forest finally ran out and lumber production hit a fifty-year low.[2]

What makes these factoids relevant to the novel is of course the relation of forest history to social history. Initially, the rise of the lumber industry (which in the early 1900s rivalled and in some areas exceeded cotton as the Deep South's major cash crop) seemed, as historian Thomas D. Clark puts it, to act "as social and economic safety valves by drawing away from cotton tenancy surplus laborers who had no alternative source of employment." But, as the same writer adds, most workers wound up trading "peonage to the sharecropper landlord and the country furnishing store for peonage to the lumber company commissary."[3] In his study of the Mississippi lumber industry, Nollie W. Hickman notes: "The sawmill worker was underpaid, lived in a nondescript house, and was able to obtain for himself only the plainest of food and clothing. Few were ever able to rise in the social and economic scale. Many were without ambition, easily satisfied with living only in the present, and little concerned about the future of themselves or their children. [Even] had the average worker been dissatisfied with the life he knew, he had little opportunity for improvement."[4]

Here we have the social frame in terms of which to understand a great many things about the characters to whom Faulkner introduces us early on: the anxious stolidity of Lena's unromantic brother and sister-in-law with their too-large family, the rootless dysfunctionality of the seducer Lucas, the reluctant mobility of Lena herself, and the counterpoint between Lucas and his hard-working quasi-namesake Byron Bunch—the super-conscientious, repressed, but warm-hearted schlemiehl who falls in love with Lena to the point that he quits *his* job at a Jefferson planing mill and thereby forfeits the precarious social standing he has so pain-stakingly built up. All these characters are what they are not just because of who they are but because of where they fit in the history of Mississippi lumbering. Lucas's placelessness, which becomes a stalking horse for his partner Joe Christmas's placeless-ness, is as much a product of his culture's shortsightedness about its natural resources as Christmas's is a product of the culture's shortsightedness about race.

That environmental history can illuminate Faulkner's fiction in unexpected ways is only to be expected of a person whose enthusi-asm for taking his annual hunting trip to the Mississippi Delta was far greater than his enthusiasm for tripping to Stockholm to re-ceive the Nobel Prize. Not only did Faulkner know at least as much about hunting and farming as any of the other major Ameri-can modernists, he was also a pretty fair natural historian: "the best scoutmaster [Oxford] ever had," according to the man who was Chancellor of Ole Miss during the 1920s,[5] and a close observer in his fiction, too, as others have shown, of regional weather, "its vegetable and animal life, its trees, flowers, insects, birds . . . —as well as of the sounds of nature and the many changes in the play of light."[6] It's symptomatic that the title of *Light in August* refers to a specific seasonal atmospheric effect.[7]

Not that we do full justice to the place of the natural world in Faulkner's work merely by inventorying landscape items and proving their historical or geographical accuracy. For one thing, the physical environment in Faulkner's work gets filtered through the lens of literary convention: stock romantic imagery of pastoral retreat from Andrew Marvell to A. E. Housman, American mascul-inist wilderness narrative from Cooper to Melville and Twain. In

Faulkner's juvenilia especially, the evocation of landscape is always passionate but often almost entirely literary: *The Marble Faun,* his early poetic sequence, looks at landscape and sees rooks and nightingales.[8] Such excrescences get tamed down, but it remains a crucial part of Faulkner's mature aesthetics to infuse facticity with myth, legend, and poetic rhetoric. In the previously quoted passage from the first chapter of *Light in August,* the imaging of Lucas and especially Lena as vernacularized versions of ancient literary types (the faithless seducer and the Madonna/Earth Mother) is interwoven with the environmental realism already stressed. Likewise, the passage quoted earlier starts with an almost photographic approach but then metamorphoses into a highly stylized regional gothic, with the "gaunt, staring" wheels rising up in a way "profoundly astonishing," and the "stubborn, baffled and bemused" look of the "gutted boilers."

Yet when Faulkner stylizes like this he by no means "loses touch" with environmental actuality, either—any more than Thoreau can be said to lose touch with environmental actuality when he overstates the seclusion of his retreat at Walden. In our passage, for example, the stylized "exaggeration" underscores both the ugly wastefulness of industry's leavings and also (no less strikingly) the environment's power to fight back in its own way, as the machinery disintegrates in "the red and choked ravines beneath the long quiet rains of autumn and the galloping fury of vernal equinoxes." It is striking how Faulkner's surrealistic image of the blighted landscape is uncannily anticipated by a passage from a 1921 report by Mississippi State Geologist E. N. Lowe describing how "cutover areas" in this part of the country tend to degrade:

> Whenever the slightest furrow concentrates the flow of rain a gully begins to form; when this deepens so as to reach the sand beneath, undercutting and slumping begins and progresses with remarkable rapidity, so that a graceful slope in an old field may in an incredibly short time present a maze of gullies and washes, some of which soon attain enormous proportions. I have seen a pig-trail down a hill slope develop into a chasm in the hill-side that would engulf a two-story house.[9]

Neither Lowe's nor Faulkner's visions of blighted nature's re-surgence are pretty pictures. This is not Gerard Manley Hopkins bouncing back in his poem "God's Grandeur" from the depressing thought that the world is "bleared" and "smeared" with toil by the upbeat affirmation that nature will always regenerate. Rather what we have here is a version of a typical insight in Faulkner's work of a special intensity to subtropical Southern nature that potentially gives it as much power over its human inhabitants as vice versa. It is like Bayard Sartoris's impression in *The Unvanquished* of the railroad that has been destroyed by Union armies as having quickly become "a few piles of charred ties among which green grass was already growing, a few threads of steel knotted and twisted about the trunks of trees and already annealing into the living bark, becoming one and indistinguishable with the jungle growth which had now accepted it."[10] Or it is similar to the hallucinatory experience of the tenderfoot protagonist in the early story "Nympholepsy," who is used to thinking of trees as timber, but suddenly feels the forest gazing on him threateningly, and "above all brood[ing] some god" regarding him "as a trespasser where he had no business being."[11]

The primordialist vision in these passages concerning natural forces bound to assert themselves gets worked out most fully in two later works: the "Old Man" sequence of *The Wild Palms* and *Go Down, Moses*. It is notable that these two narratives come to opposite conclusions, however. The first is Faulkner's strongest presentation of Nature untrammeled—a gripping narrative of man against flood (probably reminiscent of the great Mississippi Flood of 1927, which Faulkner believed wiped out the last bear in the Delta).[12] The protagonist in "Old Man"—who is simply called the "tall convict," as if the text deliberately refuses to grant him full personhood—despite almost superhuman endurance can do no more than just barely cope with the brute force of nature. By contrast, *Go Down, Moses*, just a few years later, elegiacally anticipates the death of nature. Had Faulkner given thought to the possibility that the flood might have been exacerbated by unwise manipulations of the river and its tributaries, the difference might

have been less,[13] but in any case, the contrast of nature as independent, irresistible force in "Old Man" versus the comparative senti-
mentalization of the "doomed wilderness" (through Ike McCaslin's
eyes) in *Go Down, Moses* suggests some possible reasons why he
never fully formulated an environmental ethic. First, like most
precontemporary people, his knowledge of environmental cause-
and-effect was spotty: he understood deforestation as a social problem better than he understood flooding as such. Second, the notion
of natural force as potent human adversary continued to run strong
in his thinking at some level. And third, he was first and foremost
a professional writer with at least one eye pragmatically on the
literary marketplace. He would have been well aware of the dramatic power of both man-versus-natural disaster stories and wilderness initiation stories; and if they cut in opposite directions so
far as environmental ethics was concerned, he wasn't going to go
out of his way to try to reconcile the contradiction.

Perhaps the best evidence of this pragmatism on Faulkner's part
is his readiness to dumb down episodes in his death of the wilderness saga for mass market consumption: for example, to interrupt
the completion of "Go Down, Moses" in order to crank out and
sell a compressed version of the early portions of "The Bear" to
the *Saturday Evening Post*; to dish up "Race at Morning" for the
Post in the 1950s; and to collect his more user-friendly hunting
stories in *Big Woods*. This does not mean, however, that Faulkner
was not even more deeply committed in another part of his being
to exfoliating the historical and thematic complexities of his saga,
including a serious and sustained work of environmental reflection. A closer look at *Go Down, Moses* shows that such in fact was
the case.

Go Down, Moses was one of those books that grew far beyond
its author's first conscious intent. Faulkner initially thought of it as
a short story collection on the " 'general theme [of the] relationship
between white and negro races here,' " to be got up like *The Unvanquished* so that it would thereby reap the double harvest of
magazine pieces and book publication. His first working table of
contents included only five of the eventual seven items: "The Fire

and the Hearth," "Pantaloon in Black," "The Old People," "Delta Autumn," and "Go Down, Moses."[14] According to Joseph Blotner, only after revising down to the middle of "Delta Autumn" (which portrays what may well be the last hunt for Ike McCaslin, here figured as a quasi-senile octogenarian) did he decide to write "The Bear," even though in 1935 he'd previously published a shorter proto-version of the hunting sequence under the title of "Lion" in *Harper's*.[15] He also added "Was," the farcical tale of Ike Mc-Caslin's father, Uncle Buddy, being temporarily rescued from the clutches of Ike's future mother, Sophonsiba Beauchamp, when his twin brother Uncle Buddy beats Uncle Hubert in a poker game. Therefore the completed novel (as Faulkner came to think of it: not story collection, but novel: he was irked when Random House entitled it *Go Down, Moses, and Other Stories*) focuses much more on the nineteenth century relative to the twentieth and also fore-grounds environmental reflection to a greater degree than initially. In particular, Faulkner invented the figure of young man Ike. Until he interrupted his revision of the original story sequence well past the halfway point in order to compose "The Bear," Ike McCaslin seems hardly to have existed for Faulkner except as the crusty old codger of "Delta Autumn" and the farcical 1935 story "The Bear Hunt" (which has virtually no resemblance to the later novella "The Bear"). For both "The Old People" and "Lion" had initially been Quentin Compson stories. From *Go Down, Moses* on, however, it is young man Ike who dominates old man Faulk-ner's imagination. Ike's evolution partially resembles that of the primal ancestor of Faulkner's hero, James Fenimore Cooper's Natty Bumppo—the Leatherstocking—who also grew younger as his author grew older.

In the original group of five stories, the historical center of grav-ity is the near present, save for a brief retrospection via the middle story ("The Old People") back to the age of the big virgin forests, where the boy novice is vouchsafed a glimpse of the enormous buck by Sam Fathers. The stories that bracket this one, "Pantaloon in Black" and "Delta Autumn," record chapters in the demise of the wilderness in black and white. In "Pantaloon," the protagonist,

a colossal John Henry-like figure named Rider, who heads a gang
of black timber workers at a saw mill, goes haywire when his wife
dies and gets lynched after slashing his white foreman in a game
of craps: crunched up like the huge logs he prides himself on being
able to sling around from truck to mill down the skidway. What
sawmilling does to the woods, what skidway gouges do to the hill-
sides,[16] is what the social system does to uppity black workers—
and vice versa. Rider's logs come from the same hardwood forests
of cypress, gum, and oak whose disappearance old Ike McCaslin
laments in "Delta Autumn." Here too the fate of the main character gets likened to the fate of the woods, in this case by Ike himself—who can take consolation only in the escapist fancy that the
lives of both himself and wilderness are exactly coeval, "the two
spans running out together, not toward oblivion, nothingness, but
into a dimension free of both time and space where once more the
untreed land warped and wrung to mathematical squares of rank
cotton for the frantic old-world people to turn into shells to shoot
at one another, would find ample room for both—the names, the
faces of the old men he had known and loved and for a little while
outlived, moving again and again among the shades of tall unaxed
trees and sightless brakes where the wild strong immortal game
ran forever before the tireless belling [sic] immortal hounds."[17]

Given that the character of Ike McCaslin has been picked apart
by several generations of Faulkner critics, I need not belabor the
point that Ike's voice here is not to be taken as identical to the
authorial voice, even though he is the book's main protagonist.
Faulkner critics have stated the case for dramatic irony persuasively, as indeed has Faulkner himself. The evidence for this does
not rest only on Ike's rhetorical senilities; "The Bear" has already
laid the groundwork by exposing, for example, the prim Ike's se-
duction, the formal parallels between his moral bookkeeping and
commissary discourse, and his impotence and Boon's fecklessness—not to mention the novella's implication of Ike in the forest
products industry via his decision to follow a carpenter's trade
(which he rationalizes as Christ-like).[18]

Indeed, if Faulkner had not gone on to compose "The Bear,"

and thereby shift the center of gravity in *Go Down, Moses* so pro-
nouncedly, readers probably would not even have surmised that
Ike is the book's central figure, any more than either his cousin
Roth Edmonds or his black sharecropper and cousin (via Old
Carothers) Lucas Beauchamp, nor that Ike's romantic primordial-
ism and puristical rejection of landowning might be the book's
center of values. Rather, the main emphasis, at least so far as the
environmental history theme is concerned, would have been exposure of the parallel impotence and victimage of both black and
white before the juggernaut of Delta enterprise. In the original
sequence, not only is the romantic flavor of the wilderness initiation narrative in "The Old People" bracketed by "Pantaloon" and
"Delta Autumn," it is neutralized in advance by the satirical novella that comes first, "The Fire and the Hearth," whose central
section contains a parody of hunting narrative, when Lucas Beauchamp becomes obsessed (as Roth Edmonds puts it) with " 'poking
around in the bottom . . . hunting for' " buried treasure with his
metal-detecting gadget from Memphis.[19] This seems a wry ac-
knowledgment of the link between hunting rituals and extraction
of wealth from the woods.

The addition of "The Bear" and "Was" to the original sequence
obviously places much more emphasis on the romance of old pre-
industrial days versus the comparatively shabby present, on wilderness versus settlement culture, and on white innocence versus
hard-bitten middle and old age, with the latter no longer chiefly
represented by the cranky Lucas, but by the more idealized figure
of Sam Fathers.

It is quite unlikely that the greater romanticization of the revised *Go Down, Moses* was nothing more than a strategy for playing to middlebrow readerly nostalgia. On the contrary, there is
every reason to believe that with one side of his mind Faulkner
shared a considerable measure of Old Ike's grief at the demise of
the traditional hunting grounds (which were Faulkner's own hunting grounds too), and that this prompted him to evoke more fully
the memory of a more pristine past.[20] What's more, Faulkner's
nostalgia was not just centered on the transformation of nature

but with cultural transformation as well. In a polite version of the sardonic banter about politics by the hunters in "Delta Autumn," Faulkner himself later addressed the Council of archconservative Delta planters on the evils of government interference and the virtues of the personal freedom and civic responsibility exemplified by " 'the old fathers in the old strong, dangerous times.' "[21] Faulkner's affectionate dedication of Go Down, Moses to his family's Mammy is another indicator of his reverence for traditional social arrangements.

Still, the additions he made to Go Down, Moses also tried—at least somewhat—to qualify and offset any such idealization of premodernity, of a Southern primordium: to make clear that the space of the hunt, the space of the wilderness, was no safe refuge: that it was not immune from village and town institutions any more than Ike himself could maintain his dream of extricating himself from economic entanglements. In addition to devising the long fourth part of "The Bear" as a counter to the hunting sequence (the dialogue between Ike and McCaslin in the family commissary store when Ike turns twenty-one, in which the "original sins" of the patriarch—Old Carothers McCaslin, Ike's grandfather—are revealed: the double sins of miscegenation and incest with his female slaves), in addition to making sure that these serpents were injected into the hunting narrative, Faulkner revised the denouement of the hunting sequence itself, so as to have Major DeSpain sell the timber rights to his Big Bottom tract to a Memphis logging company—a highly significant detail not in the original story, "Lion."

In so doing, Faulkner may or may not have been revisiting a real-life event: the demise of his own Big Bottom happy hunting ground, bought and held as an investment property by his friend Phil Stone's father, a successful timberland speculator until the Depression caught up with him and he died debt-ridden.[22] Big Bottom failed the year after "Lion" was published, and a year after Faulkner and a group of other local men tried to protect the game on General Stone's holdings (simultaneously reserving the right to hunt it for themselves) by incorporating the "Okatoba Hunting

and Fishing Club."[23] But even if there was no intentional link between the historical Stone's fortunes and the fictional DeSpain's
eventual decision to turn a buck on his holdings of virgin timber,
Faulkner's revisions of *Go Down, Moses* pretty clearly reflect some
of the major crosscurrents in 1930s Mississippi so far as treatment
and attitude toward forest lands are concerned. On the one hand,
during this decade conservationist thinking was gaining ground in
the Deep South more rapidly than before the advent of large-scale
timbering in the 1880s, owing to the depletion of the accessible
big virgin timber tracts and the advent of such New Deal conservationist initiatives as the Soil Conservation Bureau and large-scale
Civilian Conservation Corps and other tree-replacement programs.[24] In retrospect, if one's key criterion is the maintenance of
a sufficiently large harvestable acreage, the U.S. timber history in
the South and indeed the nation can be read as melodrama rather
than as tragedy: the feared and perhaps threatened extinction of
forestlands averted by resourceful implementation, albeit sometimes belated, of prudent conservationist measures.[25] On the other
hand, during the 1930s Mississippi lagged behind the rest of the
South in this regard. Throughout the decade, it "ranked first
among southern states in lumber production and last in reforestation": 50 percent more wood was cut than replaced.[26] The Delta
region, furthermore, was the most retrograde in the state, the
slowest to reverse itself; in the '30s, '40s, and '50s, forest acreage
in Mississippi as a whole increased, but in the Delta it continued
to decline.[27]

Thus, I would draw three inferences from Faulkner's treatment
of the loss of wilderness in "The Bear" in the revised *Go Down,
Moses*. First, clearly, to a large degree the finished novella projects
back upon the late nineteenth century both a plot of wilderness
destruction and an ethos of forest preservation that look in some
respects anachronistic when measured against the record of
Southern environmental history and environmentalism—more
like 1930s attitudes than late nineteenth-century attitudes. Few, if
any, late nineteenth-century Southerners were as ecocentric as
young Ike McCaslin, partly because the really large-scale exploita-

tion of the Deep South's forests ("the years of frantic harvest," Southern forest historian Thomas Clark calls them) was only just beginning. (Part 5 of "The Bear" is set on the eve of this phase of really intensive logging, right after the end of Reconstruction.)[28]

The second inference is that, as a prophetic intervention reflecting the rising tide of environmentalist concern in Faulkner's own day, "The Bear" makes good historical sense. It makes sense that at that particular moment in local, regional, and indeed national history the death of wilderness should have loomed up for Faulkner personally as a pressing concern. It is logical that he would have assumed an audience with a more protectionist twist than even just a decade before. But given the still quite feeble and incipient state of environmentalism in the Deep South, it also made sense that Faulkner would take the apocalyptic approach of linking together the eve of late nineteenth-century rapacity in "The Bear" with the scenes of thoughtless exploitation in "Pantaloon" and environmental deterioration in "Delta Autumn."

Third and finally, Faulkner chose hunting narratives as his preferred vehicle for dramatizing an environmentalist commitment for a reason. Not only did this come naturally to Faulkner as an old sportsman himself, it is arguably the case that since the birth of organized environmentalism in the late-nineteenth-century United States, "sportsmen, those who hunted and fished for pleasure rather than commerce or necessity, were the real spearhead of conservation"; and it is undeniably the case that through their organizations and magazines the retelling of hunting and fishing stories in wilderness-friendly ways had become institutionalized as a significant cultural/literary vehicle for raising public environmentalist consciousness. Conversely, with very few exceptions, before 1930 virtually all significant male writers supporting conservation and preservation were or had in their early lives been seriously attracted to hunting and fishing.[29]

A prime exemplar is the today-acknowledged "father of modern environmental ethics," Aldo Leopold, whose greatest period of productivity as a writer coincides almost exactly with Faulkner's. Leopold's most enduring book, *A Sand County Almanac* (1949), outlines a "land ethic" (as he calls it) that's based on "kindly" or conscientious human use of land, in the spirit of awareness that all species have a right to exist as a matter of biotic right. One of his main sources of exempla of how to treat nature properly are narratives about hunting and fishing—narratives in which, like Faulkner, Leopold stresses proper process (mastery of woodcraft knowledge requisite to hunting, for example) as vastly more important than product (bagging the game).

From a present-day standpoint, Leopold's didactic stories of how to conduct sport-hunting in nature-sensitive ways seem a bit naive, androcentric, and boy scoutish—as do Faulkner's to some extent. Indeed, to many late twentieth-century city-folk and sub-urbanites, the whole notion of hunting seems profoundly atavistic. (My Yankee students are perpetually at odds over this issue with my students from rural places in the South and West.) But when one considers that the (sub)urbanite assumption that hunting is by definition morally evil was far less ingrained in the educated read-ing public half a century ago, particularly among the male readers that certainly were Leopold's and I suppose also Faulkner's pri-mary intended audience, then the attempt to instill respect for the natural world via retelling hunting stories (in both "The Old Peo-ple" and "The Bear") in such a way as to make fulfillment come to the main character when he sees the big critter, and tragedy when it's shot—such an attempt ought to seem more bold and construc-tive even to an inveterate anti-gun-and-hunt person. Granted, this kind of narrative doesn't come anywhere near approximating the much more pronounced ecocentrism one finds in, say, *Bambi* (1924), the Disney film version of which was almost exactly con-temporary with *Go Down, Moses*, and which predictably caused a storm of protest in sport-hunting circles.[30] But there certainly is a strong family resemblance between "The Bear" and Leopold's narrative of autumn grouse-hunting in *Sand County Almanac*, where the speaker gets so preoccupied by the pleasures of nature study that he never pulls the trigger—or if he does, he never tells us. For Faulkner and Leopold both to take this middle ground of commemorating hunting experience via works that regulated hunting practice was to take a high ethical ground and not to succumb to some wimpy or unholy compromise. As Leopold, for example, declares at the end of his *magnum opus*, *Game Management*:

> Twenty centuries of 'progress' have brought the average citizen a vote, a national anthem, a Ford, a bank account, and a high opinion of himself, but not the capacity to live in high density without befouling and denuding his environment . . . a conviction that such a capacity, rather than such density, is the true test of whether he is civilized. The practice of game management may be one of the means of developing a culture which will meet this test.[31]

In analogizing between Faulkner and Leopold, I do not mean to equate. Leopold was a professional forester for whom environmental ethics became *the* central commitment; for Faulkner, environmental issues were usually a secondary concern. Enough so, in fact, that to some it may seem perverse to put such emphasis on them as I have done in my account of *Go Down, Moses*, which I would agree not only began but even ended more as a race book than as an environment book. However, I would also want to resist the claim that race or any other social issue should be held up as *the* master theme of this or any other Faulkner book: the master referent in terms of which the text's environmental representation (for example) must be decoded—as if the latter didn't have even a semi-autonomous interest and claim in itself, and on all else. The history and finished state of *Go Down, Moses* shows otherwise: that although the claims of the natural world were seldom paramount in Faulkner's fiction, they could take on a life of their own and produce unexpected changes in an original design: furthermore, that Faulkner was no mere literary pastoralist or primitivist in his reflections on Southern environmental history, but ventured them against the background of considerable knowledge of its economic, social, and racial ramifications—even if these get sometimes bent or eclipsed somewhat for the sake of his narrative.[32] In particular, the sense of postbellum and early twentieth-century Southern history as a history of environmental degradation was not simply an epiphenomenon but an integral part of Faulkner's declensionary vision of Southern history generally.[33] It is not just windowdressing then, that has led Southern historians of environmentalist persuasion to cite Faulkner as one of the great harbingers and prophets of Southern environmentalism.[34]

Although Faulkner's status as a sometime and amateur environmentalist, lacking the professional expertise and investment of a Leopold albeit a wilderness enthusiast as well as a master of narrative, limited the horizons of his perception of environmental issues, by the same token it enabled him to deal more profoundly with some aspects of their common interests. Leopold was a rhetor chiefly in the vein of documentary exposition; Faulkner, at the level of the psychohistorical case study—a mode better suited to the dramatization of split allegiances, self-deception, and ironic unintended consequences. Of all these, Leopold too was aware; but nowhere in his work, or the literature of conservationism generally, is there such a profound awareness as there is in *Go Down, Moses* of how those who genuinely value wilderness can become, without fully reasoning through the implications of their acts, active coconspirators with those who value it only as cash crop—and how sometimes, in fact, as with Ike McCaslin, they can become such even when they are excruciatingly scrupulous casuists and self-examiners. Indeed, not only in his role as "great novelist," but also also in his capacity as thinking person and environmental amateur, Faulkner was better positioned to bring to consciousness how individuals divide into contradictory parts, how environmental concern manifests itself typically as a part-time concern in competition with other concerns that may well work to undermine it, how factical and fantastical visions of the natural world exist in uneasy and ever-shifting symbiosis.[35]

One thinks for example of how, at the start of part 5 of "The Bear," the narrator chuckles at the flimsiness of the scheme cooked up by General Compson and Walter Ewell "to corporate themselves, the old group, into a club and lease the camp and the hunting privileges of the woods—an invention doubtless of the somewhat childish old General but actually worthy of Boon Hogganbeck himself." For, adds the text, "even the boy"—even Ike, the perpetual naïf—"recognized it for the subterfuge it was: to change the leopard's spots when they could not alter the leopard," the leopard in this case being DeSpain's decision to sell the timber rights to a "Memphis lumber company," a decision the hunting confrères hope against hope he may be persuaded to revoke."[36] Faulkner here constructs a multi-layered ethical dilemma around the phenomenon of environmental doublethink: the experience of being caught between ecocentric and tribal or purely selfish values, partly because one's commitment to something is always muddled and compromised by one's other commitments, distractions, or sheer inanity. In one of its several mimetic registers, the passage is a bit of self-parodic roman-à-clef: Faulkner good-humoredly mocking the quixoticism of his own recent Okatoba Hunting Club scheme.[37] More obviously, at the level of the nominal narrative, Faulkner exposes the chuckleheadedness of his fictive wilderness lovers: their inability to think straight about wilderness issues. De Spain shows this just as clearly as Compson and Ewell: he wants the Memphis entrepreneurs' money but hates himself for selling out. At the level of the plot's deeper ideological structure, the passage—reproducing the schizoid dichotomy between the wilderness of parts 1–3 and the Southern history-in-microcosm of part 4—ensures that the logic of the novella's denouement will mirror the phenomenon of environmental doublethink by setting up an ironic distinction between the spiritual teleology (Old Ben's death means end of wilderness), and the propertarian teleology (Major De Spain's sale means death of wilderness) without resolving the issue of whether the former is a mystification of the latter or whether the former produces the latter. That both of these teleologies are both invoked at distinct moments in the text and also shown to be interdependent, while leaving the question unresolved as to which has priority (either as putative catalyst to human behavior, or as the preferred epicenter around which the text's implicit ideology is presumed to gravitate), ensured that "The Bear" and indeed Go Down, Moses as a whole would become exceptionally rich meditations in environmental ethics. Who can cavil at Faulkner's inability to reach closure on the ethical issues, or even at his inability to keep the issue of Southern environmental degradation consistently in focus, when the same failures continue to plague us more than a half-century later?

NOTES

1. William Faulkner, *Light in August* (New York: Random House, 1950), 4.

2. Nollie W. Hickman, "Mississippi Forests," *A History of Mississippi*, ed. Richard Aubrey McLemore (Jackson: University & College Press of Mississippi, 1973), 2: 217, 224.

3. Thomas D. Clark, *The Greening of the South* (Lexington: University Press of Kentucky, 1984), 34.

4. Nollie Hickman, *Mississippi Harvest: Lumbering in the Longleaf Pine Belt, 1840–1915* (University: University of Mississippi, 1962), 250–51.

5. Joseph Blotner, *Faulkner: A Biography* (New York: Random House, 1974), 1:662.

6. Ilse Lind, "Faulkner and Nature," *Faulkner Studies* 1 (1980): 115.

7. Frederick L. Gwynn and Joseph Blotner, ed., *Faulkner in the University* (New York: Vintage, 1965), 199.

8. Faulkner, *The Marble Faun* and *A Green Bough* (New York: Random House, n.d.), 28–29.

9. E. N. Lowe, "Notes on Forests and Forestry in Mississippi," *Proceedings of the Third Southern Forestry Congress* (Atlanta, 1921), 195.

10. Faulkner, "Raid," *The Unvanquished* (New York: Vintage, 1966), 109.

11. Faulkner, "Nympholepsy," *Uncollected Stories*, ed. Joseph Blotner (New York: Vintage, 1981), 334.

12. Malcolm Cowley, *The Faulkner-Cowley File: Letters and Memories, 1944–1962* (New York: The Viking Press, 1966), 111.

13. Faulkner characterized the flood in the story as "inherent in the geography and the climate" (*Faulkner in the University*), 176.

14. Faulkner to Haas, May 1941, in Blotner 1: 1078.

15. Ibid., 1: 1080.

16. Hickman emphasizes that "logging with skidders brought complete destruction of young timber of unmarketable size. . . . No trees or vegetation of any kind except coarse wire grass remained on the skidder-logged hill and ridges. For miles and miles the landscape presented a picture of bare open land that graphically illustrated the work of destruction wrought by the economic activities of man" (*Mississippi Harvest*, 165–66).

17. *Go Down, Moses* (New York: Random House, 1942), 354.

18. My thanks to Noel Polk and Thomas McHaney for pointing out to me the irony of Ike's occupation in present context.

19. *Go Down, Moses*, 102.

20. N.B. such comments to University Virginia students that the evanescence of wilderness is "to me a sad and tragic thing . . . , providing you have the sort of background which a country boy like me had" (*Faulkner in the University*, 68).

21. Faulkner, "Address to the Delta Council" (1952), *Essays, Speeches, and Public Letters*, ed. James B. Meriwether (New York: Random House, 1965), 130. For the cultural context, see James C. Cobb, *The Most Southern Place on Earth: The Mississippi Delta and the Roots of Regional Identity* (New York: Oxford University Press, 1992), 254.

22. Susan Snell, *Phil Stone of Oxford: A Vicarious Life* (Athens: University of Georgia Press, 1991), 51, 220, 236.

23. Blotner, *William Faulkner*, 1:879, 885. Charles S. Aiken, "A Geographical Approach to William Faulkner's 'The Bear,'" *Geographical Review* 71 (1981): 446–59, meticulously reconstructs (with maps) the close relationships between the geography of the novel's fictive world and Stone's camp, as well as the camp farther up the Tallahatchie, closer to Jefferson/Oxford, which Faulkner had known as a child from his father's hunts. Faulkner's

late-life (1954) essay, "Mississippi," *Essays, Speeches, and Public Letters*, deliberately montages autobiography with fiction ("he had shared in the yearly ritual of Old Ben" [p. 37]).

24. See for example Clark, *The Greening of the South*, chapters 5–11; Albert E. Cowdrey, *This Land, This South: An Environmental History*, rev. ed. (Lexington: University Press of Kentucky, 1996), 149–66.

25. See for example Sherry H. Olson, *The Depletion Myth: A History of Railroad Use of Timber* (Cambridge: Harvard University Press, 1971), and Douglas W. MacCleery, *American Forests: A History of Resiliency and Recovery* (Durham, North Carolina: Forest History Society, 1993).

26. Hickman, "Mississippi Forests," 226.

27. Ibid., 227–29.

28. Clark, *The Greening of the South*, 24.

29. John F. Reiger, *American Sportsmen and the Origins of Conservation* (New York: Winchester Press, 1975), 21 and passim. For examples of popular-culture-level hunting narratives with a conservationist agenda contemporary with Faulkner, see for example Weldon Stone's 1938 story, "That Big Buffalo Bass" (the youthful fisherman wins the narrator's admiration by releasing the Moby-Dick of the Ozarks after catching him), *The Field and Stream Reader* (Garden City, New York: Doubleday, 1946), 106–16; and Nash Buckingham's "The Comedy of Long Range Duck Shooting," *Blood Lines: Tales of Shooting and Fishing* (New York: Derrydale Press, 1938), 151–72, which contrasts old-time skill with the bad sportsmanship of greedy, protocol-insouciant hunters with more modern high-powered weaponry.

30. Matt Cartmill, *A View to a Death in the Morning: Hunting and Nature Through History* (Cambridge: Harvard University Press, 1993), 178–85.

31. Leopold, *Game Management* (New York: Scribner's, 1937), 423.

32. Lewis P. Simpson, "Faulkner and the Southern Symbolism of Pastoral," *Mississippi Quarterly* 28 (1975): 401–15, makes the strongest case against Faulkner as a traditional American pastoralist, although to my mind he tries a little too hard to extricate Faulkner from pastoral influences.

33. This interconnection manifests itself with special force in Faulkner's 1954 essay, "Mississippi," *Essays, Speeches, and Public Letters*, 11–43.

34. See for example Albert E. Cowdery, *This Land, This South*, 199.

35. Again, this is by no means to say that Leopold lacked a sense of irony, of self-reflexivity, and of awareness at the mixed motives and changing agendas of human beings toward nature, including himself. See for example, H. Lewis Elman, " 'Thinking Like a Mountain': Persona, Ethis, and Judgment in American Nature Writing," *Green Culture: Environmental Rhetoric in Contemporary America*, ed. Carl G. Herndl and Stuart C. Brown (Madison: University of Wisconsin Press, 1996), 46–81; and my discussion in *The Environmental Imagination: Thoreau, Nature Writing, and the Formation of American Culture* (Cambridge: Harvard University Press, 1995), 171–74.

36. *Go Down, Moses*, 315–16.

37. Noted by Aiken, "A Geographical Approach to William Faulkner's 'The Bear,' " 450–51.

Oversexing the Natural World: *Mosquitoes* and *If I Forget Thee, Jerusalem [The Wild Palms]*

THOMAS L. MCHANEY

A great deal of William Faulkner's interest in the natural world—at least insofar as he was a writer—takes erotic form. One reason for this is his training as a poet, a symbolist, and an early exploiter of the standard tools of the modernist aesthetic, especially Freudian psychology. Faulkner fashioned and largely held to an ironic urban sense of pastoral that was derived from classical and nineteenth-century verse but shaped by his immersion in the stream of modernist poetics and thought: Freud, Eliot, Joyce, Bergson, Proust first, of course, but also, and by more than cultural osmosis, Expressionist and Cubist renderings of consciousness in painting, theater, and prose fiction. This is not to say that he preferred the urban pastoral to whatever is meant by direct apprehension of a truly natural environment, but that his times, his poetic sensibility, the traditions of writing that he chose to explore and ultimately to advance, and even the Mississippi in which he lived, offered him little alternative. His earliest uses of the natural—as opposed to the built—environment, his earliest presentations of literary landscapes, and, as well, many of his best uses of nature in mature work are stylized, condensed, extremely limited in naturalistic vocabulary, and bent to comic and dramatic purposes. Before I offer some speculations as to why this may be so, I want to demonstrate aspects of Faulkner's characteristic practice in one very early novel, for in the early work his condensations are baldly showy, making their purposes apparent. Later, after I have built a case for the inevitability of Faulkner's particular transformations of the natural environment into literary devices, I will cite a mature novel. Both novels are very personal, which makes them doubly interesting, and both share many themes, settings, images, and details of character. But in his mature work, Faulkner is more concrete with the natural world, more in sympathy with it, more in awe of it, though it is also true, to use a phrase Deborah Schnitzer wrote about Ernest Hemingway, that his presentations of the natural world invariably also function to reveal the "archetypal dimensions of his protagonists' experience of the landscape."[1] Still, his later work acknowledges that the natural world is not simply a palette for the artist, and he is far from indifferent regarding its plight at the hands of humankind.

The first Faulkner novel I've chosen evokes the natural world even before readers enter its text. The title of *Mosquitoes* is obvious, but not so obvious that it doesn't deserve some preliminary attention. As we know, the title word does not appear in any form, plural or singular, anywhere else in Faulkner's second novel, which he wrote in New Orleans, Paris, and Pascagoula, Mississippi, a small resort town on the Gulf coast, and published in 1927. But in case we should miss Faulkner's *tour de force* regarding the title, he provides a one-page, italicized epigraph evoking the pesky insects in dulcet mock-romantic:

> In spring, the sweet young spring, decked out with little green, necklaced, braceleted with the song of idiotic birds, spurious and sweet and tawdry as a shopgirl in her cheap finery, like an idiot with money and no taste; they were little and young and trusting, you could kill them sometimes. But now, as August like a languorous replete bird winged slowly through the pale summer toward the moon of decay and death, they were bigger, vicious; ubiquitous as undertakers, cunning as pawnbrokers, confident and unavoidable as politicians. They came cityward lustful as country boys, as passionately integrated as a college football squad; pervading and monstrous but without majesty: a biblical plague seen through the wrong end of a binocular: the majesty of Fate become contemptuous through ubiquity and sheer repetition.[2]

It should interest us that the future author of *The Sound and the Fury, Sanctuary,* and *Light in August* already had on his mind so

early the peculiar resonance of the words "idiotic" and "idiot,"
that he personifies his unnamed mosquitoes as lustful country boys
who come from no pastoral arcadia, apparently, but from Calvinist
gardens, and that he specifically sets them on their way to the
city's commodified sexuality, and that he evokes the deep Southern summer in terms of languorous menstrual repletion, August
moving like Omar's bird of time toward the moon of "decay and
death." Two of these terms are sexual enough, all the similes in
the passage are self-conscious and, as we might say, unnatural,
and the novel's opening scene, which follows in a section entitled
"Prologue," proposes immediately a hopped-up Freudian slant on
fin de siècle symbolist decadence. The first words of the first chapter are " 'The Sex Instinct,' repeated Mr. Taliaferro in his careful
cockney, with that smug complacence with which you plead guilty
to a characteristic which you privately consider a virtue, 'is quite
strong in me.' " He is in the French Quarter studio of the New
Orleans artist Gordon, who brushes away the phony aesthete
much as Mr. Taliaferro slaps "vainly about himself with his handkerchief" to ward off the unnamed natural nuisances of the title.
Gordon, a brawny and taciturn sculptor, works with natural materials: wood and stone; and right now he applies himself vigorously
with maul and chisel to a block of wood. Taliaferro talks, expanding
the novel's opening assertion: "frankness compels me to admit,"
he insists, "that the sex instinct is perhaps my most dominating
compulsion" (9). The scene is, of course, comic, parodic—a way of
visualizing it, perhaps, is to imagine T. S. Eliot in his banker's suit
reciting "The Lovesong of J Alfred Prufrock" to Marlon Brando's
Stanley Kowalski during the poker scene in "Streetcar." Prufrock-
like, Taliaferro muses on his host's physique, speculating "briefly
upon which was more to be desired—muscularity in an under-
shirt, or his own symmetrical sleeve." Taliaferro, we will learn, is
in ladies underwear—that is, he sells women's undergarments at a
department store downtown in New Orleans, and in a novel where
fetich (37) and Freud (248) are mentioned and their implications
are paraded, the joke arouses more than comedy. Freud teaches
us that there are no innocent jokes and that the fetichist clings to

his slipper or female undergarment out of a suspicion, or fear, of castration.[3]

At this point Gordon, finding the lingerie salesman in the way again, drives a powerful hip into Taliaferro with such force that the visitor is knocked across the room and into a wall, from which he rebounds with "repressed alacrity," his carefully tailored coat sleeve now dusted with the gritty leavings of Gordon's stone carving. He decides to sit out of Gordon's way, but finds that he must rise and put his handkerchief on the dusty upturned wooden block he has chosen. Taliaferro recalls that he "invariably soiled his clothes" when he came to Gordon's studio, a double entendre that feeds off of Taliaferro's musing "with regret," a few lines earlier, "on the degree of intimacy he might have established with his artistic acquaintances had he but acquired the habit of masturbation in his youth. But he had not even done this" (10).

Given so much initial expression of the sexual brag that followed the heels of the Freudian revolution—a brag made necessary by the fear that one would appear repressed unless she or he talked "frankly"—it is not surprising that *Mosquitoes* becomes a sexual comedy in which the natural world takes on an expressionist cast reflecting the characters'—and the author's—preoccupations with the great Victorian taboo, sex. We have known for a long time that just such a sexual comedy, Aldous Huxley's *Chrome Yellow*, which is also a kind of *kunstlerroman*, was a source for Faulkner's novel. Just how much it was a source is evident from remarks about Huxley's novel made by the American essayist and critic Henry Seidel Canby in *The Century Magazine* in 1922. In a piece entitled "Sex in Fiction," Canby wrote: "the relativity of Einstein may influence our philosophy of life profoundly before we have finished absorbing it; so far, however, it is a little remote from the science of human nature, and fiction is unaware of it. Not so with the new psychology of sex complexes and neuroses."[4] In *Chrome Yellow*, for example, he notes, Huxley "tosses together half a dozen of his contemporaries in an imagined house party and lets them talk and act the sex that is in them. . . . Nothing important happens . . . the story floats and sails upon the turbid intensity of restless sex" (100).

This is a nearly perfect description of *Mosquitoes*. As Faulkner's voluptuous ingenue Jenny Steinbauer observes of her boating companions, "They are not going anywhere, and they don't do anything" (75). The central episodes—four days on Lake Pontchartrain—indeed float upon the turbid intensity of restless sex more than upon a nominal amount of water. Lake Pontchartrain, the encompassing natural world of river and swamp, as well as the sparse vegetation and meteorological phenomenon seen from the New Orleans French Quarter in the Prologue and Epilogue chapters that frame the lake excursion are presentations of the natural world that express the sexual moods of the characters or substitute for sex itself.

To portray the natural world, Faulkner resorts to a style of expressionism that emphasizes the stasis and decadence of the novel's environment and the sexual confusion and powerlessness of its characters. What we see in the city are "stencilled palms" in a violet twilight and "mimosa and pomegranate and hibiscus beneath which the lantana bled and bled" (14), or "tired looking stars of the fourth magnitude" framed in the high windows of Gordon's studio—windows so high that, as he observes, he would have to be eight feet tall to enjoy a view. For a short time, the excursionists on Mrs. Maurier's yacht enjoy a change in atmosphere from the sweltering, mosquito-plagued unreal city of depletion and ennui they have fled. They even attempt a spirited sexual romp in the lake: the writer Dawson Fairchild and the Scottish entrepreneur Major Ayers pinch some of the women under the cover of water, driving them into the yacht's lifeboat, but Patricia Robyn, the nymphlike niece of the yacht's owner, gets revenge by ducking the men, pulling them down from below and then standing on their heads until they are left choking and must flee the water themselves before they are drowned. Like Eliot, Faulkner found it easy to inscribe mermaids on the flappers of the twenties; in the allegorical story *Mayday* and the sketch "Nympholepsy," both written not long before *Mosquitoes*, he treated male fear of female envelopment similarly—as a suffocating consequence of seeking pleasure with women.[5] The yacht from which Faulkner's characters

carry on such shenanigans and by virtue of which they are supposed to escape nature—the heat and mosquitoes of the city—by
entering a more primal version of it—the vast lake and its surrounding swamps—is aptly named the *Nausikaa*, for the Phaeacian
nymph who brings Odysseus out of the water to the palace of
her father where Odysseus tells—and perhaps exaggerates—his
watery misadventures with symbolic perils. In Faulkner's novel,
Dawson Fairchild tells a tall tale about life in the swamps, a travesty of American commerce concerning descendants of Andrew
Jackson—whose terrific equestrian effigy is centerpiece of the
French Quarter's Jackson Square. Commidifying nature with a
pragmatic vengeance, Al Jackson notices how rife vegetation is in
the swamp, and he takes up sheepherding, thinking the wool will
grow with equal abundance. When the sheep start to drown, he
makes life belts for them out of bamboo, and when the alligators
eat the ewes and lambs, he gives them artificial horns made of
cypress, because the alligators don't eat the rams. As the sheep
learn to swim better, and even dive and stay under water, they
also grow scaly and then completely metamorphose, so Al goes
into fish-ranching, but he loses his son Claude, the wild one, when
Claude's increasingly long hours in the water catching the sheep
cause him to metamorphose, too, into a shark who thereafter both-
ers the blonde lady bathers along the Gulf Coast. They know it's
Claude, though they have not seen him in months, because he
"was always hell after blondes" (281). Faulkner, the actual inventor
of this tale in a series of exchanges with Sherwood Anderson preceding the making of his novel, is exploiting a tradition that seems
relatively innocent but is not: the raw and bawdy frontier humor
of one of his (and his mother's) favorite literary characters, Sut
Lovingood.[6] Faulkner's backwoods variant upon Ovid undeniably
ends in an erotic twist: one might even say, in a contemporary
mode, that Claude's failure to succeed in commodifying nature
turns him to sexual harassment.

After a heartily sexual romp in the water, in which the virgin
nymph Patricia Robyn defeats the lecherous mermen Ayers and
Fairchild (who, when on deck, prance about like satyrs) stasis sets

in on the *Nausikaa*. (We are doubtless invited to remember that the magic boat Nausikaa's father gives Odysseus is turned to stone by the vengeful gods who oppose the hero's return home). The yacht raises land, but the natural world here appears no less decadent than in the bohemian part of the city: "while the last of day drained out of the world the Nausikaa at half speed forged slowly into a sluggish river mouth, breaching a timeless violet twilight between solemn bearded cypresses motionless as bronze. You might, by listening, have heard a slow requiem in this tall nave, might have heard here the chanted orisons of the dark heart of the world turning toward slumber" (82–83). The passage is, in fact, written in such a way as to suggest that the presence of the *Nausikaa* transforms nature into a decadent stage set: "The world was becoming dimensionless, the tall bearded cypresses drew nearer one to another across the wallowing river with the soulless implacability of pagan gods, gazing down upon this mahogany-and-brass intruder with inscrutable unalarm. The water was like oil and the Nausikaa forged onward without any sensation of motion through a corridor without ceiling or floor." Then, without preliminary warning, the unnamed insects "were all about them, unseen with a dreadful bucolic"—that is, pastoral—"intentness; unlike their urban cousins, making no sound" (83).

Plagued, the *Nausikaa* must return to open water, and as night falls, the exiles languish in various poses of ennui. The poet Eva Wiseman—who has written a book called "Satyricon in Starlight"—apostrophizes the moon in appropriately decadent form: "Ah, Moon, poor weary one. . . . By yon black moon," and the poet Mark Frost replies, "No wonder it looks tired. . . . Think of how much adultery it's had to look upon." "Or assume the blame for," the widowed Eva amends, wishing aloud that she were in love and that the effete Frost and the prissy Taliaferro were "more . . . more . . ."—an unfinished thought, though the message is clear: she wishes the two aesthetes were more sexually aggressive, though she has, not long before, fled the bold sexual playfulness of Dawson Fairchild and Major Ayers (96).

By midnight, the sky is hazed over, obscuring the stars, and a storm is brewing up the lake—but the literary moon is still visible, "still undimmed, bland and chill, affable and bloodless as a successful procuress, bathing the yacht in quiet silver; and across the southern sky went a procession of small clouds, like silver dolphins on a rigid ultramarine wave, like an ancient geographical woodcut" (99). The visual arts vocabulary freezes the scene into expressionist theater. In the night, Patricia's twin brother Josh disables the steering mechanism of their aunt's yacht by borrowing a metal linking-piece to assist his work on a newfangled pipe, a three-inch cylinder of wood he carries with him everywhere—yet another fetich? As a consequence, the following dawn, the *Nausikaa* is not only rudderless, like many of the people on it, but also aground. Patricia Robyn looks toward the shore with the captain's binoculars: "she saw a blur in two colors, but presently"—as she adjusts the lenses—"the blur became trees startlingly distinct and separate leaf by leaf and bough by bough, and pendants of rusty green moss were beards of contemplative goats ruminating among the trees and above a yellow strip of beach and a smother of foam in which the sun hung little fleeting rainbows" (121). She likewise magnifies the ship's steward, whom she's hardly noticed until now, and begins to plot a romantic escape from boredom, tempting the steward to run away with her to the shore, where they will strike out for the town of Mandeville, the terminus of a regular excursion route from the city and a kind of Gretna Green—that is, a place where runaway marriages and sexual liaisons without benefit of marriage also were easily made (220).

The episodes devoted to the adventures of Patricia and David in the swamp are among the most sexually suggestive in the novel. In Faulkner's handwritten manuscript for *Mosquitoes*, which turned up only a few years ago,[7] the narrative of Patricia and David's inconclusive flight from the *Nausikaa* takes a different form from the way it is presented in the novel's typescript and first edition. In the manuscript, which appears to be a first draft and has numerous interlineations and marginal revisions, the episode in the swamp is continuous, an unrelenting flight through enveloping heat, stagnant water, and assaults of punishing insects by two half-dressed and unprepared young people. Read as Faulkner penned it his manuscript, especially, the episode compounds the effect for which Faulkner was reaching in the novel: that is, to eroticize nature variously as a dark trope expressing sexual exhaustion or futility. In the typescript that is the basis for the published book, Faulkner broke the episode into many parts, alternating, or counterpointing, short spans of the couple's experience with largely comic scenes back on the yacht.

The episode begins with a naked Patricia taking a predawn swim in mist that temporarily obscures the *Nausikaa*. Alone, she swims beyond where she can see the boat, nearly panics, but succeeds in coming back, and then must climb aboard and walk across the deck beneath the spellbound David's doglike gaze at the "startling white bathing suit" of her nakedness. When she comes back on deck in her flapper's short linen dress, Patricia orders David to grab bread, bacon, and oranges from the ship's galley, to row ashore and contrive with a rope that the boat is returned to the yacht. They eat the food immediately, but not before the vast primality of the forest nearly overpowers them:

> Trees heavy and ancient with moss loomed out of it hugely and grayly: the mist might have been a sluggish growth between and among them. No, this mist might have been the first prehistoric morning of time itself; it might have been the very substance in which the seed of the beginning of things fecundated; and these huge and silent trees might have been the first of living things, too recently born to know either fear or astonishment, dragging their sluggish umbilical cords from out the old miasmic womb of a nothingness latent and dreadful. . . . "Gee," she said in a small voice. (169)

They wait for the mist to clear, wraithlike, "swaying and swinging like hugh spectral apes from tree to tree" and they move away from the lakeshore, so they won't be seen from the yacht. David makes a fire while Patricia "paused at the edge of a black stream to harry a sluggish thick serpent with a small switch" and a "huge gaudy bird came up and cursed her, and the snake ignored her with a sort of tired unillusion and plopped heavily into the thick water," a symbolist scene evoking sexuality (huge spectral apes), the puniness (a "small switch") of Patricia's ability to repel the ancient signifier of sin and guilt and youth's enemy, time, and a mockery of deity that might have come out of Flaubert, the gaudy bird that curses her for playing with the snake (171). Then, like furies, the mosquitoes descend upon them like a cloud of fire and drive them away. They see a road, but between them and the raised road is "a foul sluggish width of water and vegetation and biology"—certainly not diction a naturalist would use—and trees that pay little regard to the "puny desecration of a silence of air and earth and water ancient when hoary old Time himself was a pink and dreadful miracle in his mother's arms" (174). The affair envisioned by the two young people grows worse and worse, more punishing, more exhausting. "The swamp did not seem to end, ever. On either side of the road it brooded, fetid and timeless, somber and hushed and dreadful . . . beneath a sinister brass sky"(177). David cannot take his eyes off the blotches of dead blood on Patricia's stockings; she grows faint and distraught, crying out "They hurt me, they hurt me" in an "impossible spasm of agony," and David is powerless to help her, though he tries to find drinking water and he gives her his shirt to repel the insects after she has "dragged her dress up about her shoulders, revealing her startling white bathing suit between her knickers and the satin band binding her breasts" (179–80). This is a far cry from Odysseus's encounter with Nausikaa and her maidens, who are washing their underclothes when the hero emerges from the water, and perhaps it is also a wry commentary upon the underwear scene Joyce made of this in the Nausikaa chapter of *Ulysses* where, sitting at the shore, the onanist Bloom—Faulkner's lingerie salesman Taliaferro, recall, "had never even" learned to masturbate—spies Gerty MacDowell's underwear, and Gerty spies him spying. It is Patricia who has arranged this tryst, however, and it's she who remains in charge, despite her discomfort, taking much from David and conventionally promising to make it up to him someday, though she does not. After succumbing to exhaustion himself, he finds that she has, indeed, taken them in the wrong direction, but at this moment a local boatman comes along to carry them back to the *Nausikaa,* insulting David's manhood all the way until Patricia curses him roundly and shuts him up. Back aboard the yacht, David is left to sit on a coiled rope holding one of Patricia's "cracked and stained . . . disreputable" slippers, the same fetich Faulkner will later put into the hands of Benjy Compson, as he stares "across the dark water and its path of shifting silver" (235). The boat is repaired and returns to port. Like most of the passengers, David goes his own way as soon as they dock. In the aftermath, the three wisest men on the trip—Fairchild, the semitic man Julius, and the sculptor Gordon—share a drunken walk through the French Quarter, encountering prostitutes, priests, and beggars, but the natural world dissolves into a hallucinatory darkness.

In the novel, it is Patricia's brother Josh who observes that "literature is art and biology isn't," and Dawson Fairchild who makes Wildean claims for the superiority of fiction-making over the untidiness of the natural world, so they would doubtless agree with the modernist precept that Nature does not construct reality, and that "the many appearances in the world are less 'true' than the abstract design produced by their juxtaposition."[8] Clive Bell's famous essay on art[9] is paraphrased and makes yet another useful exposition of the antinature aesthetic:

> Surely, it is not what I call an aesthetic emotion that most of us feel, generally, for natural beauty. . . . I am satisfied that, as a rule, most people feel a very different kind of emotion for birds and flowers and the wings of butterflies from that which they feel for pictures, pots, temples, and statues. (20)

Faulkner's point of view regarding the natural world, then—at this juncture in his career, at any rate—is doubtless that he may do whatever is necessary with the natural world to render the world according to art.

Though we hardly yet know how much, Faulkner read a great deal and he remembered everything, so our Mississippi writer (who spent so many crucial years receiving a literary education) is, like many poets, one of those who entered nature, as Lawrence

Buell has reminded us, as a writer, through a literary sensibility, not as a naturalist.[10] As he constructed that literary sensibility, Faulkner entered nature more and more through his own previous perceptions, judgments, and expressions of nature. If, as he sometimes tries to convince us, Faulkner grew up in the rural South and was barely half-educated—both untruths, of course, but let us suppose that he was rural but could read—why doesn't he come on in a more naturalistic and less literary mode? Why isn't he the agrarian nature poet Cleanth Brooks wanted him to be?[11] One explanation lies in a clearer perspective on the environment in which Faulkner was born and matured. The historian Jack Kirby, in his marvelous study of cotton agriculture in the South, *Rural Worlds Lost*, has written that the minute Southern planters sold their first bales of cotton on the world market they lost any claim to the term agrarian. Then the Civil War, as many historians have shown, brought the first modern war—long before The Great War—onto Southern ground, and, to quote Kirby at some length:

> The ravages of Civil War and the emancipation without compensation of southern slaves presented profound problems and wrung some structural changes [in Southern culture], but the South remained a plantation society. Cultivation of cotton, tobacco, and other export staples actually expanded, as did the dependency of the region upon outside capital and markets. Commensurately, southern subregions previously independent of the world system, shrank. The former slaves, and ultimately hundreds of thousands of whites who had formerly lived outside the plantation districts, were drawn into an American version of labor and credit dependency known in virtually all the regions of the world after the end of slavery. Towns and cities and certain manufactures grew throughout the late nineteenth and early twentieth centuries, but most were of a special sort. Urban centers acted as regional branches of northern and European sources of credit, supply, and transportation; factories specialized in preliminary processing of minerals (as with the Birmingham, Alabama, steel complex) or of forest products or made textiles in the piedmont near newer cotton fields. Before World War I there was little outside the region to attract southern migrants. Farm tenancy, especially the lowest, most dependent kind, sharecropping, expanded at dismaying rates through the 1920s, then worsened during the early 1930s.[12]

"So," he concludes, "the South in the second quarter of the twentieth century was more modern, in the traditional sense of the word, than ever" and expansion of "plantation production areas"— that is, large one-crop farms—"always amounted to an expansion of 'modernity' and the end of isolated, 'premodern' rural life in southern subregions where the plantations and staple culture spread," gradually destroying "the traditional structure of life in the hill country" as timbermen followed railroaders and in turn were followed by planters and crop-lien merchants and bankers. "Open lands were alienated, squatters and landless herdsmen were converted into tenants, and the local barter and labor-exchange economy was wrecked" (27).

Lest we think these are modern, revisionist opinions, consider the words of the 1938 Works Progress Administration Mississippi Guide, which, recall, was supposed to be an upbeat advertisement for state tourism, regarding the part of north Mississippi where Faulkner grew up and wrote:

> When the war completely upset the economy upon which ante-bellum prosperity had been based, it not only destroyed surplus capital but also fixed on the state the share-cropping and credit system—the enemy of diversification and the chain that binds the tenant to the merchant-banker and to poverty. The merchant-banker has continuously demanded that cotton, and cotton alone, be grown to repay his financial advances. Yet, repeated sowing of this basic crop on clay hillsides caused sheet erosion. Great red gullies have consumed the fertility of the land, until today an occasional ante-bellum mansion teetering crazily on the edge of a 50-foot precipice offers mute evidence of the decay Faulkner has seen fit to depict in his novels.[13]

This experience of what happens when materialism, not good agricultural practice, tries to rule over nature, Kirby points out, "was a southern version of a process known to most of the peoples of the world" (118).

As his fellow Mississippians could attest in 1938, William Faulkner was witness to and a product of this process of the transformation and degradation of the natural world in north Mississippi and throughout the South. For all the neo-Agrarian assumptions to the contrary, Faulkner did not rise up out of what we might, with large capitals, call Pastoral Southern Nature. He experienced the boy life of small-town north Mississippi, to be sure, but several factors made this less bucolic than it might have been had he grown up in a more remote or more rural place. Oxford was a university town and a county and regional judicial center linked by rail and roads and newspapers to the burgeoning modern world. Faulkner's great-grandfather may have been a Civil War legend to him and his brothers when they were young, but to northern Mississippi he was also a legend of post-Civil War enterprise, a lawyer, planter, railroad builder, and local and regional booster. Faulkner's grandfather was a lawyer, banker, a member of the Board of Trustees of the University of Mississippi. His father was the quintessential small-town entrepreneurial dabbler of the twentieth century, town-bred himself yet out of step with the changing economic life around him. Rather like the younger Jason Compson—but, remember, growing up in a region now suffering from the results of environmentally thoughtless modern capitalism—he seems to have lived out a life in which success was just behind him or just ahead—the diminutive family railroad he wasn't allowed to bid for when it went on the market or the livery stable he opened, after giving up the Standard Oil Company franchise, just as the automobile came into vogue. (Someday we might see that as an heroic defiance.)

William Faulkner spent his life in towns and cities, and while he early on adopted the habit of worshipping Nature as found in other people's poems, he left no evidence that he was, at least in the first half of his career, an inveterate student or even a close observer of the natural world. Its general rhythms—cycles of seasons, cycles of the day—with a preference for the twilit and the autumnal, sufficed for the purposes of the psychological dramas he drove himself to write. Though at a few points in his life he was a prodigious walker, some of it was on golf courses, and it seems clear that he covered the most ground in automobiles and trains, later briefly in airplanes, and that he used these modes of modern transportation to visit not spots of unspoiled nature but cities where urban pleasures were his goal. Not for Faulkner the fair and often isolating summers in the upper peninsula of Michigan, with canoe and rod and rifle, of Ernest Hemingway. I don't remember it being recorded that Faulkner ever caught a difficult fish— though he had a fishing license—or felled a noble game animal, or kept a close record of the ecology of the woods. As his stepson's memoir *Bitterweeds* recalls, he was a strict game warden regarding Bailey's Woods, where he liked to ride his horses later, but he was apparently never tempted to investigate the minutiae of its flora in what we would call a Thoreauvian manner.[14]

Faulkner's doom, instead, as he would put it later, was to transfer his ambitions from simply trying to be *different* in a small town where, because of his father's lack of professional success, he felt déclassé in the face of well-to-do lawyers' and doctors' families, to becoming an aviator in World War I, to writing books. In "Verse Old and Nascent," published in the New Orleans *Double Dealer* in April 1925, after he had been in the city several months, he confesses that he tackled verse first for "advancing various philanderings" in which he was engaged, but that Housman's "Shropshire Lad" closed the period of his search for a poetic style because in it he found what he was seeking: "the splendor of fortitude" and "the beauty of being of the soil."[15] The last phrase is, however, almost an advertisement for Faulkner's first book, *The Marble Faun*, in the preface to which Phil Stone claims that these are "poems of youth and a simple heart," "poems of a mind that reacts directly to sunlight and trees and skies and blue hills," poems "drenched in sunlight and color as is the land in which they were written, the land which gave birth and sustenance to their author" who has "roots in this soil as surely and inevitably as has a tree."[16] One wonders whether Stone had read the poems he had paid to publish. But Stone, we know, would say anything to advance Faulkner in whatever direction he wanted Faulkner to take. Stone, after all, had impersonated the nonexistent Rev. Twimberly-Thorndyke in order to write Faulkner a spurious recommendation so that he could enter the Royal Air Force as a displaced Briton, and, according to Susan Snell in her brilliant life of Stone, the

Oxford lawyer later penned numerous letters of introduction to literary figures in Europe whom he actually did not know for Faulkner to carry and use when he went abroad[17] (105, 180). The poplar trees in the grey garden of Faulkner's prologue to *The Marble Faun* are not the familiar tulip poplars of Southern woods, but the phallic and regularly spaced Lombardy poplars, set like shrubs, that he stylized in drawings that accompany the 1920 dream play *Marionettes*. *The Marble Faun* evokes otherwise a world of craggy mountains, snow, copses, heaths, rooks, and nightingales not common in north Mississippi, along with generalized references to more usual fauna: oak, beech, cherry, and so on, and all, of course, from the point of view of a dissatisfied piece of statuary in an urban garden. At this stage of his career, and on through *Soldiers' Pay*, *Mosquitoes*, and *Flags in the Dust* (a.k.a. *Sartoris*), Faulkner, then, is one of those writers who, as Buell suggests, is more likely to abstract us from physical nature than direct us toward it. *Mosquitoes* does, however, as *The Marble Faun* does not, satirize the "hyper-civilization of urban life." As urban pastoral, the portrayal of "playful exuberance and amatory despair" among the idle in *Mosquitoes* hardly represents what Buell could call a "green consciousness" (Buell 31–32), yet its satiric portrayal of the excesses of modernity spares almost nothing, including that peculiar shepherd of the swamps, Claude Jackson, who turns into a shark. Unlike William Bartram, whom Buell exonerates from complicit utopianism in a "settler pastoral" to inspire immigration into new territories, Faulkner does not absolve the wilderness of its alligators and mosquitoes. Faulkner does achieve another thing that Buell remarks, that is, the dramatization in *Mosquitoes* of something like D. H. Lawrence's judgment that "nature-quest narratives" acted out "struggles between libidinal and repressive forces" (Buell 33). It seems likely that Faulkner read Lawrence's 1923 *Studies in Classic American Literature*, which may, in fact, have influenced his reading of a 1922 copy of *Moby-Dick* purchased by Phil Stone.[18] Lawrence's view, Buell points out, was that such dramatizations were unconscious expression in writers such as Melville, but Faulkner's is certifiably conscious and deliberate, as his reference to Freud and his use of the Freudian vocabulary prove.

Reference to such a psychological struggle reminds us, I think, of Faulkner's main topic, not nature but human nature, and leads naturally to consideration of the remarkable mature novel by Faulkner I alluded to earlier. About a decade—and eleven novels—after writing *Mosquitoes,* Faulkner returned (actually, for the second time: *Pylon* of 1935 was the first) to the setting of his second novel, New Orleans, to the site of some of its writing, Pascagoula, Mississippi, and to many of its themes and formal devices. He did so with much greater artistic success. *If I Forget Thee, Jerusalem,* as Faulkner wished to call it—evoking the 137th Psalm and *The Brothers Karamazov*[19]—is another novel about the "unnatural" natural behavior of humans in highly sexualized environments. As we all know, it presents two intricately related stories in deliberate counterpoint, both with titles that function like the title *"Mosquitoes."* That is, the "wild palms"—which, at his publisher's insistence became the title of the published book as well as of the primary story—are, like the mosquitoes, a troubling and symbolic natural background noise—specifically, the wild dry clashing of cabbage palm fronds in the persistent coastal winds of Pascagoula, Mississippi. The term also refers to the complicated work of human hands, work that includes a perverse satiric art and a botched abortion as well as the compelling pull of desire and romantic hope. The "old man" of the secondary story is both the Mississippi River in a terrific out-of-bounds one hundred year flood—historically, the 1927 inundation of the Delta regions of Mississippi and Arkansas—and the archetypal adventures of one of the South's nameless tall men—a former hill country farm boy whose romantic hopes have resulted in a ten-year jail sentence for a botched train robbery. The tall convict, as he is known only, expresses a Jungian primality that is exposed when he is released from his comfortable open-air prison (good bunks, square meals, cameradie, baseball, and his own mule) and sent out upon the torrent to rescue flood victims. The flood will sweep him hither and thither through a mad landscape where rules of order are violated, where he must struggle with atavistic beasts and the terminal pregnancy of his one passenger until he is deposited in New Orleans and starts to make his way back upriver through a devastated but refecundated landscape.

Mosquitoes and *If I Forget Thee, Jerusalem* share cities, rivers, swamps, even the French Quarter haunts of artists, for it is in such a place that the fated lovers of "Wild Palms" meet. Though both novels use the natural world to dramatize libidinal conflict and sexuality in general, in *Mosquitoes* nothing really happens. In fact, the skein of affairs that begins with Mr. Taliaferro announcing that the "sex instinct" is his strongest compulsion ends with Mr. Taliaferro putting his tin box of condoms—the same Three Merry Widows (Agnes, Mabel, Becky) brand that Luster finds evidence of in *The Sound and the Fury*—unused, back into their accustomed place in his bureau drawer (Arnold 152). But in *If I Forget Thee, Jerusalem,* acts with or against nature have severe consequences. That nothing happens in *Mosquitoes* was doubtless one of Faulkner's main points about the milieu he portrayed. By the time he wrote *If I Forget Thee, Jerusalem*, obviously he understood much more about what made for dramatic writing, and he was far more skilled at evoking the natural and symbolic power of the environment. What Faulkner had done in *Mosquitoes* by inscribing sexual entanglement upon nature, by signifying the lure of sex as an endless, painful, debilitating flight through a miasma of responsibility and betrayal, brooded over by indifferent gods, he does realistically in *If I Forget Thee, Jerusalem* by dramatizing directly the odyssey of adulterous runaway lovers who flee New Orleans by train, having sex in a hastily procured sleeping cubicle, and go to Chicago, where their "bitching," as Charlotte Rittenmeyer is prone to call sex, is increasingly confounded by the respectability and routine into which the lives of working people fall. In this novel, Faulkner uses the old vulgarities—that is, the specific forbidden names of sexual organs and basic human acts—to address the old verities. When his couple escapes north of Chicago into the kind of nature that bred Ernest Hemingway's love of the outdoor life, the autumnal scene gives his central character Harry morbid thoughts out of the philosophy of Schopenhauer and the poems of Sara Teasdale—dead leaves embracing their images in the still waters—and Charlotte, a smart urban artist, finds that she cannot capture the motion of animals in the woods. So, mouthing hedonism, they go to what must be the worst possible environment: a frozen Utah mining camp, where Harry—who isn't really a doctor yet—takes a job as the required medical person and becomes part of the mine owners' plot to exploit the foreign workers. In this frozen wasteland, Charlotte's douche bag freezes and bursts and so she becomes pregnant and that, as Hemingway might have put it, starts to ruin everything.

In *Mosquitoes*, Faulkner had the instinct, apparently after writing his swamp piece one way, to divide the episodes of his young lovers' symbolic flight and to alternate the little sections in counterpoint with scenes back on the yacht. His purpose—or at least his effect—was not so much to heighten either set of episodes and probably not even to use one set of events to play off the other, but to create artificial suspense for anticlimactic material. He might have done better, had he been more skilled, counterpointing the adventures of lost youths fetching up in increasingly hot, wet, painful, exhausting swampland with a little more bedroom farce on the yacht. *If I Forget Thee, Jerusalem*, by contrast, employs contrapuntal design brilliantly in a thoroughgoing way. The psychological story of the lovers certainly portrays the natural world in which they move to symbolize the sexuality that is central to their story—from the romantically decaying fountain in the New Orleans courtyard where they fall in love, to the snowbound Utah landscape with its barren gash of a mine where they conceive a child, to the barren illicit cottage on the burning Mississippi beach where Charlotte dies of septicemia. But the primary job of using nature to concretize an archetype of what is going on with the lovers is in the contrapuntal story, "Old Man," where Faulkner also does some of his best nature writing. In "Old Man" nature displaces humankind so thoroughly that Faulkner gives his characters nothing but generic names—the tall convict, the plump convict, the woman in the boat. As dramatic counterpoint, the con-

vict's being hauled out in the middle of the night to fight an ep-
ochal flood, his being swept away with a pregnant woman in a
small boat on rivers going backwards, and his struggle through
snake- and alligator-infested landscapes in an atmosphere always
dissolving beneath him read as the awful power of sex and the
paradoxical human predicament under its rule, not just libido versus repression, but desire versus disappointment, bondage versus
freedom, even life versus death, in the sexual relationship between
woman and man.

Nature, in *If I Forget Thee, Jerusalem*, as is said of the Mississippi River in a hundred-year flood by the beleaguered convict,
actually is "now doing what it liked to do"[20] (135). An observation
like that doesn't make *If I Forget Thee, Jerusalem* a green novel,
yet many elements of the book do reflect Faulkner's evolving critique of things that were occurring in the natural environment that
he knew best. The flood on which he draws is the great 1927 flood
of the Mississippi, occurring in the spring that *Mosquitoes* was
published, but there had been a serious flood in 1917 and another
in 1937, the year he wrote his novel. The cause of these floods can
be traced to the lumbermen and railroads that stripped the Southern watersheds starting after the Civil War, part of that commercial nexus, as Jack Kirby explains to us in detail in *Rural Worlds
Lost*, that imposed modernity upon the rural South. The tall convict ironically has a better life working the crops of the Mississippi
state prison farm than he would have if he had become a sharecropper, and so his one taste of freedom during the flood convinces
him that it is better to abjure romance and even his successful—
though absurd—struggles with primal nature and return to a simpler bondage in the regimented prison with its warm bunkhouse
and fields that could, as far as he is concerned, contain papier-
mâché crops (26). He had, by the way, gotten his original prison
term by trying to rob a train, inspired by pulp fiction. Modernism
in rural Mississippi indeed.

Harry and Charlotte flee through late-Depression-era America,
and the barren mining camp, where Harry is the spurious medical
authority, doubtless seems even bleaker for the exploited work-

ers—a place that the then-trapped Hollywood film writer Faulkner describes as conceived by Sergei Eisenstein to depict Dante's
hell (157). In San Antonio, where they go next, Harry gets a WPA
job as a school crossing guard but we see nothing of the landscape,
and their final and pregnable refuge, a cottage on the Gulf coast,
is more truly nature according to Dante than even the mining
camp: as Charlotte lies dying they are on a burning beach where
Harry gathers needless firewood and the wind—something, the
novel tells us, you let into the womb to produce an abortion—
makes for the nerve-wracking arid rattle of the wild palms. Once
Harry is jailed for causing Charlotte's death by botching the abortion, he can see the source of the bad smell that naturalizes one of
Charlotte's metaphors—she had said that if you weren't good
enough for love, it was like the ocean and threw you up on the
beach to become a bad smell, and she had even made a papier-
mâché figure by that name, The Bad Smell, a kind of mojo to ward
off their fate; Harry sees now that what he smells arises from the
dumps of commercial fisheries. It is an environment where modernity has conquered, his landlord the kind of person who "born and
bred in sight of the sea had for taste in fish a predilection for
the tuna, the salmon, the sardines bought in cans, immolated and
embalmed three thousand miles away in the oil of machinery and
commerce" (9). Contrast this with the convicts' first glimpse of the
flood:

> It was perfectly motionless, perfectly flat. It looked, not innocent, but
> bland. It looked almost demure. It looked as if you could walk on it. It
> looked so still that they did not realise it possessed motion until they
> came to the first bridge. There was a ditch under the bridge, a small
> stream, but ditch and stream were both invisible now, indicated only
> by the rows of cypress and bramble which marked its course. Here
> they both saw and heard movement—the slow profound eastward and
> upstream . . . set of the still rigid surface, from beneath which came a
> deep faint subaquean rumble. . . . It was is if the water itself were in
> three strata, separate and distinct, the bland and unhurried surface
> bearing a frothy scum and a miniature flotsam of twigs and screening
> as though by vicious calculation the rush and fury of the flood itself,
> and beneath this in turn the original stream, trickle, murmuring along

in the opposite direction, following undisturbed and unaware its appointed course. (53–54)

Going backward, going forward, sitting still, nature overtakes and
overwhelms the tall convict again and again, doing what it liked to
do. Though satiric, and often comic, *If I Forget Thee, Jerusalem* is
not urban pastoral nor does it abstract us from physical nature.

Faulkner's next two novels following *If I Forget Thee, Jerusalem*
are *The Hamlet* and *Go Down, Moses,* his works the most identified with his sympathetic and realistic treatment of the natural
world. He was, in fact, working on the material eventually collected into these two books when he took time out to counterpoint
"Wild Palms" with "Old Man." The three books are not so different as one might suppose. What occurred in Southern agriculture
from the 1870s to the turn of the century is brilliantly presented
in *The Hamlet*, but Faulkner portrays the results not so much in
economic and agricultural terms as in erotic ones, where the fecund yet indifferent Eula Varner at one level represents nature as
tragic pawn in a world of feckless farmers and sharecroppers, some
too venal, others too dispirited, to approach and use nature or sex
properly. *Go Down, Moses,* in a measure similar to *The Hamlet*,
makes the fate of the natural world—the plantation and the wilderness—a direct reflection, and even a result, of erotic events: dou-
bled incest, marriage bed politics, philandering, as well as lasting
married love. Good farming is like good sex: it doesn't require
a piece of paper denoting ownership, but it does require good
husbandry, and for that one must have a decent political and economic environment, a sense of self-worth, as well as respect for
the rhythms of the natural world. Violation of simple and observ-
able natural relations—whether erotic, racial, or ecological—
produces negative human results with long-lasting consequences.
The farm and the hunting ground are intertwined, interrelated,
and you cannot live a good life in one without living a good life in
the other, and vice versa. The reluctant celibate messianist Ike
McCaslin is wrong about land and agriculture because he is wrong
about sex and race, whereas the successful Lucas Beauchamp is,
with an occasional struggle, generally right about them all.

If William Faulkner eroticized nature practically out of existence in such early novels as *Mosquitoes*, and used the landscape
solely as a background to reflect the mood of his characters, in *If I
Forget Thee, Jerusalem* he did not. Any materialization of nature is
limiting—and the special pleading of any fiction necessarily prog-
nosticates the "kind" of nature that can appear in it. Nature, as an
abstraction constructed by those who imagine or write about it and
even from the perspective of observant naturalists, is ideologically
constructed. The way nature is "oversexed" in *Mosquitoes* says
much about the importance of sex—and cleverness about sex—to
William Faulkner, but recall this is a novel in which sex itself is
manifested chiefly by the sexually dysfunctional. Where sex is
more directly manifested, without romantic idealization, it often
becomes grotesque in the way that Mikhail Bakhtin speaks of the
grotesque—vital and productive, polluted and taboo, a carnivaliza-
tion of the misty ideology of romantic sex. This is what we see in
If I Forget Thee, Jerusalem—and in *The Hamlet* and *Go Down,
Moses*. In *If I Forget Thee, Jerusalem* and the two subsequent
books, nature is similarly constructed by Faulkner as antic, perverse, powerful, mysterious, but nowhere is nature as grotesque,
as carnivalesque as in the "Old Man" section of *If I Forget Thee,
Jerusalem* where the crazy streams, the hither and thither tributaries of the Mississippi finally erupt the tall convict and his pregnant
anonymous passenger, the carnivalesque mock-king and mock-
queen, into the great river itself:

> Sometime about midnight, accompanied by a rolling cannonade of
> thunder and lighting like a battery going into action, as though some
> forty hours' constipation of the elements, the firmament itself, were
> discharging in clapping and glaring salute to the ultimate acquiescence
> to desperate and furious motion, and still leading its charging welter
> of dead cows and mules and outhouses and cabins and hencoops, the
> skiff passed Vicksburg. . . . But he didn't see Vicksburg; the skiff, trav-
> elling at express speed, was in a seething gut between soaring and
> dizzy banks with a glare of light above them but he did not see it; he
> saw the flotsam ahead of him divide violently and begin to climb upon
> itself, mounting, and he was sucked through the resulting gap too fast
> to recognise it as the trestling of a railroad bridge; for a horrible mo-

ment the skiff seemed to hang in static indecision before the looming
flank of a steamboat as though undecided whether to climb over it or
dive under it, then a hard icy wind filled with the smell and taste and
sense of wet and boundless desolation blew upon him; the skiff made
one long bounding lunge as the convict's native state, in a final paroxysm, regurgitated him onto the wild bosom of the Father of Waters.
(134)

The equivalent moment in the love story is Harry and Charlotte's
nearly naked idyll on the Wisconsin Lake and their decision to
leave civilization and head for the frozen mining camp where they
will not be able to make love for a long time, because they share
the bunkhouse with a couple who play in bed like wild horses, and
when the young couple from the South finally do make love, after
the Buckners have left, Charlotte conceives because their
wretched gas heater goes out and her douche bag freezes and
bursts and so she has no birth control. The juxtaposition—like all
those in *If I Forget Thee, Jerusalem*—is stunning, and it does not
allow us to forget, or abstract, either nature or human affairs.

This is, I believe, how Faulkner understood the natural world.
The tour de force of the later novel is, of course, understandably,
the kind of thing the author of *Mosquitoes* could not do. That he
learned to do it, however, is why his work remains so important to
writers of all genders all over the world who have meditated in
fiction on the natural world.

NOTES

1. Deborah Schnitzer, *The Pictorial in Modernist Fiction from Stephen Crane to Ernest
Hemingway* (Ann Arbor: UMI Research Press, 1988), 87.

2. *Mosquitoes* (New York: Boni & Liveright, 1927), [8].

3. As in his first novel, *Soldiers' Pay*, Faulkner demonstrates a well-controlled, if wry,
awareness of Freud's *The Psychopathology of Everyday Life* and *Three Essays on the Theory of Sexuality*.

4. Canby, "Sex in Fiction," *Century* 105 (1922): 98–103.

5. The fragment "And Now What's to Do," possibly written at this time also, expresses
a similar fear in terms of spiderwebs and quicksand: "Like going after something you
wanted, and getting into a nest of spider webs. You got the thing, then you had to pick the
webs off, and every time you touched one, it stuck to you. Even after you didn't want the
thing anymore, the webs clung to you. . . . No. Quicksand. That was it. Wade through once,
then go on. But a man won't. He wants to go all the way through, somehow; break out on
the other side" (reprinted in *Mississippi Quarterly* 26 [Summer 1973]: 399–402).

6. In a letter to his mother from New Orleans, Faulkner specifically identified the Al

Jackson stories with the Sut Lovingood tales (James G. Watson, *Thinking of Home: William Faulkner's Letters to His Mother and Father, 1918–1925* [New York: Norton, 1992], 193).

7. William Faulkner, *Mosquitoes: A Facsimile and Transcription of the University of Virginia Holograph Manuscript* (Charlottesville: Bibliographical Society of the University of Virginia and the University of Virginia Library, 1997). This manuscript is not complete, though it constitutes more than a third of the novel. It differs structurally in several respects from the subsequent typescript and the published book. Though I have not been able to trace the provenance of these sheets beyond the Philadelphia dealer who sold them to the University of Virginia Faulkner Collection—a dealer who writes only that they came from the heirs of a deceased collector—it would not surprise me to learn that they passed at some time through the hands of the woman on whom Patricia Robyn was based, Helen Baird.

8. Jewel Spears Brooker, *Mastery and Escape: T. S. Eliot and the Dialectic of Modernism* (Amherst: University of Massachusetts Press, 1994), 31. The richness of allusion in *Mosquitoes* is revealed in Edwin Arnold's *Mosquitoes: Annotations to the Novel* (New York: Garland, 1993), a reference on which I have depended frequently in this discussion.

9. Arnold, page 23, points out the paraphrase to Clive Bell, *Art* (1913; New York: Capricorn, 1958).

10. Lawrence Buell, *The Environmental Imagination: Thoreau, Nature Writing, and the Formation of American Culture* (Cambridge: Belknap Press of Harvard University Press, 1995).

11. Brooks's chapter on "Faulkner as Nature Poet" is filled with idealizations that a close reader does not find in many of Faulkner's novels, including the wildly comic and, dare one say, oversexed *The Hamlet*, for which Brooks must write a chapter entitled "Faulkner's Savage Arcadia," a title more in keeping with the natural world we find in *As I Lay Dying, Sanctuary, Light in August, Absalom, Absalom!*, and *Go Down, Moses*, as well as *Mosquitoes* and *If I Forget Thee, Jerusalem* [*The Wild Palms*]. Brooks, *William Faulkner: The Yoknapatawpha Country* (New Haven: Yale University Press, 1963).

12. Jack Temple Kirby, *Rural Worlds Lost: The American South, 1920–1960* (Baton Rouge: Louisiana State University Press, 1987), 26–27.

13. *Mississippi: A Guide to the Magnolia State* (New York: Viking, 1938), 7.

14. Malcolm Franklin, *Bitterweeds: Life with William Faulkner at Rowan Oak* (Irving, Texas: The Society for the Study of Traditional Culture, 1977).

15. Faulkner's expression about seeking to be "different" in a small town occurs in "Verse Old and Nascent," published in the New Orleans *Double Dealer* in the spring of 1925 and reprinted in *William Faulkner: Early Prose and Poetry*, ed. Carvel Collins (Boston: Little, Brown, 1962), 114–18. The development of his "doom"—set in motion by reading books his grandmother had purchased on shopping trips to Memphis—is recounted in the introduction to *The Faulkner Reader* (New York: Random House, 1954). The account of feeling self-conscious about his father's business in the face of "genteel professions" is in the fictional fragment "And Now What's to Do," which appears to be very autobiographical.

16. Phil Stone, Preface to William Faulkner's *The Marble Faun* (1924). *The Marble Faun and A Green Bough* (New York: Random House, 1965), 6.

17. Susan Snell, *Phil Stone of Oxford: A Vicarious Life* (Athens: University of Georgia Press, 1991), 105, 180

18. Faulkner's brief but brilliant summary of the symbolic plot of Melville's novel was published in the summer of 1927, not long after the publication of *Mosquitoes*, in response to a request from the book editor of the *Chicago Tribune*, who wrote a number of recent authors to ask what book they would like to have written. Faulkner admired the "Greek-like simplicity" of the book and saw it as a "sort of Golgotha of the heart"—a phrase echoing *Mosquitoes*, where the character Dawson Fairchild speaks grandly about the "Passion Week of the Heart," as well as Sherwood Anderson's *Winesburg, Ohio*, wherein Dr. Parcival propounds his idea that everyone in the world is Christ and they are all crucified ("The Philosopher"). (Letter to the book editor of the *Chicago Tribune* reprinted in *William Faulkner: Essays, Speeches, and Public Letters*, ed. James B. Meriwether [New York: Random House, 1965], 197–98). Phil Stone had ordered *Moby-Dick* from the Brick Row Book

Shop in New Haven in 1922 (Joseph Blotner, comp., *William Faulkner's Library: A Catalogue* [Charlottesville: University Press of Virginia, 1964], 125).

    19. For evidence of these and other allusions in the novel, see my *William Faulkner's "The Wild Palms: A Study"* (Jackson: University Press of Mississippi, 1975).

    20. *If I Forget Thee, Jerusalem.* Corrected text, established by Noel Polk (New York: Vintage International, 1995), 35.

Unsurprised Flesh: Color, Race, and Identity in Faulkner's Fiction

THERESA M. TOWNER
For Jim Carothers

Cholly and Mrs. Breedlove fought each other with a darkly brutal formalism that was paralleled only by their lovemaking. Tacitly they had agreed not to kill each other. He fought her the way a coward fights a man—with feet, the palms of his hands, and teeth. She, in turn, fought back in a purely feminine way—with frying pans and pokers, and occasionally a flatiron would sail toward his head. They did not talk, groan, or curse during these beatings. There was only the muted sound of falling things, and flesh on unsurprised flesh.[1]

This passage from Toni Morrison's first novel describes perfectly the hopeless cycle of violence that characterizes the marriage of Pecola Breedlove's parents. Caught in the grinding small-town poverty of 1941 America, both Pauline and Cholly come to depend on these arguments to provide structure and meaning in life: her "tiny, undistinguished days" as a maid are redeemed by these "violent breaks in routine that were themselves routine" (41); and his "myriad . . . humiliations, defeats, and emasculations" are relieved temporarily by his chance to "touch and therefore hurt" his wife (42). In the Breedlove marriage we have a portrait of symbiotic cruelty that I think the creator of Caroline and Jason Compson would have appreciated, and I invoke it at a conference on Faulkner and the Natural World in order to begin an extended illustration of the ways in which Faulkner repeatedly investigates the concept of "the natural" in his representations of race. One of his

continuing appeals to me—a student of African-American literature and culture as well as of Faulkner—is his refusal to accept as
"natural" anything that is not literally of the flesh. Everything else
but that is somehow humanly constructed and hence infinitely
constructible. This constructedness is especially evident in and
characteristic of identity and culture, and we see that trait particularly in the various racial portraits throughout Faulkner's fiction,
in characters white and black.

Recent literary theory on the subject of race has taught us a
great deal about how such theories in the past have often been
dressed out as "natural" manifestations of either divine or human
will that, nevertheless, served some very concrete human economic ends. Henry Louis Gates, Jr., reminds us of the racial legacy
of the Enlightenment:

> Since the beginning of the seventeenth century, Europeans had wond-
> erered aloud whether or not the African "species of men," as they most
> commonly put it, could ever create formal literature, could ever master
> "the arts and sciences." If they could, the argument ran, then the Afri-
> can variety of humanity and the European variety were fundamentally
> related. If not, then it seemed clear that the African was destined by
> nature to be a slave.[2]

To the Europeans of the seventeenth, eighteenth, and nineteenth
centuries, writing was "the visible sign of reason itself"; its absence, evidence of inability to reason (9). The African and his descendants in the New World thus occupied a lower place on the
Great Chain of Being that classified all the elements of Nature
than the white man did, and for proof that the ranking was correct
all one need do was point tellingly to the absence of African writing. By the mid-eighteenth century, Gates says, philosophy itself,
in the voices of Hume and Kant, asserted "the fundamental identity of complexion, character, and intellectual capacity":

> [Hume wrote:] There never was a civilized nation of any other com-
> plexion than white, nor even any individual eminent either in action
> or speculation. No ingenious manufactures amongst them, no arts, no
> sciences. . . . Such a uniform and constant difference could not happen,
> in so many countries and ages, if nature had not made an original
> distinction between these breeds of men.

[Kant elaborated:] "So fundamental is the difference between [the black and white] races of man, . . . it appears to be as great in regard to mental capacities as in color." (10)[3]

In such ways did European philosophy seek to explain the "natural" relationship between color and intelligence.

Of course we can see at this remove that such a conflation was anything but natural; and if we still doubt its usefulness as a tool to reinforce the economic advantage of the white man of reason, we should recall that by the early eighteenth century teaching slaves to read and write was illegal in some parts of the United States. Frederick Douglass writes movingly of the moment that his mistress was forbidden by her husband to teach young Frederick the alphabet:

> I now understood what had been to me a most perplexing difficulty—to wit, the white man's power to enslave the black man. It was a grand achievement, and I prized it highly. From that moment, I understood the pathway from slavery to freedom. It was just what I wanted, and I got it at a time when I the least expected it. Whilst I was saddened by the thought of losing the aid of my kind mistress, I was gladdened by the invaluable instruction which, by the merest accident, I had gained from my master. Though conscious of the difficulty of learning without a teacher, I set out with high hope, and a fixed purpose, at whatever cost of trouble, to learn how to read.[4]

Douglass understood instantly upon being forbidden to read that there was nothing "natural" about the condition of life known as slavery—that it was a system instituted of man and thus one that could be escaped and ultimately dismantled. By the middle of the nineteenth century in Mississippi, however, this system had been very carefully inscribed as natural and race-mixing as unnatural: "Amalgamation is incest," Henry Hughes's *A Treatise on Sociology* proclaimed in 1854; "Impurity of race is against the law of nature. Mulattoes are monsters. The law of nature is the law of God. The same law which forbids consanguinous amalgamation forbids ethnical amalgamation. Both are incestuous."[5] By 1904, during Governor James K. Vardaman's administration, this radical journalist-turned-politician would assert, "You can scarcely pick up a news-

paper whose pages are not blackened with the account of an un-
mentionable crime committed by a negro brute, and this crime, I
want to impress upon you, is but the manifestation of the negro's
aspiration for social equality, encouraged largely by the character
of free education in vogue."[6] Nine years later (and now a Senator)
he elaborated: "I unhesitatingly assert that political equality for
the colored race leads to social equality. Social equality leads to
race amalgamation, and race amalgamation leads to deterioration
and disintegration."[7] Color, as Douglass knew, is biological; but
the racial category to which he belonged was culturally constructed and maintained, to the specific benefit of people like
James Vardaman. Similarly, Gates notes that scientifically speaking
(or "naturally" speaking, in the language of this conference), "race"
is a fiction, a term that "pretends to be an objective term of classification, when in fact it is a dangerous trope." Presently "we care-
lessly use language in such a way as to will this sense of natural
difference into our formulations [of issues]. To do so is to engage
in a pernicious act of language, one which exacerbates the complex
problem of cultural or ethnic difference, rather than to assuage or
redress it" (5).

I don't think Gates's analysis of "race" as a metaphor operating
within a certain ideological position would have surprised William
Faulkner, who was nothing if not an astute observer of the ways
human beings "engage in pernicious acts of language."[8] In fact,
there is throughout his work a deep suspicion of language and a
wariness on this issue of its meaning, its relationship to life. When
Addie Bundren says that "words dont ever fit even what they are
trying to say at"; when the narrator of "All the Dead Pilots" says
that human life "can be preserved and prolonged only on paper
. . . that any match . . . can obliterate in an instant"; and when the
direct result of Benjy's failed attempt to say his sister's name is his
castration: we see in each instance evidence of a writer writing
anxiously about the very vexed question of what "trying to say"
means.[9] Noting this more general obsession with language (spoken
and written), I would like now to analyze a few of Faulkner's specific representations of the kind of racial metaphors Gates has de-

scribed—the dangerous tropes of difference that appear at key junctures in his fiction. By doing so I hope finally to explain Faulkner's treatments of race as evidence of his interest in the ways that humans try to invent, and reinvent, themselves and their neighbors according to willful and carefully tended conceptions of "the natural."

Dumping the Body

When Mink Snopes shoots Jack Houston in *The Hamlet*, he is convinced that he acts upon high moral principle. Upon seeing the body, he has to suppress the desire "to leave a printed placard on the breast itself: *This is what happens to the men who impound Mink Snopes' cattle*, with his name signed to it."[10] Practical instincts of self-preservation tell Mink that he must not sign his action. Instead,

> He must rise and quit the thicket and do what he had next to do, not to finish it but merely to complete the first step of what he had started, put into motion, who realised now that he had known already, before he heard the horse and raised the gun, that that would happen which had happened: that he had pulled trigger on an enemy but had only slain a corpse to be hidden. (242)

Following this passage is the lengthy scene in which Mink hides Houston's body by shoving it into a hollow tree, only to have to remove it later and try to hide it permanently from Houston's howling dog. In those passages we see how stubborn flesh is, living or not, human or not:

> . . . he knew now it was not imagination he had smelled and he dropped the axe and began to tear at the shell with his hands, his head averted, his teeth bared and clenched, his breath hissing through them. . . .
> When the body came suddenly free, he went over backward, lying on his back in the mud, the body across his legs, while the hound stood over it, howling. He got up and kicked at it. It moved back, but when he stooped and took hold of the legs and began to walk backward, the hound was beside him again. [Mink fights off the dog temporarily.] He picked up the ankles, facing forward now, and tried to run.

... He stooped; once more he raised the body which was half again his size, and hurled it outward into the mist and, even as he released it, springing after it, catching himself back just before he followed it, seeing at the instant of its vanishing the sluggish sprawl of three limbs where there should have been four, and recovering balance to turn, already running as the pattering rush of the hound whispered behind him and the animal struck him in the back. (280–82)

First-time readers are struck by the gruesomeness of these scenes, by the steadily accumulating details of Mink's effort to rid himself of Houston's corpse. Returning to them in the context of an examination of the natural world, I note Faulkner's evenhanded distribution of stubbornness: Mink, the dog, and the body itself all seem to struggle against one another; the dog and the body are just as determined to resist and expose Mink as he is to conceal and dispose of each of them.

I think of this episode as the equivalent in Faulkner's natural world of a primal scene. Mink brings the ordeal on himself because he has "pulled trigger on an enemy"—what in Gates's terms we might call a "dangerous trope"—but has instead "only slain a corpse to be hidden"; consequently, he faces the monumental problem of what to do with what his "enemy" really is—a collection of bones and flesh, subject to death and decay.

In Faulkner's fiction we see characters repeatedly facing Mink's problem of what to do with a body. Addie Bundren's beleaguered corpse is the obvious example, but think too of how the Compsons solve the various problems presented by Benjy's growing body, which whimpers, cries, and bellows uncontrollably and more loudly as he matures. In *Intruder in the Dust*, Chick Mallison, Miss Habersham, and Aleck Sander try to exhume Vinson Gowrie's body to prove Lucas Beauchamp innocent of his murder; in *Light in August*, the mutilation of Joe Christmas's body ends a life full of uncertainty and violence, and the man who wields the knife himself moves in "blind obedience to whatever Player moved him on the Board"[11]; *Sanctuary* depends wholly on Temple's violated body; and even *Soldiers' Pay* has at the center of its action the mute and wounded person of Donald Mahon. My point is that

Faulkner's eye is never far from the one constant natural element of the human—the body itself—and his attention is everywhere engaged by the problem of how individual characters respond to that one constant natural human element.

Coffee and Milk

Flesh in Faulkner's natural world comes in many colors. Uncle Buddy McCaslin looks "like an old gray rock or a stump with gray moss on it"[12]; Tomey's Turl has "saddle-colored hands" (*GDM* 26); Clytie Sutpen is "coffee-colored"[13]; Three Basket is "dust-colored" (*CS* 331); Philip Manigault Beauchamp is "a complete and unrelieved black"[14]; Charles Etienne de Saint Valery Bon's skin has a "smooth faint olive tinge" (*AA* 161). These many colors are categorized racially by the one-drop rule, according to which "one drop" of African ancestry defined the black slave and citizen alike. (Though Faulkner's fiction treats three races, his representations of the Americans native to Yoknapatawpha tend, as Cedric Gael Bryant has argued in another context,[15] to throw the behaviors of the black and white races into relief. They are, to paraphrase Quentin Compson, obverse reflections of the two races they live between.[16]) This one-drop rule is a vestige of the slaveholders' law that children born to slaves "follow the condition of their mothers" for, as Frederick Douglass puts it, "the slaveholder, in cases not a few, sustain[ed] to his slaves the double relation of master and father" (3). Sensitive to the history of the South's peculiar institution and to the precarious means by which any individual's identity forms and develops, Faulkner repeatedly probes the terrifying moments wherein culture and identity collide.

Go Down, Moses begins with a figure ruined by such a collision. Isaac McCaslin, "a widower now and uncle to half a county and father to no one" (3), frames a tale that happened long before his birth. In the short frame, Faulkner emphasizes the absences in Ike's life at nearly eighty years of age: this "father to no one" has "owned no property and never desired to" and lives in a house that is "not his," and the story he introduces is "not something he

had participated in or even remembered himself" (4). A reading
of the novel that follows reveals just how much of his life Ike has
forfeited to his idealism,[17] and next to Ike's life as an old man
Faulkner sets a black life that opposes and reflects Ike's in every
major respect. Lucas Beauchamp faces and conquers a challenge
to his marriage, which counters Ike's disastrous marriage; Lucas
fathers and successfully raises children; Lucas learns from his mis-
takes: to his new son-in-law he says, "George Wilkins, I don't give
no man advice about his wife" (75). That line revises in humorous
miniature the scene in which Lucas agonizes over Molly's stay in
Zack Edmonds's house.[18] Afraid that Molly has been more to Zack
than a nurse for his son, he says, "How to God . . . can a black man
ask a white man to please not lay down with his black wife? And
even if he could ask it, how to God can the white man promise he
wont?" (58). Lucas struggles with exactly the kind of ethical issues
Ike does, but his struggle takes place within what W. E. B. DuBois
called the Veil of Blackness:

> . . . the Negro is a sort of seventh son, born with a veil, and gifted with
> second-sight in this American world,—a world which yields him no
> true self-consciousness, but only lets him see himself through the rev-
> elation of the other world. It is a peculiar sensation, this double-
> consciousness, this sense of always looking at oneself through the eyes
> of others, of measuring one's soul by the tape of a world that looks on
> in amused contempt and pity.[19]

By situating Lucas both within this veil and at such obvious counterpoints to Ike, Faulkner implies that Ike indulges in a culturally
privileged gesture when he gives up the McCaslin patrimony.
Lucas would never do such a thing. Life as a poor man with non-
white skin has taught him that a man "can want a heap in [his
lifetime] and a heap of what he can want is due to come to him, if
he just starts in soon enough" (127). But he must "start in"—and
this of course Ike does not do.

In Rosa Coldfield's contorted narrative in *Absalom, Absalom!*,
Faulkner investigates more specifically the relationship between
race and identity. As Rosa describes to Quentin how she reacted

to the news that Henry shot Charles Bon, she focuses on the moment at which Clytie stopped her on the stairs at Sutpen's Hundred, forbidding her to go up to Judith. All of the "despair," "shock," and "outrage" that Rosa felt pours out of her in one "instinctive" sentence: *"Take your hand off me, nigger!"* (112). On the stairs, she reveals her fear of the blackness of the *"Sutpen coffee-colored face"*: *"he chose well,"* she thinks; *"he bettered choosing, who created in his own image the cold Cerberus of his private hell"* (109). Faulkner shows us that for all her "outrage," Rosa, who spent her childhood avoiding touching objects that Clytie had touched, was not even very surprised to feel her hand. However much she fears Clytie's blackness and Sutpenness—the two "dangerous tropes" that threaten her most directly—Rosa cannot deny the simple power of Clytie's human presence. She speaks to the power of the physical:

> *I know only that my entire being seemed to run at blind full tilt into something monstrous and immobile, with a shocking impact too soon and too quick to be mere amazement and outrage at that black arresting and untimorous hand on my white woman's flesh. Because there is something in the touch of flesh with flesh which abrogates, cuts sharp and straight across the devious intricate channels of decorous ordering, which enemies as well as lovers know because it makes them both:—touch and touch of that which is the citadel of the central I-Am's private own; not spirit, soul; the liquorish and ungirdled mind is anyone's to take in any darkened hallway of this earthly tenement. But let flesh touch with flesh, and watch the fall of all the eggshell shibboleth of caste and color too.* (111–12)

Clytie's hand on Rosa's arm is the touch of flesh upon unsurprised flesh; it represents the simple fact of common humanity in midst of the many barriers constructed to deny or restrict that humanity.[20] Rosa's body has its cultural function—it is "white woman's flesh," not just "my white skin"—but that function disintegrates even as Rosa tries to assert it by calling Clytie a nigger. It is a remarkable passage in which Faulkner shows both how white racial privilege attempts to control challenges to its power and how precariously that privilege is situated.

Dumping the Coffee and Milk

I will bring these comments to a close by examining how, in three important instances, Faulkner racializes a character's identity in ways that call attention to the culturally constructed nature of race and of language's role in its construction. With Frederick Douglass and DuBois, Faulkner knew that racial epithets, for example, erase an individual name and identity and replace them with a categorizing insult.[21] Much as Gates's critical work does, Faulkner's fiction represents "race" as a metaphor for human difference and as a trope of great power in the world.

I think we see Faulkner's understanding of the great power accorded whiteness in America most movingly in *Sanctuary* in his rendering of Temple's story of the night she was raped. That novel contains perhaps his most brutal representations of sexuality and violence, and in Horace Benbow's consciousness the two coalesce most problematically:

> In an alley-mouth two figures stood, face to face, not touching; the man speaking in a low tone unprintable epithet after epithet in a caressing whisper, the woman motionless before him as though in a musing swoon of voluptuous ecstasy. Perhaps it is upon the instant that we realise, admit, that there is a logical pattern to evil, that we die, he thought. . . .[22]

Epithets as endearments, victims as beloveds, and lovers as assailants, "face to face" but "not touching": structurally and thematically, *Sanctuary* depends upon the kind of "darkly brutal formalism" with which Morrison's Breedloves fight one another. Every move of Temple's to flee before the rape increases Popeye's awareness of her and his determination to have her; every attempt of Horace's to discover the truth behind Tommy's murder moves Lee Goodwin closer to death. Temple tells Horace what really happened in the corn crib, but at Goodwin's trial she tells another story—not because she either loves or fears Popeye, but to cover up the violent pleasure the lover Popeye supplied for her. Any mention of her own pleasure would negate her word on the horror of the rape, and our recognition of this increases our sense of the strange free-floating evil at the heart of *Sanctuary*. The evil that Horace describes has an inexorability about it in this novel, even if it is not exactly the logic he claims. Yet it has no discernible source, for every person is complicit in it. That complicity accounts for what Horace sees as Temple's "actual pride" in telling her story, "a sort of naive and impersonal vanity, as though she were making it up" (226).[23] What she makes up, of course, is the lie she recounts at Goodwin's trial—the lie that her father and brothers and Jefferson itself all demand. Temple wants to conceal her affair with Red, and Jefferson must believe, in the words of its district attorney, that "these good men, these fathers and husbands, [can] hear what you have to say and right your wrong for you" (299).

They cannot right her wrong, of course, because they misunderstand it. In the gap that exists between any of the stories that Temple tells and the version that Faulkner supplies us of the crimes against her, we find the sources of this misunderstanding. She tells Horace most graphically about the night before her rape, "which she had spent in comparative inviolation." "Now and then Horace would attempt to get her on ahead to the crime itself," Faulkner writes tellingly, "but she would elude him and return to herself sitting on the bed, listening to the men on the porch, or lying in the dark while they entered the room and came to the bed and stood there above her" (225). "The crime itself," Faulkner would have us know, is not so much Tommy's murder as the murder of Temple's "inviolation" at the hands of all the men on the Old Frenchman place.

As her story unfolds we realize that during this night Temple strove mightily to exert some control over her situation. We see her terror when she tells Horace that "You can feel people in a dark room" and that she wished for a chastity belt with spikes on it: "I'd jab it into him. I'd jab it all the way through him and I'd think about the blood running on me. . . . I didn't know it was going to be just the other way" (228). With Gowan drunk asleep beside her, Temple tried to become in effect her own protector by changing herself (as Popeye groped her) first into a (white) boy,

then a (white) corpse, then a forty-five-year-old (white) school-
teacher, and finally and most desperately, an old (white) man. Temple's imagination tried to cope with Popeye's hand on her belly by
becoming first something Popeye would not expect—a boy—then
something that reflects her own grief—a corpse with shucks in the
coffin (227–29). The last two projections, however, in which Temple believes she could fight and beat Popeye, Faulkner casts in
specifically racial terms:

> I'd think what I'd say to him. I'd talk to him like the teacher does in
> school, and then I was a teacher in school and it [Popeye] was a little
> black thing like a nigger boy. . . . And I was telling it what I'd do, and
> it kind of drawing up and drawing up like it could already see the
> switch.
>   Then I said That wont do. I ought to be a man. So I was an old
> man, with a long white beard, and then the little black man got littler
> and littler and I was saying Now. . . . Then I thought about being a
> man, and as soon as I thought it, it happened. (230–31)

The only way Temple can control any part of her situation the
night before the rape is to make Popeye—who, as Michel Gresset
argues, is associated with black and blackness throughout *Sanctuary*[24]—into a small black male presence who gets steadily smaller
and less threatening to whatever white persona Temple inhabits.
She will not relinquish her whiteness; she cannot visualize Popeye
as female. At Temple's very core stands the belief that violating
presences are black and male, "inviolation" limited likewise to the
white and male. To Temple, her femaleness guarantees her violation, and even her whiteness cannot protect her from that.

Her "transformation" occurs just as Popeye's hand becomes especially threatening, and it allows her to shut down emotionally:
"I just went to sleep," is how she puts it (231). Even Horace, who
listens so sympathetically, does not understand either "the crime
itself" (the rape) or what Faulkner would have us see as the real
crime against her (the "murder" of her "inviolation"). Horace dismisses her tale. He dismisses her except as a means to clear his
client, but he cannot avoid comparing this violated young woman
with his own stepdaughter of about the same age.[25] As he holds

Little Belle's photograph in his hands and sees there "a soft and fading aftermath of invitation and voluptuous promise and secret affirmation," the unsteady truce between physical desire and step-fatherly restraint disappears. So too does Horace's sense of himself as male. He becomes both violator and violated as he vomits, "leaned upon his braced arms while the shucks set up a terrific uproar beneath her thighs . . . [and] watched something black and furious go roaring out of her pale body" (234). In this curious passage, as Noel Polk has argued,[26] the line between rapist and victim, between male and female dissolves for Horace just as surely as it does for Temple during the night at the Old Frenchman place. Faulkner also complicates the imagery of whiteness and blackness that falls so neatly into place in Temple's consciousness. The "black and furious" something of vomit and blood turns into a "black tunnel" through which the pale victim, "like a figure lifted down from a crucifix," shoots into a "darkness" that contains the victim's only liberation from grief and terror: "an interval in which she would swing faintly and lazily in nothingness filled with pale, myriad points of light" (234–35). Horace's nausea, exhausted, mirrors Temple's detachment after her rape (142–43) and presages his response to Lee Goodwin's lynching (311). Because of all of these complications of black and white imagery, I cannot agree with Gresset when he argues that "it is as if there were a double evil potential in undersize linked with blackness—as if, indeed, the two images put together became synonymous with impotence, especially when the latter's objective correlative is immobility."[27] Popeye may be sexually impotent, but he is extremely powerful in almost every other way that matters, especially in his willingness to maim and destroy. In the world of this novel, "sanctuary" exists only in the numb reaches after trauma; and in linking the episode of Horace's nausea so closely with Temple's story of the night before Tommy's murder, Faulkner systematically dismantles race- and gender-based explanations of human behavior. This dissolution implies that, to Faulkner, human identity is shifting, nebulous, malleable, and hence infinitely corruptible.

It is, in a word, *constructed*, and of many elements. If Temple's

story shows us how powerfully whiteness works in the white identity, then in the style and themes of "That Evening Sun," we see
Faulkner's examination of what black powerlessness means to one
particular white identity. As narrator, the twenty-four-old Quentin
Compson recounts an episode in which the black sometime-cook,
sometime-prostitute Nancy either is or is not killed by her husband, Jesus. Quentin begins his story ornately, describing the Jefferson of "now":

> Monday is no different from any other weekday in Jefferson now.
> The streets are paved now, and the telephone and electric companies
> are cutting down more and more of the shade trees—the water oaks,
> the maples and locusts and elms—to make room for iron poles bearing
> clusters of bloated and ghostly and bloodless grapes, and we have a
> city laundry which makes the rounds on Monday morning, gathering
> the bundles of clothes into bright-colored, specially made motor cars:
> the soiled wearing of a whole week now flees apparitionlike behind
> alert and irritable electric horns, with a long diminishing noise of rub-
> ber and asphalt like tearing silk, and even the Negro women who still
> take in white people's washing after the old custom, fetch and deliver
> it in automobiles. (CS 289)

James B. Carothers has noted how Quentin's style changes between this beginning paragraph and the story's end, as the result
of his becoming involved again in the experience he describes.[28] I
would add that Quentin becomes just as terrified in the narrating
as he was in the living of this traumatic exposure to Nancy's terror;
his narrative degenerates by story's end into a simple recounting
of the dialogue between the Compsons as they walk home from
Nancy's cabin—a "Caddy said," "Jason said" singsong. And this
change from mature to childish voice occurs abruptly after Quentin recounts the episode between Jesus and Nancy in the kitchen,
in which they discuss Nancy's pregnancy. The nine-year-old
Quentin understands what the adults are talking about, but the
seven-year-old Caddy is still trying to make sense of it all:

> [Nancy says]: ". . . You want Mr Jason to catch you hanging around his
> kitchen, talking that way before these chillen?"
> "Talking what way?" Caddy said. "What vine?"

"I cant hang around white man's kitchen," Jesus said. "But white
man can hang around mine. White man can come in my house, but I
cant stop him. When white man want to come in my house, I aint got
no house. I cant stop him, but he cant kick me outen it. He cant do
that."

Quentin realizes at this moment the truth of what Jesus says:
"When white man want to come in my house, I aint got no house."
Whether Nancy is pregnant by the white Mr. Stovall or someone
else, white or black, with Quentin we know that what Jesus says is
true. And it is the shock of that recognition of truth that propels
Quentin backward in time to nine years old:

> Dilsey was still sick in her cabin. Father told Jesus to stay off our
> place. Dilsey was still sick. It was a long time. We were in the library
> after supper. (CS 292)

Nancy's utter powerlessness mirrors Jesus's, and in recognizing
that and feeling it so deeply, Quentin comes to understand also
that Nancy's condition results directly from his own family's privileged place in the world. Not for nothing, then, is little Jason so
busily engaged throughout the story with the word *nigger*; Faulkner is subtly demonstrating that the color of Nancy's flesh may be
some very natural shade of brown, but the racial difference between her and the Compsons is very deliberately constructed and
maintained:

> "I aint a nigger," Jason said. "Are you a nigger, Nancy?"
> "I hellborn, child," Nancy said. "I wont be nothing soon. I going
> back where I came from soon." (CS 298)

Jason is trying to trace what DuBois called "the problem of the
twentieth century" (209 ff.), the color line that divides white and
black, while Quentin has felt and fully understood its terrible effects.

Standing perhaps as Faulkner's greatest example of the constructedness of racial categories and their relationship to individual identity is Joe Christmas, who murders and is murdered
because of the American color line, yet who never knows where
he stands in relation to it. In his example we see the heartbreaking

consequences not of not knowing what "color" his "blood" is, but of knowing all too well how the contending races expect the members of each to think, feel, and behave. Joe has been an apt student of those expectations and comes to share them so completely that he can pass equally well in either race. Unsure of what label to assume, he tries to manipulate the color line itself to his own advantage—telling white prostitutes, for instance, that he is black so he will only get maybe a beating but assuredly a woman at no charge. When this trick no longer works, it makes him "sick," Faulkner says, and pushes him to try to cross the line completely:

> He was in the north now, in Chicago and then Detroit. He lived with negroes, shunning white people. He ate with them, slept with them, belligerent, unpredictable, uncommunicative. He now lived as man and wife with a woman who resembled an ebony carving. At night he would lie in bed beside her, sleepless, beginning to breathe deep and hard. He would do it deliberately, feeling, even watching, his white chest arch deeper and deeper within his ribcage, trying to breathe into himself the dark odor, the dark and inscrutable thinking and being of negroes, with each suspiration trying to expel from himself the white blood and the white thinking and being. And all the while his nostrils at the odor which he was trying to make his own would whiten and tauten, his whole being writhe and strain with physical outrage and spiritual denial. (*LIA* 225–26)

Joe's flesh is white, and in response to his attempts to get rid of "the white blood," his body just gets whiter. In this paradoxical condition Faulkner reveals that Joe is really the victim of "the white thinking and being" of his raising and background; he is McEachern's and Doc Hines's progeny, most evidently in his violent repudiations of their influence, no matter the natural color of his skin.

Yet in one crucial respect Joe Christmas is literally and symbolically black. When Percy Grimm castrates him, Joe bleeds so profusely and suddenly that the blood would appear black, rather than the oxidized red or the blue of it in the body. So much for the natural reasons for Faulkner's description of Joe's death:[29]

> For a long moment he looked up at them with peaceful and unfathomable and unbearable eyes. Then his face, body, all, seemed to collapse,

to fall in upon itself, and from out the slashed garments about his hips and loins the pent black blood seemed to rush like a released breath. It seemed to rush out of his pale body like the rush of sparks from a rising rocket; upon that black blast the man seemed to rise soaring into their memories forever and ever. They are not to lose it, in whatever peaceful valleys, beside whatever placid and reassuring streams of old age, in the mirroring faces of whatever children they will contemplate old disasters and newer hopes. It will be there, musing, quiet, steadfast, not fading and not particularly threatful, but of itself alone serene, of itself alone triumphant. (464–65)

It is the "black blast" of Joe's blood that will not leave the memories of the men who saw him castrated: he dies the way he dies because their world demands that he, in Percy Grimm's words, "let white women alone, even in hell" (464).[30] And again we see that the only thing "natural" about Joe Christmas's death is the undeniable presence of his mutilated and lifeless body on Gail Hightower's kitchen floor.

To Faulkner (and Toni Morrison, too), identity is infinitely constructible, perhaps most fluidly so in language, that slippery and often untrustworthy medium within which the writer works. For all his distrust of words that may or may not "fit what they are trying to say at," Faulkner nevertheless records the many moments in human experience when identity and culture cooperate as well as collide. In his world, after all, connectedness and communion are as possible as isolation: Byron and Lena can hit the road to raise a baby; Chick, Aleck Sander, and Miss Habersham can unite to free Lucas; Lucius Priest can ride in a horse race to try to win back Boss's automobile. Even these tenuous connections require our recognition that a Faulkner narrative is more often than not about the role of narrative itself in human life— about the story we tell ourselves about us and our place in the world, and about the places where our reflexive narrative fails. Writing on *Sanctuary*, Jay Watson sounds this theme: "[e]ven when a human life rests on the power of forensic narrative, Horace fails as a storyteller, so his arguments bow before a malevolent rhetoric, an amoral but persuasive theatricality,"[31] which accounts nicely for Horace's disappearance from Faulkner's fiction. André

Bleikasten, Stephen Ross, and Warwick Wadlington all note the
communal quality of the combined voices and reflected conscious-
nesses of the narrators of As I Lay Dying; Ross speaks most closely
to my argument here when he writes, "[v]oice in As I Lay Dying
also interrogates the metaphysics of individual consciousness, revealing characters' secret selves by immersing them in a communal
discourse, making their private thoughts a function of how they
hear, respond to, and render each other's speech."[32] Communual
or individual, both discourse: both say, or try to say, and with
enormous repercussions in the world at large. Faulkner gives
Gavin Stevens an uncharacteristically lucid moment in The Town
to reflect on the magnitude of such repercussions. He describes
the last night of Eula Varner's life on earth in terms of his own
regret at not being able somehow to foresee her suicide: "always
and forever that was remains," he thinks, "as if what is going to
happen to one tomorrow already gleams faintly visible now if the
watcher were only wise enough to discern it or maybe just brave
enough."[33] To speak, or to "try to say," as Benjy does, is "natural"
(remember, too, "man's puny inexhaustible voice" from the Nobel
Prize speech). To write is to produce the irreducible metaphor for
what I have been calling the "constructedness" of such phenomena as race, identity, and culture. To write as Faulkner does, un-
compromisingly and unflinchingly about life on the American
color line, is to be both wise enough and brave enough to confront
the processes by which human beings continue to use one another
by words.

NOTES

1. The Bluest Eye (New York: Holt, 1970; rpt. Penguin Books, 1994). Subsequent citations appear parenthetically in the text.
2. "Writing 'Race' and the Difference It Makes," in "Race," Writing, and Difference
(Chicago: University of Chicago Press, 1986), ed. Gates, 8. Subsequent citations appear
parenthetically in the text.
3. David Hume, "Of National Characters," 1753; Immanuel Kant, Observations on the
Feeling of the Beautiful and Sublime, 1764. Cited in Gates, "Race," 20, n. 12 and 13, his
emphasis removed here.
4. Narrative of the Life of Frederick Douglass, An American Slave, Written by Himself
(1845; New York: Doubleday, Anchor Books, 1989), 36–37. Subsequent citations appear
parenthetically in the text.

5. *A Treatise on Sociology: Theoretical and Practical* (Philadelphia: Lippincott, Grambo, and Company, 1854), 31, cited by Barbara Ladd, " 'The Direction of the Howling': Nationalism and the Color Line in *Absalom, Absalom!,* " *American Literature* 66, 3 (September 1994): 546.

6. "Governor Vardaman on the Negro," *Current Literature* 36 (March 1904): 270–71, cited in Joel Williamson, *William Faulkner and Southern History* (New York: Oxford University Press, 1993), 157.

7. Vardaman's comments were brought to my attention most recently by Ladd's insightful essay cited above. See " 'The Direction of the Howling,' " 545. See also Joseph Blotner, *Faulkner: A Biography* (New York: Random House, 1974), 129–32, 145.

8. Gates argues that we should bracket the word *race* consistently in quotation marks to reflect in our texts the cultural difference that the unbracketed word would leave unmarked. I take the point to respond to Noel Polk's recent argument that race has been overemphasized in Faulkner studies (usually at the expense of examinations of gender issues). He asks us to note that "only four of Faulkner's novels—*Light in August, Absalom, Absalom!, Go Down, Moses,* and *Intruder in the Dust*—and that at most three of well over a hundred short stories . . . are in any way 'about' race, and you will have some sense of how relatively little of his work Faulkner invested in race-consciousness" (*Children of the Dark House: Text and Context in Faulkner* [Jackson: University Press of Mississippi, 1996], 143; see also 234). As I believe my discussion of *Sanctuary* in this essay indicates, Faulkner did not need specific racial issues in order to racialize his subject matter; in fact, Toni Morrison would argue that his racialization of the white subject's imagination is even more telling than his representations of black characters. (See *Playing in the Dark: Whiteness and the Literary Imagination* [Cambridge: Harvard University Press, 1992].) In Polk's shorthand, then, Faulkner's work might not be "about" race, but it is nearly always about "race."

9. *As I Lay Dying* (1930; corrected text, New York: Vintage International, 1990), 157; *Collected Stories* (New York: Vintage, 1977), 531; *The Sound and the Fury* (1929; corrected text, New York: Vintage International, 1990), 53. References to these texts appear parenthetically in this essay, preceded by the standard title abbreviations where necessary.

10. *The Hamlet* (1940; corrected text, New York: Vintage International, 1991), 242. Subsequent parenthetical page citations refer to this edition.

11. *Light in August* (1932; corrected text, New York: Vintage International, 1990), 462. Subsequent citations of this edition appear parenthetically.

12. *Go Down, Moses* (1942; corrected text, New York: Vintage International, 1990), 25. Subsequent parenthetical page citations refer to this edition.

13. *Absalom, Absalom!* (1936; corrected text, New York: Vintage International, 1990), 110. Subsequent page citations appearing parenthetically refer to this edition.

14. *A Fable* (1954; in *William Faulkner: Novels 1942–1954;* [New York: The Library of America, 1992], 1011.)

15. In "Mirroring the Racial 'Other': The Deacon and Quentin Compson in William Faulkner's *The Sound and the Fury*," Bryant observes that Quentin's "discovery that black and white people are 'forms of behavior,' obversely and unalterably trapped within socially constructed identities and 'voices' like the word 'nigger'." See *Southern Review* 29, 1 (Winter 1993): 37 (my emphasis).

16. I agree with Polk's assessment of critics who would read Faulkner's Indians as "innocents in some New World Eden" of a better American past, a position that puts the critic too close philosophically to Isaac McCaslin. See Faulkner's *Requiem for a Nun: A Critical Study* (Bloomington: Indiana University Press, 1981), 255–56. James B. Carothers has also noted the similarities between the Indians' stereotypes of the black slave and those of the white culture they imitate; see *William Faulkner's Short Stories* (Ann Arbor: UMI Research Press, 1985), 75–77.

17. John Duvall puts matters this way: "Ike McCaslin fails to provide the key to a nonpatriarchal society because his renunciation—his refusal to profit from a system of male power that perpetuates racial injustice—is just that, simple negation and refusal, a withdrawal from life. He generates no alternative vision of how to live in the world, and the transmission of patriarchal authority is in no way disrupted by Ike's refusal to be its embodiment."

I would add that the absence in the text where Ike's child should be reflects this very failure. See "Doe Hunting and Masculinity in *Go Down, Moses* and *Song of Solomon*," *Arizona Quarterly* 47, 1 (Spring 1991): 110.

18. This technique of repetition-with-a-difference has a long history in the African American literary tradition known as signifying; the most well-known explication of this tradition appears in Gates's *The Signifying Monkey: A Theory of African-American Literary Criticism* (New York: Oxford University Press, 1988). Ralph Ellison's essay "Change the Joke and Slip the Yoke" speaks to some of the uses to which black Americans have put signifying differences: "Very often, however, the Negro's masking is motivated . . . by a profound rejection of the image created to usurp his identity. Sometimes it is for the sheer joy of the joke; sometimes to challenge those who presume, across the psychological distance created by race manners, to know his identity." See *Shadow and Act* (1964; New York: Vintage, 1972), 55.

19. *The Souls of Black Folk* (1903), in *Three Negro Classics*, ed. John Hope Franklin (New York: Avon, 1965), 214–15.

20. Minrose Gwin demonstrates that Rosa's subsequent slapping of Clytie "seals Clytie's black Otherness to the white South just as Clytie's touch becomes an unforgettable metaphor for what [Margaret] Walker would call 'black humanism,' which seeks human dignity in a racist world." Moreover, "in the articulation of [Rosa's] epiphany—'And you too? And you too, sister, sister?'—she implicitly acknowledges her own sisterhood with Clytie and with the dark side of her self and her culture." See *Black and White Women of the Old South: The Peculiar Sisterhood in American Literature* (Knoxville: University of Tennessee Press, 1985), 17, 123.

21. Here I am thinking most particularly of DuBois's "Of the Passing of the First-Born," where the deliberately crafted prose describing the morning of his son's funeral stands in telling contrast to the one-word comment of the white passersby: "Blithe was the morning of his burial, with bird and song and sweet-smelling flowers. The trees whispered to the grass, but the children sat with hushed faces. And yet it seemed a ghostly unreal day,—the wraith of Life. We seemed to rumble down an unknown street behind a little white bundle of posies, with the shadow of a song in our ears. The busy city dinned about us; they did not say much, those pale-faced hurrying men and women; they did not say much,—they only glanced and said, 'Niggers!' " (*The Souls of Black Folk*, 352–53).

22. *Sanctuary* (1931; corrected text, New York: Vintage International, 1987), 232. Subsequent parenthetical page citations refer to this edition.

23. I believe Laura E. Tanner errs when she pushes her provocative analysis of rape and reader-response theory in *Sanctuary* to include Temple as a violator of herself and the reader and Temple's willing violator as well. She reads this passage as proving that Temple is making up the story, whereas I maintain that Faulkner keeps us fastened on Horace's limited perspective, thus adding him (but not us, and certainly not the traumatized Temple) to the list of those who injure her. See "Reading Rape: *Sanctuary* and *The Women of Brewster Place*," *American Literature* 62, 4 (December 1990): 559–82.

24. "Faulkner's Self-Portraits," *Faulkner Journal* 2, 1 (Fall 1986): 2–13.

25. Jay Watson argues persuasively that Horace's attempted surveillance of Little Belle at the novel's end represents "a powerful coda to the communicative inadequacies that have plagued the hapless attorney throughout the novel." *Sanctuary* in this reading evidences "the ascendancy of silence, the power of rhetorical deception, and the unconditional surrender of spoken language" on many levels. *Forensic Fictions: The Lawyer Figure in Faulkner* (Athens: University of Georgia Press, 1993), 74, 73.

26. "The Space Between *Sanctuary*," *Intertextuality in Faulkner*, ed. Michel Gresset and Noel Polk (Jackson: University Press of Mississippi, 1985), 16–35.

27. "Faulkner's Self-Portraits," 5.

28. *William Faulkner's Short Stories*, 12.

29. For a description of Nelse Patton's lynching in Oxford, upon which Faulkner based Joe's, and an important eyewitness account of it, see Arthur F. Kinney, "Faulkner and Racism," *Connotations* 3, 3 (1993/94): 265–78.

30. I agree with Diane Roberts's reading of Joe's death: "In the end Joe incorporates

both white and black, both male and female, both the ability to menstruate and to ejaculate, and is present yet erased; the myriad play of self and desire is obliterated in the face of the community need for conformity and unity, for the hierarchies of white/black, male/female to remain undisturbed"—to which I would add that no one needs those hierarchies more desperately than Joe himself, and therein lies another layer of the ideology of whiteness that his life both illustrates and challenges. Joseph R. Urgo makes a similar point: "Racism functions in *Light in August* as a primary example of a strained relation with physicality. . . . If the cultural code is violated, it is the man and not the system which must give. . . . When Joe's blood is released from his 'pale body' he is finally cleansed of the 'filth' by which he has been defined and caged: the filth of racial and sexual exclusiveness, the filth of the cultural nexus which has imprisoned the spirit of his flesh." See Roberts, *Faulkner and Southern Womanhood* (Athens: University of Georgia Press, 1994), 184; Urgo, "Menstrual Blood and 'Nigger' Blood: Joe Christmas and the Ideology of Sex and Race," *Mississippi Quarterly* 41, 3 (Summer 1988): 398, 401. For provocative insights into the ideology of whiteness, see Laura Doyle, *Bordering on the Body: The Racial Matrix of Modern Fiction and Culture* (New York and Oxford: Oxford University Press, 1994); and David R. Roediger, *Towards the Abolition of Whiteness: Essays on Race, Politics, and Working Class History* (London: Verso, 1994).

31. *Forensic Fictions*, 75.

32. Bleikasten, *Faulkner's "As I Lay Dying"* (Bloomington: Indiana University Press, 1973); Wadlington, *"As I Lay Dying": Stories Out of Stories* (New York: Twayne, 1992); Ross, *Fiction's Inexhaustible Voice: Speech and Writing in Faulkner* (Athens: University of Georgia Press, 1993), 125.

33. *The Town* (1957; New York: Vintage, 1961), 334.

This essay contains some material that appears in a volume of essays on Faulkner and Morrison (Jackson: University Press of Mississippi, 1997). I would like to thank the editors of *Unflinching Gaze: Morrison and Faulkner Re-Envisioned*, Carol Kolmerten, Stephen M. Ross, and Judith Bryant Wittenberg, for helping me to develop that argument, and Seetha A-Srinivasan of the Press for permission to use the material here.

Writing Blood:
The Art of the Literal in *Light in August*

JAY WATSON

There is only one thing that makes a race and that is blood.
—BENJAMIN DISRAELI

It is possible to kill the human body with an idea.
—THOMAS DIXON

Blood makes noise.

—SUZANNE VEGA[1]

For its August 1995 issue, the alternative music magazine *Spin* sends a correspondent to San Francisco to explore an emerging sexual subculture, an offshoot of the S/M scene whose members, mainly women, engage in what they call "blood sports." In local sex clubs promoting "safe blood play," *Spin*'s reporter, appropriately named Eurydice, watches as young women insert open-topped hypodermic needles into the veins of their arms, splattering the room, and each other, with their jetting blood. "We love blood," one proclaims. "It drives us mad." A twentysomething Ivy League graduate tells Eurydice, "I get off being bitten"; she lets the blood dry in streaks on her body. A "vampire stripper" and her boyfriend hire themselves out to clubs, sipping each other's blood out of insulin syringes and inviting audience members to do the same. Eurydice talks to couples who practice "cutting" as a form of foreplay, ritualistically—and strange as it may seem, lovingly—slicing and scarring each other with razors, scalpels, hunting knives. Some drink the blood they spill during their lovemaking; others finger-paint on walls or the bodies of their partners. Still others find in scars a highly coveted means of adornment. At piercing salons with names like Gauntlet and Body Manipulations, professional cutting artists carve elaborate designs into the skin of their customers, making blood prints of the patterns and collecting them in portfolios: Celtic knots, runic and tarot figures, flower buds, even, incongruously, Hello Kitty. Some share tricks of the trade, like the seasoned pro who eschews the scalpel in favor of a heated knife-tip that "cauterizes as it cuts."

None of the erotic ceremonies witnessed by Eurydice involves incapacitating pain or debilitating blood loss. Even the exorbitant spectacle with the needles involves only a small fraction of the pint we are routinely called upon to donate to the Red Cross. Still, she explains, these ceremonies carry a visceral power, because the blood "is uncontained and it colors everything." So much so that on returning from this underworld Eurydice finds herself alternately "enchanted" and "haunted" by her subjects, whose blood continues to color her dreams.[2]

By contrast, what has haunted me most about the world captured by Eurydice is how uncannily its basic elements seem to reproduce central motifs from *Light in August*. It is as if the razors, knives, and scalpels, the repeated, *public* acts of cutting into—and open—the human body, and especially the primal, ubiquitous blood, were lifted straight from the pages of Faulkner's 1932 novel, surely his bloodiest. The echoes are no doubt unintentional, but they are, I think, significant, especially when we take a moment to reflect further on the strategic value of cutting for the young women and men who participate in blood sports. In an appeal to the reader near the end of her article, Eurydice directly addresses this value: "We all know the impulse to cross the line from the metaphorical into the literal . . . from the outside to the inside" (SL 110). The terrain to be recaptured once this line is crossed, or cut, is the body itself, the body appropriated and alienated by metaphor. And the metaphor, in this case, is blood. Blood, after all, has emerged in the popular discourse of the last decade as one of the leading metaphors for AIDS. Over and over we are warned that blood can give you AIDS. It must not be spilled. It must not be shared. It must not be uncontained. Blood = AIDS. And as the members of ACT UP reminded us throughout the 1980s, AIDS = Death. The transitive property of equality suggests a third and final metaphor: Blood = Death.

In this context, cutting functions as an impassioned, politically charged, and wickedly mimetic[3] response to the discourse of AIDS-era America, an attempt to recapture the literal value, the physical presence, and even the numinous force of blood from a set of popular metaphors that implicitly and sometimes explicitly equate it with death. Cutting brings about an eruption of the natural world into the midst of a discursive field. Materially and *pointedly* grounded in the body, it reappropriates blood as one's own vital fluid rather than someone else's figure of speech.

The devotees of cutting culture include homosexuals and prostitutes. The basic equipment includes syringes and needles. Blood is exchanged and shared. And yet, as Eurydice observes, participants report finding it not only relatively safe but exhilarating. In this way cutting represents an almost point-by-point rejection of the way AIDS discourse links homosexuality, prostitution, and drug use with virulent social contagion and death. In AIDS America, "blood" makes difference, as if applying Disraeli's formula in my epigraph to sexual preference, sex work, and chemical dependency rather than to race. Thanks to AIDS and the semantic field that has coalesced around it, "blood" can fashion these categories into sources of deadly alterity that must be quarantined for their, and "our," own good.

In cutting culture, however, blood functions in a dramatically different way. Instead of making difference, it literally makes *noise*, as in the following lesbian encounter recorded by Eurydice:

> The razor breaks the skin. Blood trickles out. The strokes become shorter, quicker, and deeper, like sexual thrusts, until Daddy [the dominant partner] moans, then cuts, with firm precision, small parallel X's from shoulder to shoulder. The rest of us watch and sip our drinks. Some women make out.
>
> Daddy now slashes at random. Blood spurts, painting them pagan. "I open you like no fist can open you," Daddy says in a controlled waspish tone.

As if that were a cue, [her] torn [partner] starts to scream. She screams for mercy, and yet I've never heard such a scream; it is wild and celebratory and it fears the bloodletting may stop. It is the scream of having crossed over to the other side. (SL 63)

This is noise in more than a simple acoustic sense. The young woman's scream makes cybernetic noise as well, disrupts an information system. It jams the interpretive circuitry, takes one aback. (The attending journalist is certainly taken aback.) Its celebratory intensity resists assimilation into the reigning paradigms of AIDS discourse, where blood, as one young woman remarks, is "a dangerous sport these days," the most dangerous thing going in AIDS America. The scars of Eurydice's subjects point beyond the metaphorical and political liberties our society routinely takes with "blood" and toward a fuller engagement with the human body in its materiality and urgency. The art of blood sports is an art of the literal, forging an affirmative, somatic link between identity and blood. It makes human skin into a canvas for hard-won portraits and self-portraits rather than crudely imposed caricatures.

Here again it is as if we have never left *Light in August*. As I hope to demonstrate, cutting surfaces at crucial points in Faulkner's novel as an oppositional practice and trope, a writing (in) blood that is also very much an art of the literal in the cultural context of the early twentieth-century Deep South—a world where, as in our own AIDS-haunted moment, blood is the most dangerous thing going, the culture's most loaded and coercive metaphor. Only this time, of course, it is a metaphor for race. Turn-of-the-century Southerners were fond of saying that "blood tells," that race determines character and breeding always wins out in the end. In *Light in August*, however, where the phrase "blood tells" fails to appear even once, blood is just as likely to make noise, to disturb reigning social fictions rather than to corroborate them. By repeatedly bringing blood to the surface of the human body, cutting in *Light in August* mobilizes the power of literal meaning and the natural world as a rejoinder to the discursive system that puts "blood" in service of racial exploitation and violence.

This system, of course, has a history. With all due respect to Disraeli, blood has not always made race, but before exploring how it came to do so, I want to offer a few remarks on what I mean by the literal. I'm not attempting a systematic definition or theory here, just sharing some tentative impressions and working hypotheses:

1. The literal does not mark the absence of aesthetic richness, expressive force, or political interest but is instead a crucial if often neglected source of these properties. Faulkner's dazzling high modernist credentials make the temptation to discount the literal in his work a very real one. On the whole, Faulknerians have preferred to comb his novels for their occulted metaphors and elaborate symbol systems. But reading Faulkner need not be an either/or proposition, a zero-sum game. His fiction gains in complexity and immediacy when we allow for the interplay of letter and trope.

2. Literal meaning does not simply lie inert beneath metaphor but exerts an active counterpressure on it. Along with the body, with which it is so closely associated in Eurydice's San Francisco and Faulkner's Jefferson, the literal acts as a constraint on the power of figuration. A related proposition is that nature, the real, and the material all exist to some degree outside, beyond, or in *relative* autonomy from culture, representation, and discourse. The two realms overlap, but not totally. The natural world, of which body and blood are elements, exerts pressure on representation, even as it is shaped and partially constituted by representation, and even though it can never be apprehended in representation's absence, as some sort of unmediated reality. What we must try to do, if we are unwilling to grant the social complete hegemony over nature, is to read for the traces and aftereffects of the real in discourse, the rents, rifts, and ripples it leaves there, the strain it introduces into language and the noises with which it interrupts the apparently seamless functioning of representation.

3. The project I'm attempting to sketch is not a *nostalgic* attempt to regain a lost aboriginal purity of language and experience represented by the literal, a condition of language somehow prior to the "corrupting" influence of the trope. As George Lakoff and

his collaborators have more than sufficiently demonstrated, metaphor is present from the outset of human imagination and cogni-
tion and deeply constitutive of both.[4] What I'm after here is the
much timelier and more politicized effort to regain a momentary
upper hand for the literal, to reinstate it in the very heart of, and
in the teeth of, metaphorical meaning, in the specific case of the
most pernicious metaphor at work in Faulkner's South.

4. I'm trying above all to invoke the *felt experience* of literal as
opposed to metaphorical meaning, and of the material body as
opposed to the cultural field, rather than to institute some hard
and fast epistemological dichotomy between the two categories. I
would be the first to agree that, considered from a strictly theoretical point of view, the literal probably exists on a continuum with
metaphor rather than in qualitative distinction from it. The same
would go for the body and culture. I'm interested, however, in a
more personal and empirical response to the literal: that palpable
sense of meaning at home, if you will, in denotation, rather than
meaning on the prowl, ever elsewhere, off in the interstices between tenor and vehicle. A meaning right here, under your nose,
rather than a meaning you have to reach for.

With these caveats in mind, we can return to the historical question of how blood made race, how, in a gradual process stretching
over several centuries, it came to be understood in the West as the
hidden principle and *cause* of racial identity, physiognomy, and
behavior. Clearly, a complete history of the idea of blood would
range far beyond the scope of this essay. So at the risk of oversim-
plification, I want to isolate a few important developments in the
intellectual history of race that helped bring blood to the forefront
of the Euro-American racial imagination. One was a crucial shift
in the semantic field of racial terminology itself. The others took
place in the theoretical field in which racial issues were discussed.[5]

Throughout the Enlightenment period, scientists engaged in
the study and classification of racial groups were generally in
agreement that all human beings, whatever their perceived differences, were ultimately of common descent from a single pair of
original ancestors created in a single act of divine will. This view,

known as monogenism, grounded scientific inquiry in biblical authority. Monogenists typically appealed to environmental factors to account for the racial diversity of the species: the early descendants of Adam and Eve were thought to have migrated to different parts of the globe, forming distinct regional populations that, under the influence of climate, landscape, and available diet, evolved over generations into distinct races. The late eighteenth century saw the rise of a competing view, polygenism, which derived each race from a separate act of creation. Polygenists turned to heredity rather than environment to explain racial difference, assigning each race its own specific line of descent. In their view, the races had not grown apart over time; they had always been different, since each one originally sprang from a different pair of progenitors. By the middle decades of the nineteenth century, thanks in no small part to the international influence of a newly emergent "American school" of anthropology, polygenic hereditarianism had largely supplanted monogenic environmentalism as the leading scientific account of racial origins and diversity.

This shift helped "blood" acquire a new resonance in the theoretical discourse of race. Under monogenism, which assigned everyone to the same ultimate line of descent, all people would in a very real sense be of common blood. One's "blood" would simply be one's humanity, one's human descent from Adam and Eve, and "blood" would thereby be of little use as a specific racial descriptor. It is only with the advent of polygenism, with the belief that different racial groups are descended from different ancestors, that the sense of "blood" as entailing a specific heritage, a distinct racial identity, can emerge as viable, and only then that one might speak intelligibly of *mixed* blood, since mixture presupposes recognizably distinct racial "strains" of blood to begin with. Along complementary lines, the shift from environmentalism to hereditarianism was a movement from external causes of racial characteristics toward progenitive causes rooted in the somatic endowment one receives from one's biological ancestors. A movement toward the body, the province of blood, and away from air and water, light, terrain, and temperature. Moreover, under environmentalism, racial differences were by no means to be considered final, for if the races had diverged as a result of adaptation to living conditions, they could just as easily converge again in the future as a result of the same process; hence the widespread scientific and popular speculation about whether European colonists would darken with prolonged exposure to the tropics, or whether African slaves transported to northern Europe would eventually grow lighter in color, perhaps within a single life span. For hereditarians, however, race was no accident. It was destiny, an irrevocable legacy handed down from one's remotest progenitors to one's distant posterity. This sense of immutable and perhaps even irreconcilable racial difference could readily attach itself to the semantic content of "blood."

That content was itself changing during the period under consideration. As the French sociologist Colette Guillaumin observes in her pathbreaking 1972 essay, "The Specific Characteristics of Racist Ideology," "There is a subtle trap laid for us by words whose forms do not alter over time, for we tend to ascribe to them with no hesitation the identity of a fixed meaning."[6] This has been the case with the vocabulary of race, whose apparently stable signifiers have actually undergone a process of "historical drift" over their centuries of use, acquiring new layers of meaning and shedding old ones. At its "permanent semantic core," Guillaumin argues, race conveys nothing more than the idea of a "coherent group of people" (RSPI 38). But her inspired work with several centuries of French dictionaries suggests that the basis of this coherence was understood very differently by seventeenth- and eighteenth-century speakers than by their modern counterparts.

Prior to 1800, words like "race," "blood," and "inheritance" were used above all in a *juridical* sense, to indicate a legal line of descent. The emphasis was on lineage, family continuity, the power of name in an age of great aristocratic households, where nobility and title were routinely conferred via royal patent or political or ecclesiastical appointment. The language of race was what Guillaumin calls "auto-referential," used by the group in power to signify its own proudly cultivated sense of difference, a difference presumed to entail superiority, as in "the race of Bourbons," "the blood of kings," and so on. By the mid-nineteenth century, however, this entire semantic field had shifted. The same words appeared, but their emphasis was now primarily *biological* rather than juridical. What mattered most was no longer the legal continuity of relatively small, powerful families, but the genetic continuity of vast global populations. Racial terms became "alteroreferential," used by the group in power to signify the difference and presumed inferiority of others.[7] One increasingly encounters phrases like "the race of Arabs," "Jewish blood," "inherited Negro features," and so on in the popular and scientific literature of the period. Strictly speaking, one's racial identity was no longer a function of one's ancestors, those who genealogically "go before," but of one's progenitors, those who somatically "beget forth." At about this time, the adjective "black," which had denoted a physical trait in individuals (skin color), began to indicate membership in a hereditary group (the Negro race). Race had become biophysical and absolute.

With these developments, "blood" could begin to function in racial discourse not only as a descriptor, a way to invoke or even quantify one's lineage, but as a motive force behind the formation and transmission of racial characteristics. Consider, as a case in point, the issue of "mixed blood." As long as race was understood as lineage and "blood" as a fundamentally heuristic means of conveying who one is, where one comes from, and what one is entitled to, it made little sense to think of a diverse racial background as involving competing strains of "blood" that actually come together within the confines of one's body. The concept of "blood" simply assigned a bodily familiarity and immediacy to what was still intuited as an abstract and disembodied set of legal relations. But with the advent of the biological view, "mixed blood" came to be seen by many as an embodied state in which discrete bloodlines interact dynamically, with direct consequences for bodily health and psychological well-being. Note that "blood" here captures a sense of race that is no longer an inert quality of the body but an active element at work within it; the heuristic device has acquired an *explanatory* as well as descriptive power.

This brings us to a third important development in the intellectual history of race, the rise of what Guillaumin calls "endogenous determinism," a concept she discusses in two important essays, "The Idea of Race and Its Elevation to Autonomous Scientific and Legal Status" (1980), and "Race and Nature: The System of Marks" (1977).[8] For centuries, Guillaumin observes, the nature of a thing was understood to be its purpose and place in the world order as fixed by God and subsequently interpreted by theology. But from the Enlightenment forward, the nature of a thing has increasingly come to be viewed as the product of properties internal to the thing itself. Human groups defined as "natural," for instance, groups like the races and sexes, are assumed to arise from mechanical causes intrinsic to the groups themselves rather than from exogenous forces like God, history, society, or economics. Put simply, such groups exist as a result of their own logic. Guillaumin rightly associates this view with scientific development; the principle of endogenous determinism helped science carve out a disciplinary space for itself, a unique field—the study of autonomous natural principles—that it could call its own.

Guillaumin argues that the modern understanding of race rests on a *somatic* form of endogenous determinism that posits bodily characteristics as the driving force behind human capacities, social relations, and historical events. According to Guillaumin's own materialist view, racial groups are the product of specific social relationships that allow the members of each group to be first discerned and then lumped together under some sort of indexical sign or mark. This mark *could* be almost anything—a uniform, a gold star, a tattoo or brand—as long as it effectively signifies the group's status. Since the eighteenth century, however, it has almost invariably been a permanent morphological feature ascribed to "nature": skin pigmentation, skull size and shape, hair texture, and so on. Social relations, then, create race by means of the mark. Somatic determinism, however, reverses and obscures this materialist logic, making the social relationships (one's access or lack thereof to goods and services, the degree of compensation for one's labor, one's presumed or externally imposed status) into a function of the specific "nature" of the racial group, a racial "nature" in turn derived from the specific bodily features considered inherent and permanent to every member of the group and characteristic of it, the features collected under the system of marks. According to this "pseudo-materialism" (RSPI 143), the mark creates race, and race drives history and society. It is as if race is to be held "naturally" responsible for the social practices that bring it into existence in the first place. "Wherever there is a power relationship," Guillaumin writes, "a somatic trait [will be] found or invented" to serve as the putative basis of a "natural" group that can be dominated due to its "nature" (RSPI 81).[9]

In the early years of the nineteenth century, as its racial overtones became increasingly biologized, blood emerged as just such a trait. An ideal one, in fact. No longer simply an index of racial identity or a convenient way to inventory mixed ancestry, it began to be written and spoken of as the basis of racial identity. At a time when the social and taxonomic problem of miscegenation made skin color less and less viable as an indicator of race, blood acquired the status of an endogenous principle. When Immanuel Kant, for instance, declared "the composition of the human blood" to be the "seat" of "innate, natural character," he was not just locating character in blood but actively and much more problematically deriving character from blood.[10] In 1837, a French scientist named Victor Courtet de l'Isle put forward the theory "that human history was determined not merely by interracial struggles, that is to say 'physically', but also in a more intimate way through a welter of combinations or injections of different bloodstreams, or chemically," which is to say endogenously. According to historian Léon Poliakov, Courtet "seems to have been the first to clothe this idea, which was to become . . . a dogma of modern racism, in scientific language."[11] Blood was even elevated to the position of grammatical subject, as in Thomas Dixon's 1902 novel, *The Leopard's Spots*, where an authorial spokesman offers perhaps the supreme statement of endogenous racial determinism in all of American literature: "One drop of blood makes a Negro. It kinks the hair, flattens the nose, thickens the lip, puts out the light of intellect, and lights the fires of brutal passions. . . . There is enough Negro blood here to make mulatto the whole Republic."[12] Here blood is endowed with the power to transform human morphology, to benight the mind, to enflame the emotions, to redirect national history and identity, and, most crucially, to create race itself. Blood, then, makes race in two distinct senses: the concept of "blood" helps to sustain and legitimate the concept of "race," and, within that conceptual scheme, blood is understood as constitutive of race.

So how does blood make race in *Light in August*? And where does Faulkner go from there? Bearing in mind Faulkner's youthful remark about Paul Cézanne, that he painted with a brush dipped in light, it might be apropos to describe *Light in August* as written with a pen dipped in blood.[13] But blood is not only drawn and shed throughout this novel, it is also frequently and consequentially *invoked*, and invoked not only to handle the taxonomic problem of who or what someone "is," racially speaking, but also to handle what we might call the *motivational* problem of what one's race makes one *do*. On numerous occasions in *Light in August*, "blood" is held responsible for human behavior. The novel, however, offers its own critique of this view by juxtaposing scenes in which blood is invoked as an endogenous racial principle and scenes of cutting, of actual bloodshed or deliberate bloodletting. By presenting cutting as the result of a racialized discourse, as underwritten by representations of "blood" and "race," such scenes function as a subversive commentary on these representations and the violent cultural work they perform. Once again, summoning the literal, bringing blood itself forward for inspection, becomes a way to short-circuit a destructive metaphor by calling attention to its material consequences. With all this in mind, then, I want to focus on two narrative sequences from *Light in August* in which Joe Christmas is in flight from the law. The first, which ends in Mottstown, takes place over chapters 13 through 15 and represents a kind of trial run, as it were, for the second, which takes place in chapter 19, ending on the floor of Gail Hightower's kitchen.

In both of these sequences it is important to foreground the historical problem of African American mobility, which has for several centuries made white Southerners nervous enough to resort to racialized interpretations (movement as the expression of endogenous fecklessness and indiscipline) rather than the more obvious and appropriate social interpretations one would expect under regimes of slavery and institutionalized segregation. The history of this social problem would include fugitive slaves, freedmen and -women on the move in massive numbers during the Jubilee period following emancipation, and, perhaps most disturbingly, the Great Migration of the 1910s and 1920s, in which African Americans were moving out of the South altogether. Against this historical background, Joe's itinerancy renders him problematic from the moment he sets foot in Jefferson. One of the first things noticed about him at the sawmill where he finds employment is his "rootless" appearance, which should be understood not simply as a possible economic problem (how long will he perform his job before wanderlust seizes him again?) but as a definite genealogical problem, an absence of lineal roots that makes racial classification both difficult and *urgent*.[14] As the historian Joel Williamson has written of small-town white Southerners in an era of widespread anxiety about miscegenation, "The identification of newcomers in a community was always important to them, but as blackness disappeared beneath white skins and white features, it became vastly more so."[15] This anxiety pervades even the earliest spoken exchanges concerning Joe:

> The foreman and the superintendent were talking at the door. They parted and the foreman returned. "His name is Christmas," he said.
> "His name is what?" one said.
> "Christmas."
> "Is he a foreigner?"
> "Did you ever hear of a white man named Christmas," the foreman said.
> "I never heard of nobody a-tall named it," the other said. (LIA 33)

The name "Christmas" only compounds the problem of Joe's root-lessness. Insofar as the town is unable to identity anyone else "a-tall" who has ever gone by "Christmas," the name seems to present an identity independent of lineage, as if derived from the mere circumstance of a holiday, or the time of year associated with it. And indeed, the reader will learn that Joe has passionately re-jected a name, McEachern, that entailed both a line of descent and a juridical identity as adopted son, in favor of one that gives no hint of legal or biological ancestry (LIA 145, 184). It is as if from the very beginning he disavows the category of lineal "blood."

These associations will problematize Joe all over again when, in the wake of Joanna Burden's death and after three years of almost sedentary existence in Jefferson, he begins to move again, to run. Once Lucas Burch plants the seeds of racial suspicion in the white community, Joe's enigmatic history, and the social history of black movement in the region, will be enlisted in this process of raciali-zation. The farther Joe runs, the blacker he will get, the more easily he will be consigned to the black race, whatever truths his body might seem to offer to the contrary. The fact that he runs, and the *way* that he runs, pose interpretive problems for the white community: why does he neither escape nor surrender nor get caught but uncannily circulate, hover? This behavior threatens conventional racial categories, but the community will obstinately resolve the crisis by drawing on received stereotypes about black flight and invoking the racialized metaphor of "blood" as a mo-mentary stay against category confusion.

For Mottstown, the problem is that Joe went walking up and down the main street until somebody recognized him, that " '[h]e never denied' " who he was (in other words, he didn't lie about it, the way Mottstown thinks "a nigger" would), that " '[h]e never did anything' " when confronted by his captor, Halliday (in other words, he didn't try to escape, the way Mottstown thinks "a nig-ger" would), that " 'it looked like he had set out to get himself caught' " (LIA 347, 349–50). The solution, the inevitable conclu-sion, is that " 'it must have been the nigger blood in him' " that would endogenously *cause* such baffling, perverse, outrageous

conduct (LIA 349). Here "blood" emerges as the somatic characteristic that creates, fixes, and naturalizes race so that the latter
can be invoked to explain anything and everything. Even though
by rights "a nigger" ought to be a fugitive, " 'ought to have been
skulking and hiding in the woods, muddy and dirty and running' "
(LIA 350), and even though, according to one of Mottstown's anonymous narrators, Joe " 'don't look any more like a nigger than I
do' " (LIA 349), still it must have been that Negro blood. The ver-
dict echoes the earlier remark made by Hightower's grocer,
" 'Why, the fool never even had sense enough to get out of the
county. . . . Show he is a nigger, even if nothing else' " (LIA 309),
but with the additional intervention of "blood" as the mark and
source of that racial identity.

It is probably no coincidence, then, that the one thing Joe can
do that will be recognized by the Mottstown community as unam-
biguously, categorically Negro, is to bleed, to receive violence and
acquiesce to the cutting of his body. In the words of one witness,
Halliday " 'had already hit the nigger a couple of times in the face,
and the nigger acting like a nigger for the first time and taking it,
not saying anything: just bleeding sullen and quiet' " (LIA 350).
Faulkner's point here is surely that Joe's bleeding face could and
should unleash a certain demystifying potential at work in literal
meaning, that by helping to fashion Joe as the fugitive Negro who
has eluded and mocked the white community for the better part
of a week, the figure of "blood" has led directly to the very real
blood that runs down Joe's face. A racial representation has sponsored material violence. An idea has come face to face, if you will,
with its consequence. Mottstown, however, is unable to see Joe's
blood in this literal, humanizing way. The racial discourse of the
white community is here so powerful that even red blood can be
reinscribed within race, by making "bleeding" and "taking it" into
the acts of a Negro. What Mottstown sees is not the blood of a man
who has been forcibly constructed as a Negro, it's the blood of a
man who *is* a Negro . . . because he bleeds.

This perfectly circular reasoning conceals a further irony: if
being cut makes Joe black in Mottstown, *cutting* has made him

black in Jefferson, where his alleged identity as the razor-wielding murderer of a white women has already advanced him several steps toward the social category of Negro.[16] Similarly, if cutting has helped make Halliday white in Mottstown, confirming his status as a representative of a white community outraged and taunted by a fugitive black killer, being cut has helped make Joanna Burden white in Jefferson, since it is only when she is discovered to be the victim of putatively black, and putatively sexual, violence that the white community seems to recognize her as a white woman living alone among Negroes (see LIA 291–92). The list of permutations is complete: black and bleeding (Joe), white and bleeding (Joanna), black and cutting (Joe), white and cutting (Halliday). Bleeding quietly about the face, then, can only be evidence of race in confirming preexisting racial suspicions. *Any* sign can be seized upon as the mark of race, as proof of blackness; a sign, as Umberto Eco has noted, is anything that can be used to lie.[17] No matter what Joe does—if he runs or if he is caught, if he cuts or if he bleeds—he will "therefore" be black.

What to make, then, of the fact that Joe is already bleeding from the face, marked by blood, *before* he presents himself for capture in Mottstown? Bleeding, moreover, by his own hand. On the morning of his final day of flight, he kneels beside a spring and "shaves, after a fashion. His hand trembles; it is not a very good job, and he cuts himself three or four times, stanching the blood with the cold water until it stops." He then goes to stand beside the road, "his gaunt face blotched with patches of stubble and with dried blood," as he awaits the wagon that will take him to civilization and capture (LIA 336). I want to suggest that the cutting in this scene is not entirely accidental, that it is in fact as much a part of the ritual preparation for capture (and for the ordeal that will inevitably follow capture) as the acts of ablution and shaving. The (perhaps Freudian) slips with the razor transform Joe's morning toilet into a scarification rite, a stylization of the body that brings blood to its surface as if in anticipation of its expropriation by metaphor in the discourse of Mottstown. Released or perhaps unleashed by his shaky hand, Joe's blood signals his human embodiment and vulnerability, all the more so by making his body prefigure the bloody beating he will receive in Mottstown, a beating, as noted earlier, underwritten by the discourse of "blood." By tattooing himself in this way, Joe fashions his body into a somatic text that is already speaking back to that discourse, interfering with Mottstown's racial information system. He makes noise. Mottstown, of course, will be able to answer the challenge of this clamorous blood, but the fact that Joe's razor scars will soon be covered over by fresh blood and new marks should not be taken as a sign of futility or failure, for it also confirms the basic accuracy of the prediction he has carved into his face at the spring.

Whether this act reflects Joe's conscious intent is probably impossible to say. But if so, it is perhaps Joe's most Christlike act in a novel filled with such gestures, a simultaneous assertion and relinquishment of authorial control over his own body: I bleed (by my own design) . . . but what is more I *will* bleed (by the community's design, for reasons beyond my control). But whatever his intent, what Joe brings to Mottstown, and will bring again to Jefferson in chapter 19, is what his predecessor brought to Jerusalem: a political theater of violence and blood.

Chapter 19 takes these problems, strategies, and resistances and elevates them to frantic intensity. Here the discourse of "blood" grows more eloquent, coherent, and urgent, because here there is more horror to account for, more violence to legitimate, than ever before. Here also the novel's artistry in blood reaches a new level of oppositional force, as literal meaning grows harder and harder to foreclose or neutralize. Blood becomes at once more sovereign in its grip on race and noisier in its dissonance than anywhere else in the text, as demonstrated by the chapter's three defining moments: Percy Grimm's pursuit of Joe Christmas; Gavin Stevens's speculations on Joe's death; and the death scene itself in Hightower's kitchen. Once again, a great deal will be riding on the relationship between running and race, and on the part "blood" plays in articulating that relationship.

Percy Grimm, for instance, appears wildly inconsistent in chapter 19, savagely running down, killing, and mutilating the very man whose constitutional rights he has set out to protect. But what consistently motivates Grimm as he passes from peacekeeping to butchery is the logic of 1920s-era American nativism, the same belief system behind the xenophobic immigration restrictions voted into law by Congress in 1924. Throughout the entire macabre sequence in which he figures, Grimm's primary responsibility is to his country; he is, after all, a member of the *National* Guard. America is his first and truest love; his initiation into manhood occurs in a fistfight with a disillusioned World War One veteran who questions the value and wisdom of patriotic loyalty (LIA 450). But it is a particular idea of America that Grimm reveres, one defined by the nativism of the times: in his "belief that the white race is superior to any and all other races and that the American is superior to all other white races" (LIA 451), we can see the convergence of national pride and race pride. Grimm's America is a racial republic, organized not around the inalienable political rights of an Enlightenment subject but instead around white solidarity and supremacy, as if the state itself has followed Guillaumin's path from the juridical to the biological. For Grimm, then, to guard the nation is to guard the white race.

According to this way of thinking, to protect the fundamentally *American* right to due process is to insure the freedom, equality, and safety of whites under a thoroughly racialized national order. By extension, for Joe to allow himself to be guarded amounts to accepting the rights of a white man. He certainly *looks* white, after all (or to echo the Mottstown native quoted earlier, he doesn't look any more like a black man than you or I do), and as long as he agrees to *act* white, to accept the constitutional protection afforded to all whites under nativist ideology, guarding America (or as Grimm likes to put it, "preserv[ing] order," "let[ting] the law take its course") will entail guarding Joe. Thus due process can be racialized even in being extended to a suspected mulatto (see LIA 451–52).

For Joe to break and run, though, is to topple this ideological house of cards. The farther he runs from the protection Grimm offers, the blacker he will get; the blacker he gets, the more dangerous he will become; and the more dangerous he becomes, the more violence against him will be justified in the name of pre-empting the violence expected from him. We are witnessing the transformation of a mulatto from structurally white to structurally black. Joe gets blacker not only because his escape once again conjures up the troubling historical image of black movement and flight, but also because in disturbing public order and rejecting the protection of law, he now threatens the precious national community so jealously guarded by Grimm. In threatening Grimm's America, however, Joe threatens the white race. And in threatening the white race, he becomes a Negro, as Grimm will confirm with his parting shot to Joe, " 'Now you'll let white women alone, even in hell' " (LIA 464). Put simply, to be un-American is to be black. Note that this racial reasoning is largely if not completely independent of the so-called one-drop rule, which categorizes all mulattoes as Negroes. For Grimm, it is Joe's threatening behavior rather than his ostensibly mixed ancestry that racializes him. Indeed, one suspects that anyone who posed a similar threat to Grimm's racial republic would be similarly "blackened."[18]

The kind of materialist analysis practiced by Guillaumin will be obliged to conclude that here as in the earlier escape sequence the act of running makes Joe black: the social event becomes the occasion for the projection of a naturalized racial identity onto Joe, an identity that can then be invoked to explain the event. The logical trap ultimately relocates Joe outside Grimm's definition of national membership, transforming him into exactly what Grimm must guard *against*. Once Joe no longer accepts the protection of the law, the law, and America, must be protected from him. This is how the man whose mission was to keep Joe from getting lynched can wind up single-handedly lynching Joe himself.

In the aftermath of Joe's death, Gavin Stevens performs a kind of ideological mopping-up operation for white Jefferson. As evening settles upon the exhausted and perplexed town, Stevens steps forward to supply the endogenous somatic mark from which Joe's enigmatic identity and equally enigmatic behavior can be derived. That mark, once again, is blood. The intervention of "blood," and the enormous explanatory power Stevens assigns to it, will allow him to reverse the real terms of Grimm's reasoning—that Joe is black because he runs—and to suggest instead that Joe runs because he is black, that his "black blood" makes him run. I find it suggestive that the most articulate, deterministic, and fully biologized theory of "blood" put forward in the novel is the work of a blue-blood, a patrician and scion of slaveholders (though I suppose it's unfair, given the thrust of my argument, to make Stevens accountable for the behavior of his progenitors). Sophisticated, highly educated, and professionally trained, Stevens will put physical anthropology to work in service of criminal psychology with the same enthusiasm and complete lack of irony exhibited by nineteenth-century criminologists like Italy's Cesare Lombroso or England's Francis Galton:

> [T]here was too much running with him, stride for stride with him. . . . It was not alone all those thirty years . . . but all those successions of thirty years before that which had put that stain either on his white blood or his black blood, whichever you will, and which killed him. But he must have run with believing for a while; anyway, with hope. But his blood would not be quiet, let him save it. It would not be either one or the other and let his body save itself. Because the black blood drove him first to the negro cabin. And then the white blood drove him out of there, as it was the black blood which snatched up the pistol and the white blood which would not let him fire it. And it was the white blood which sent him to the minister, which rising in him for the last and final time, sent him against all reason and all reality, into the embrace of a chimera, a blind faith in something read in a printed Book. Then I believe that the white blood deserted him for a moment. Just a second, a flicker, allowing the black to rise in its final moment and make him turn upon that on which he had postulated his hope of salvation. It was the black blood which swept him by his own desire beyond the aid of any man. . . . And then the black blood failed him again, as it must have in crises all his life. He did not kill the minister. He merely struck him with the pistol and ran on and crouched behind that table and defied the black blood for the last time, as he had been defying it for thirty years. He crouched behind that overturned table and let them shoot him to death, with that loaded and unfired pistol in his hand. (LIA 448–49)

The word "blood" appears twelve times in this speech, evoking a complex, hybrid ancestry but also a causal principle actively at work in Joe, prompting instantaneous modulations of behavior that lead to outright contradictions and paralyzing impasses. Like Thomas Dixon, whom one suspects he has read, Stevens installs the word "blood" in the grammatical subject position. Blood drives, it snatches, it prevents, it deserts, it rises, it sweeps, and in the end, it devastatingly fails. To deny this sovereign force is fatal, spelling mutilation and death. It amounts to going against nature.

Stevens fashions an image of the mulatto not as a vigorous, hardy alloy of bloodlines, but as a degenerate mongrel, a self-canceling patchwork of antagonistic strains, pulled this way and that in a terrible tug of war that extends beyond the rarefied plane of consciousness to the concrete movements and gestures of the body itself. The tragedy of Stevens's mulatto is not social, the ostracism of an individual denied membership in any human community, but somatic, a matter of the organism's own grotesque rejection of itself on the physical level.[19] Borrowing an insight from Twain's *Pudd'nhead Wilson*, a novel *Light in August* is much indebted to, Stevens suggests that a man's own blood—and not, as Twain wrote, his hand—can be his deadliest enemy, as if equating mixed ancestry with something very like leukemia.[20] This view conveniently transfers the responsibility for Joe's death from Grimm, where it rightly belongs, to Joe himself (whose blood, after all, failed him). Invoking "blood" in this way allows Stevens to mystify Grimm's patriotic racism, suture over his hysterical violence, and excuse the white community for its part in that violence.

Which brings us to the butcher knife, the cutting tool that initiates the hideous, quasi-homoerotic form of blood sport between Grimm and Joe. If Grimm and Jefferson would no doubt explain that Joe must be cut and castrated because he is black (that is, because he could never be trusted to "let white women alone" otherwise), it seems to me that Joe must be marked in this way *in order* to be black, that the act of cutting contributes further to the fabrication, imposition, and perpetuation of a racial identity understood in ontological terms. The blood released from Joe's body, then, like that released earlier by Halliday's fists, is intended to help stage and construct race.[21] I want to suggest, however, that this project backfires, that the explosive emergence of Joe's blood overloads the racial circuitry and ultimately turns the power of blood *against* Grimm.

> For a long moment he looked up at them with peaceful and unfathomable and unbearable eyes. Then his face, body, all, seemed to collapse, to fall in upon itself, and from out the slashed garments about his hips and loins the pent black blood seemed to rush like a released breath. It seemed to rush out of his pale body like the rush of sparks from a rising rocket; upon that black blast the man seemed to rise soaring into their memories forever and ever. (LIA 464–65)

Everything hinges here on the way Faulkner simultaneously alludes to and renounces racial metaphor in coloring Joe's blood black. The visual effect is not unlike that achieved by Hollywood directors of the black and white era who used chocolate syrup for screen blood. The reader is meant to see, not an authorial confirmation of Stevens's racial theories, whose discourse the passage cunningly echoes, but instead the literal and material fact of blood: the thick, dark, viscous, deoxygenated fluid issuing from the massive, violently opened veins that run along the inside of the thighs and loins.[22] The rupture of the body brings the rupture of metaphor. The man on the floor is not black; if anything he is quite pale. Rather, the *blood* is black, on an immediate perceptual level; and the horror of this realization—that a racial trope like "black blood" has helped make real, dark blood flow—unsettles the white community's complacent racial thinking. The rhetorical effect is the exact opposite of the way an originally forced figure of speech, or catachresis, comes to acquire a familiar value over time, as in a phrase like "the legs of a table," which has gradually lost its ability to startle. Here, however, in a process we might call *defiguration*, it is as if we suddenly beheld a tabletop resting on four fleshy human legs; it is the restoration of literal meaning to the long-familiar figure of "black blood" that startles, forcing us to confront rather than evade the material body. As that body leaks blood, "blood" leaks as well, cracks open; the solidity and cohesion of the cultural concept is shaken with the return of the literal and the somatic.

Volatile as rocket fuel, the pent black blood mesmerizes everyone in its presence. Joe now incarnates the relationship between representation and violence. He has become an artist in blood, with his own body, and Hightower's floor, for a canvas. The black blast of his blood assaults the spectators, rocking them with its visceral impact: "They are not to lose it," Faulkner writes, even as the horror of the moment recedes. "It will be there, musing, quiet, steadfast, not fading and not particularly threatful" (LIA 465). Even more than the man, the blood is what Jefferson will remember, blood that is only blood, that doesn't stand for anything in an analogical relationship but stands only in contiguity to the violence that releases it. "[O]f itself alone serene, of itself alone triumphant" (LIA 465), it signifies nothing other than itself in its unassimilable magnitude. Once again we have witnessed the eruption of the natural world into a metaphorical field.

The reemergence of the screaming fire alarm at scene's end, "mount[ing] toward its unbelievable crescendo" before "passing out of the realm of hearing" (LIA 465), should remind us, in a characteristically Faulknerian way, that we have *not* been hearing it for quite a while now, for the entire period, in fact, that Joe has lain bleeding in Hightower's kitchen. The temporary absence of that sonic assault, which has functioned throughout the chase scene to elevate readerly and communal tension, offers further evidence of the "noise" generated by Joe's blood, its ability to crowd even the siren out of narrative consciousness and to wrestle attention to itself. "Rush," "rocket," and "blast," all explicitly noisy words, contribute to the effect. If chapter 19 confirms Thomas Dixon's claim that "[i]t is possible to kill the human body with an idea," it also illustrates how in its dying throes the body can speak back to the idea that killed it, can make plain, in the medium of its own blood, the terrible consequences of representation and thereby clear a preliminary space for its resistance.

Such resistance, in fact, is already at work in the castration scene, in the specific and entirely appropriate form of physical revulsion. "When the others reached the kitchen they saw the table flung aside now and Grimm stooping over the body. . . . [W]hen they saw what Grimm was doing one of the men gave a choked cry and stumbled back into the wall and began to vomit" (LIA 464). More than any other aspect of the scene, the nausea of this nameless weekend warrior explicitly confirms that the eruption of the literal has reached an audience alert to its significance on at least a visceral level and perhaps a cognitive one as well. All around this man, words are turning into unspeakable acts and things. "Blood" is made real. "Lynching" is no longer something you only hear about. This is what the word "castration" looks like. Nausea signals how drastically this process of literalization raises the stakes of the scene. In its near-speaking of the unspeakable, and in its complicated mimicry of Joe's bleeding (the body turned inside out, its internal fluids rocketing into the social world), it offers the text's most forceful commentary on Grimm's attempt to liquidate Joe, to reduce him to fluid and pulp as Stevens will later reduce him to "blood." Nausea here makes noise in its own right, bursting onto the scene of cutting as proof that Grimm's racial violence is not going over without a hitch, that there are limits to what he can get away with in the name of the racial republic, since even his cronies are confused and sickened by what he does. We might even say that in its very form, its undifferentiated mixture of the unassimilated elements of digestion, materials that have not been or cannot be properly absorbed, vomit directly suggests noise, that nausea is to the body what noise is to the intellect. In this sense the man's nausea would simply *be* the noise that Joe's blood and Grimm's violence have generated.

Long before the Grand Guignol of chapter 19, however, *Light in August* has already linked nausea, blood, and pervasive anxiety about human difference. Only this time the context is gender rather than race. This new context raises some interesting problems I would like to address briefly before concluding.

From the moment Joe hears his first adolescent rumors about menstruation, female blood interferes with his still incipient sense of "the smooth and superior shape" of woman's body and desire.

Not even the crude form of therapy he attempts by shooting a sheep and bathing his hands in its dying blood—yet another immersion in the literal that suggests blood sport—can reconcile Joe to the red blood of woman. Though others have associated menstrual blood with power, fecundity, and the intrauterine matrix that gives life to every human being,[23] Joe can only equate it with "periodical filth" (LIA 185). Such filth is incompatible with his idea of woman, or more precisely, with his idea of *his* woman: "All right," he thinks. "It is so, then. But not to me. Not in my life and my love" (LIA 186; emphasis removed). Thus when his first lover, Bobbie Allen, turns up "sick" on the night their relationship is to be consummated, Joe, upon learning what explicitly ails her, reacts hysterically, knocking her down and running away to the woods, where, faced with his misogynistic vision of leaking urns, he vomits (LIA 188–89).

Nor do things get much better when Joe confronts the cessation of menstrual blood in a new lover, Joanna Burden. Intuiting the problem to be menopause rather than pregnancy, he lashes out with physical and verbal violence, bloodying Joanna's face as he pronounces her "worn out" and "not any good anymore" (LIA 277–78). This view of menopause as the end of sexuality and desire reveals the vicious double standard at work in Joe's projections onto the feminine: a woman who bleeds is filthy, sickening, but a woman who no longer bleeds is used up, and a woman who is used up can be beaten, made to bleed. Either way, this personal mythology of gender makes woman's identity and value revolve around blood. But in drawing Joanna's blood, in making his hand an instrument of cutting, Joe unleashes the same unpredictable force of the literal that Grimm does in the castration scene. There, as we have already seen, Grimm tries to use blood to construct an object of contempt, but blood, the literal, gets away from him, subverting his design and ultimately exposing his brutality. One could argue that something similar happens here: like Joe's bleeding face in chapter 15, and his bleeding loins in chapter 19, Joanna's bleeding mouth embodies the relationship between representation and violence, eliciting the contradiction at work in Joe's cruelty: she must bleed because she no longer bleeds.

Here, then, are the rudiments of an art of the literal in which blood makes noise for gender. An art, however, that never quite emerges in full. To me, this is one of the great squandered opportunities of *Light in August*: the subversive potential of woman's blood, its power to unsettle pernicious representations of gender, never receives anywhere near the attention that Faulkner brings to his detailed analysis of blood and race. Though female blood is an almost constant preoccupation in the novel, it is almost never directly represented in the narrative. Joanna's bleeding face is a rare exception. More typical are three other scenes involving the traumatic rupture of a woman's body: the murder of Joanna Burden, the birth of Lena Grove's son, and Hightower's unsuccessful attempt to deliver a Negro baby. All three are scenes of cutting, in which a straight razor is present and presumably in use. And all three presumably involve large amounts of blood. Yet blood is almost completely absent from the narrative depiction of these scenes.[24] Joanna's blood, for instance, simply vanishes into the textual aporia that surrounds her death, reemerging only much later at the crime scene, in a single offhand reference (LIA 289). And Lena's puerperal blood is never mentioned at all. This reticence is especially striking when contrasted with the voyeurism of chapter 19, which all but wallows in Joe's blood.

What is equally striking is that Faulkner does stage Lena's childbed as a vivid rejoinder to the highly conventional image of womanhood held by Byron Bunch, an image whose romantic excesses are amusing at times but also capable of real harm. It is typical of Byron's colossal innocence that when Lena's time comes he cannot even think of the word "midwife" (LIA 393), so committed is he to the idea of her "physical inviolability" and purity (LIA 49). To put it mildly, this man is in denial. His idealization of Lena leaves him unable to see that her body and desire have a specific history, and that it is to this history rather than his personal fantasy that they now answer. He has never arranged for a doctor to assist Lena in birth because, as he will later acknowledge, he has never believed that he would need one, that she is not a virgin (LIA 398, 401). This fantasy persists even as Lena's labor begins. "[H]e expected to see her sitting up; perhaps to be met by her at the door, placid, unchanged, timeless." What he encounters instead is an object lesson in Lena's mutability and pain that not even he can deny. We might expect blood to deliver this lesson, rushing out of Lena's laboring body to signal her pain in yet another demystifying eruption of the somatic. Anyone who has ever been present at a childbirth knows that the event is accompanied by a great deal of blood. But here, perhaps following Byron's own modest gaze, there is a displacement upward, toward Lena's "bloodless mouth." A mouth, however, whose "wailing cry in a tongue unknown to man" directly evokes the history that has marked Lena's body and hurts it still. Hearing that wail, Byron can finally recognize the full extent of his negligence, the part his willful repression of Lena's sexuality and pregnancy has played in her present suffering. A woman finally emerges in flesh and blood from his projections. If, as so many have argued, the representation of woman as ideal, virginal, and pedestaled has caused real Southern women real pain,[25] Lena's cry, and the cry of her baby, speak back to those cultural fictions in a language of pain and need. This is why it is not merely tautological to say that Lena's wail makes noise.

Why, at this moment, does Faulkner's art of the literal abandon blood in favor of voice? Why must *Light in August* look away from the red blood of woman?[26] One answer I can suggest is not necessarily flattering to Faulkner, though that may not make it wrong either. It may be that Faulkner minimizes the material presence of blood in the novel's scenes of birth, menstruation, and sexualized violence in order to appropriate their power for Joe's death scene, as if the blood that rushes out of Joe has been *textually* as well as physically "pent," channeled from the bodies of Lena, Bobbie, and Joanna into the unforgettable eruption of chapter 19, a return of the repressed if ever there was one. I am suggesting, then, that Joe's death may acquire its truly climactic force in large part by engulfing the resonance of these earlier sequences and their un-seen but implicitly present blood. This resonance extends to gender. I have elsewhere described the castration scene as a failed attempt by Grimm to contain the uncanny masculine excess of Christmas by forcibly refiguring his body as female.[27] Joe's blood thus marks the violence that attends the construction of sex and gender as well as the construction of race. So with the vomiting man to prompt us, we can perhaps see in Joe's resexed and *visibly* bleeding genitals an image of the nauseating menstruation that we did not see when it was Bobbie Allen who bled.[28] Similarly, in the bloody slashing of Joe's body we witness the murder-by-cutting that went unnarrated when Joanna Burden was its victim. And it may even be that in the violent opening of Joe's loins, and the sudden emergence of their precious contents onto a scene dramatically altered by that arrival, we are meant to recognize a visual echo of still another image we have never directly seen in *Light in August*, the image of a woman in birth. If so, if Joe's death scene has absorbed the power of Lena's birth scene, then Grimm's cutting has ironically mutated into obstetrical work, an episiotomy, if you will, expediting delivery of the burden that Joe, like Lena, has entered the narrative already gestating. But where Lena gives birth to the literal in the form of another human life, Joe's burden—the only legacy he will ever leave—takes the material form of his pent black blood. That blood does not simply attend what is born, it *is* what is born, what will carry Joe's name forward into communal memory in the same way that a child could have.

Faulkner did not invent the art of the literal, the writing (in) blood, that I have here called defiguration. The South's obsession with the subject and trope of blood often led its writers to experiment with scenes of bloodshed and bloodletting. In Edna Ferber's *Showboat*, for instance, a novel published several years before *Light in August*, a white man circumvents miscegenation law by cutting the hand of his mulatta wife and sucking her blood, an act that allows him to claim that the couple's marriage is legitimate because he, too, is now of "mixed blood." With its clever defiguration of the racial metaphor, this loving version of blood sport proves effective, keeping at bay the sheriff who has come to arrest the wife.[29] *Light in August*, of course, can offer no equivalent to such unqualified success, only a series of Pyrrhic victories in which the subversive potential of cutting and defiguration goes largely unrecognized among the characters but still remains for the reader to contemplate. All the same, Faulkner's use of this strategy remains particularly meaningful, the stakes particularly high, given his decision to make racial identity purely hypothetical in Joe's case. Since the narrative finally offers no "firm" or "factual" basis for it, Joe's race can *only* be a matter of representation, even for him. He may be (part) black, he may not; no one, including the reader, will ever know for sure. With the issue of Joe's racial identity pointedly unresolved, Faulkner isolates discourse—the rumors and theories circulated by a community all too eager to read from a glance, a remark, or a gesture to race—as the ultimate ground of the novel's pervasive racial violence: but for the power of metaphors like "black blood," the blood and vomit of *Light in August* might never have flowed. "Race does not exist," writes Guillaumin. "But it does kill people" (RSPI 107). *Light in August*'s artistry in blood drives that point home with a vengeance, recording the hard facts that attend the South's defining social fiction.

NOTES

1. Disraeli quoted in Hannah Arendt, *Antisemitism* (New York: Harcourt Brace Jovanovich, 1968), 73. Dixon, *The Leopard's Spots: A Romance of the White Man's Burden, 1865–1900* (1902; Ridgewood, N.J.: Gregg Press, 1967), 340. Vega, "Blood Makes Noise," *99.9F°* (A & M, 1992).

2. See Eurydice, "Scar Lovers," *Spin* 11.5 (August 1995): 60–66, 110. Further references to this essay, abbreviated as SL, will be included in the text.

3. In using the term I mean to evoke Luce Irigaray's sense of *parodic* imitation, mimicry, rather than the more straightforward concept discussed by Aristotle and Auerbach. See for instance Irigaray, *This Sex Which Is Not One* (1977), trans. Catherine Porter with Carolyn Burke (Ithaca: Cornell University Press, 1985), 131, 136–37.

4. See for instance Lakoff and Mark Johnson, *Metaphors We Live By* (Chicago: University of Chicago Press, 1980), and Lakoff and Mark Turner, *More Than Cool Reason: A Field Guide to Poetic Metaphor* (Chicago: University of Chicago Press, 1989).

5. The discussion in the following two paragraphs attempts to synthesize ideas found in the following sources: Michael Banton, *Racial Theories* (New York: Cambridge University Press, 1987); Elazar Barkan, *The Retreat of Scientific Racism: Changing Concepts of Race in Britain and the United States between the World Wars* (New York: Cambridge University Press, 1992); Michel Foucault, *The History of Sexuality: Volume I: An Introduction* (1976), trans. Robert Hurley (New York: Vintage, 1978), 124–26, 147–50; George Frederickson, *The Black Image in the White Mind: The Debate on Afro-American Character and Destiny, 1817–1914* (1971; Middletown: Wesleyan University Press, 1987); David Theo Goldberg, *Racist Culture: Philosophy and the Politics of Meaning* (Cambridge, Mass.: Black-

well, 1993); Stephen Jay Gould, *The Mismeasure of Man* (New York: Norton, 1981); Ivan Hannaford, *Race: The History of an Idea in the West* (Baltimore: Johns Hopkins University Press, 1996), especially 187–324; William Stanton, *The Leopard's Spots: Scientific Attitudes toward Race in America 1815–59* (Chicago: University of Chicago Press, 1960); Nancy Stepan, *The Idea of Race in Science: Great Britain 1800–1960* (Hamden, CT: Archon Books, 1982); and George Stocking, *Race, Culture, and Evolution: Essays in the History of Anthropology* (1968; Chicago: University of Chicago Press, 1982).

6. Guillaumin, "The Specific Characteristics of Racist Ideology" (1972), *Racism, Sexism, Power, and Ideology* (New York: Routledge, 1995), 37. Future references to this book, abbreviated as RSPI, will be included in the text. For the essay specifically, see RSPI 29–60.

7. "Before, a dominant class which literally did not see other people; after, a dominant class which literally did not see itself" (RSPI 55).

8. See RSPI, 61–98 and 133–52, respectively.

9. The dominant race(s) must also be invented and naturalized in much the same way. See for example Theodore W. Allen, *The Invention of the White Race, Volume One: Racial Oppression and Social Control* (New York: Verso, 1994), and Noel Ignatiev, *How the Irish Became White* (New York: Routledge, 1995).

10. Kant quoted in Léon Poliakov, *The Aryan Myth: A History of Racist and Nationalist Ideas in Europe* (1971), trans. Edmund Howard (New York: Basic Books, 1974), 171.

11. Poliakov, 228–29. A century later, this view still persisted in the work of scientists like J. B. S. Haldane, who in 1931 proposed the hypothesis that blood groups (hematological categories) could serve as the basis for racial classification. Similar projects were carried forward into the 1950s as more and more about the genetics of blood groups became known. See Stepan 102–3.

12. Dixon, 244.

13. For the Cézanne comment, see William Faulkner, *Selected Letters of William Faulkner*, ed. Joseph Blotner (New York: Random House, 1977), 24.

14. William Faulkner, *Light in August* (1932; New York: Vintage International, 1990), 31. Future references to the novel, abbreviated as LIA, will be included in the text.

15. Joel Williamson, *New People: Miscegenation and Mulattoes in the United States* (New York: Free Press, 1980), 103.

16. For fuller elaborations of this logic, see Hoke Perkins, "'Ah Just Cant Quit Thinking': Faulkner's Black Razor Murderers," in *Faulkner and Race: Faulkner and Yoknapatawpha 1986*, ed. Doreen Fowler and Ann J. Abadie (Jackson: University Press of Mississippi, 1987), 222–35; and Martha Banta, "The Razor, the Pistol, and the Ideology of Race Etiquette," in *Faulkner and Ideology: Faulkner and Yoknapatawpha 1992*, ed. Donald M. Kartiganer and Ann J. Abadie (Jackson: University Press of Mississippi, 1995), 172–216, especially 204–6.

17. Umberto Eco, *A Theory of Semiotics* (1976; Bloomington: Indiana University Press, 1979), 7.

18. Including the demonstrably white. As Williamson explains, the fear of "invisible blackness" circulating among turn-of-the-century white Southerners meant that one's character could be in the most serious and literal sense "blackened" regardless of one's "actual" (genetic) racial background. "By about 1900 it was possible in the South for one who was biologically pure white to become behaviorally black. Blackness had become not a matter of visibility, not even, ironically, of the one-drop rule. It had passed on to become a matter of inner morality and outward behavior. People biologically black in any degree could not openly aspire to whiteness; but whites could easily descend into blackness if they failed in morality. Thus there was created in the white mind a new and curious kind of mulatto—a mulatto who was in fact genetically white but morally black. In sum, 'Negro' became an *idea*. Here in our very midst, the Southern white might say, there are unseen 'niggers,' men who might marry our daughters, who might thus in effect secretly rape them and spawn a despicable breed. Such men were the ultimate hidden enemies, and bound to raise fevers of paranoia. . . . Thus by the early twentieth century the color line actually reached into the white world to include white people who behaved in a black way" (108). Grimm

simply expands the ideological dimensions of this racial litmus test, making national loyalty into a "behaviorally white" trait.

19. Such a rejection was even thought to extend to the reproductive sphere by the many authorities on race mixing who considered mulattoes infertile—a view that seems to have originated with Edward Long of Jamaica in 1774. See Poliakov, 178; and George Fredrickson, *White Supremacy: A Comparative Study in American and South African History* (New York: Oxford University Press, 1981), 142. We should not overlook the irony that the scene Stevens is attempting to interpret culminates in a savagely imposed sterility that suspiciously resembles the medico-legal procedure referred to in contemporary eugenics discourse as compulsory sterilization, the same procedure presumably employed on Benjy Compson. For a fascinating account of the eugenics movement in the South, including compulsory eugenic sterilization laws and procedures, see Edward Larson, *Sex, Race, and Science: Eugenics in the Deep South* (Baltimore: Johns Hopkins University Press, 1995).

20. For the Twain quotation, see Samuel Langhorne Clemens, *Pudd'nhead Wilson and Those Extraordinary Twins*, ed. Sidney E. Berger (New York: Norton, 1980), 52.

21. A list to which we might add the blood released by the two accomplices of Bobbie Allen who slash open Joe's face to "see if his blood is black" (LIA 219; emphasis removed).

22. Here I take issue with the more cautious assessment of the passage offered by James A. Snead: "Whether 'black' is here a figurative or literal term is crucial, but impossible to determine." More to the point, I think, is Snead's earlier suggestion that "[t]he more blood is spilled to distinguish black from white blood" in *Light in August*, "the more difficult it is to see the difference; at a considerable price it becomes clear that black and white 'blood' are the same." See Snead, *Figures of Division: William Faulkner's Major Novels* (New York: Methuen, 1986), 97, 93.

23. See for instance Irigaray's characteristic panegyrics upon "red blood" in *This Sex Which Is Not One* (76–77, 151, 185–86) and in *Speculum of the Other Woman* (1974), trans. Gillian C. Gill (Ithaca: Cornell University Press, 1985), 125–27.

24. At the conference, Terrell Tebbetts of Lyon College alerted me to another one of these bloodlessly narrated scenes: the death in childbirth of Joe's mother, Milly Hines, who presumably expires from blood loss because her father, Doc Hines, will allow no one to attend to her during and after labor. As Mrs. Hines recounts the scene, " 'I tried to get out the back way and he heard me and run around the house with the gun and he hit me with the barrel of it and I went back to Milly and he stood outside the hall door where he could see Milly until she died' " (LIA 379). No word, though, on the somatic specifics of what either Hines saw. I have omitted this episode from the discussion proper only because it lacks the explicit element of cutting shared by the other three scenes.

25. One could begin with Lillian Smith, "The Women," *Killers of the Dream* (1961; New York: Norton, 1978), 138–55, proceed to Anne Goodwyn Jones, *Tomorrow Is Another Day: The Woman Writer in the South, 1859–1936* (Baton Rouge: Louisiana State University Press, 1981), and arrive at Diane Roberts, *The Myth of Aunt Jemima: Representations of Race and Region* (New York: Routledge, 1994), and have barely scratched the surface of the literature on this issue.

26. At one particularly egregious point just after the birth of Lena's son, Hightower is talking to the girl "in his cheerful, testy voice while his hands are busy" (LIA 403). Busy indeed, and we can easily guess doing what. Once again, however, the narrative willfully misdirects us from the scene of female blood.

27. See Jay Watson, "Overdoing Masculinity in *Light in August*; or, Joe Christmas and the Gender Guard," *Faulkner Journal* 9.1–2 (Fall 1993/Spring 1994): 149–77, especially 164–70.

28. As several people pointed out to me at the conference, the explicitly noted blackness of Joe's blood only reinforces this connection with menstrual blood. For other comments on the castration scene's visual allusions to menstruation, see John Duvall, "Faulkner's Crying Game: Male Homosexual Panic," *Faulkner and Gender: Faulkner and Yoknapatawpha 1994*, ed. Donald M. Kartiganer and Ann J. Abadie (Jackson: University Press of Mississippi, 1996), 62–64; Diane Roberts, *Faulkner and Southern Womanhood* (Athens:

University of Georgia Press, 1994), 184; and Joseph R. Urgo, "Menstrual Blood and 'Nigger' Blood: Joe Christmas and the Ideology of Sex and Race," *Mississippi Quarterly* 42 (1989): 401.

29. An episode I have cribbed from Roberts, *The Myth of Aunt Jemima*, 163.

Getting Around the Body: The Matter of Race and Gender in Faulkner's *Light in August*

MARY JOANNE DONDLINGER

"My, my. A body does get around," exclaims Lena Grove at both the beginning and the end of Faulkner's *Light in August* (1932).[1] Initially, her statement seems rather insignificant and simple-minded, but her declaration is profound. At a moment when the human body has become a topic of much discussion in both theory and praxis, particularly the gendered and racialized body and the cultural restrictions imposed upon it, Lena Grove's calm amazement resonates meaningfully. How and to what extent is a "body" able to "get around," despite the limitations imposed upon it by cultural categorizations? Can a body get around these very restrictions or at least get around within them? In her work on gender identity and the materiality of the body, feminist philosopher Judith Butler addresses these issues. In discussing the performative nature of gender and race, Butler posits that the very materiality of the body is produced discursively through the citation and reiteration of cultural norms.[2] She also points out that because those norms require continuous reiteration, they are open to "repetition with a difference"—repetitious performances which can disrupt or parody the regulatory norm. In other words, sometimes "a body gets around" the regulatory system through repeating the very laws of the system.

Bearing these ideas in mind, I will examine how the body of Joe Christmas, the novel's central protagonist, is discursively materialized. Despite all his literal "getting around" in the novel, Christmas cannot circumvent his culturally racialized body—"culturally" racialized because in spite of his white skin, he is labelled black. Nevertheless, the ways that he is able to "get around" the law and to violently "get through" that law at the end of the novel, show the extent to which he disrupts that regulatory system. In contrast to Joe Christmas, the way that Lena Grove does "get around" in the novel reveals how her gendered body also "gets around" the regulatory system which aims to restrain it. It also shows the extent to which she disrupts that system without experiencing the violence which attends Joe Christmas.

Before proceeding, however, I must pause at Lena's exclamation and discuss its connotative and denotative resonances. "Getting around" not only calls to mind the travel through or navigation of physical space and time and the effect that this movement has upon the formation of identity; it also suggests bypassing, or circumventing, getting past an obstacle, sidestepping the law. The phrase also refers to sexual promiscuity; one who "gets around" is one who "gets it" often and with various partners. "Getting around" also evokes the word "passing" and the meanings ascribed to it in a work like Nella Larson's *Passing*, a novel that Butler analyzes to exemplify her theory about bodies. "Passing" itself is a word that suggests getting around or getting by, and is also used in evaluation of performance, as in a passing grade. While I wish to invoke all of these meanings when using the term, I think that "getting around" goes beyond merely "passing." The shade of difference between the two terms is perhaps best illustrated by invoking Faulkner's Nobel Prize acceptance speech. To "pass" is to "endure"; to "get around" is to "prevail." I also suggest that the traveling or literal "getting around" in *Light in August* is a metaphor for "passing" and bypassing the restrictions that are imposed upon the body.

Indeed there is much "getting around" in the novel. Joe Christmas literally gets around the whole country on a road that ran "for fifteen years" (*LIA* 223). Before, during, and after that journey Joe "gets around" sexually. These experiences have much to do with the shaping of his identity, contouring his understanding of his body. Lena Grove also "gets around" literally, travelling from Alabama to Mississippi and then on to Tennessee by the end of the novel. Her story (or narrative strand as previous critics have called it) even "gets around" the strand of Christmas, providing the opening and the closing of the novel, with a few narrative loops into the lengthier story of Christmas which occupies much of the middle of the book. While both characters "get around" in the novel, this getting around has different productive effects on their bodies. In the end, Christmas is only more tightly bound in the "circle" of cultural circumscription, while Lena's experience is more liberating. Lena "gets around" and "prevails."

Joe Christmas's body is materialized discursively in *Light In August*. Despite his white skin, Christmas is said to be black, not because he actually is black either in appearance or by heritage, but simply because his grandfather, Doc Hines, says he is. The events preceding Christmas's birth and how Hines interprets them constitute Christmas's racial categorization—a categorization named by a Father. Christmas is racialized by others as well— namely the orphanage dietitian and Joe Brown/Lucas Burch. I will also examine how Christmas racializes himself, reading those moments in the novel where he calls himself black as citational reiterations of Doc Hines's original performative.

The reader is not told the events preceding Christmas's birth until nearly the end of the novel. At that time Byron Bunch and Mrs. Hines narrate to Reverend Hightower that Christmas is the son of Milly Hines and a circus performer of indeterminate race. When Milly informs her father, Doc Hines, that the circus performer is Mexican, he already "knew somehow that the fellow had nigger blood" (374). It is clear that Doc Hines is crazy and that the community considers him crazy. His craziness expresses itself as religious fanaticism, violent misogyny, and violence in general. Nevertheless, when he says that Joe Christmas is black, he is believed. He is believed because the sexual myths that Hines invokes are cultural myths to which the community subscribes, even though the community realizes that Hines is fanatically obsessed with them. To be more specific, the white communities of Mottstown, Jefferson, and the rest of Yoknapatawpha County fear miscegenation because it "taints" white blood and white superiority, and because it confuses the distinctive categories of white and black. Consequently, this community fears black men and stereotypes them as rapists and defilers of Southern womanhood.

Given these social constructions, when Milly is "seduced" by the circus performer and gets pregnant, Doc Hines "naturally" assumes that the circus performer has "nigger" blood, since both Hines and his community see the bestial sexual appetite of the black man for white women as part of his "nature." As Byron Bunch points out, "[Hines] aint never said how he found out, like that never made any difference" (375). In fact, it does not make any difference. A white girl is pregnant out of wedlock; therefore, the offspring, regardless of the race of the parents, has the blackness of sin, "bitchery and abomination," and illegitimacy in its blood. Christmas's racial categorization is constituted not by the color of his skin or by biological heritage, but by a father's outrage at the lawless sexual behavior of his daughter. Milly's refusal to adhere to the sexual regulations of a patriarchal economy—her "bitchery"—constitutes the "abomination" of her son's blood. His blood is tainted with the "blackness" of illegitimacy.

The sexual lawlessness of his mother is not the only illegitimate act that materializes Christmas's race. After allowing his daughter to die in childbirth as punishment for her sexual lawlessness, Hines places the infant Joe in an orphanage. The dietitian there pays no attention to Christmas or the possibility of his having "nigger blood" until she discovers him hiding in the closet while she is having illicit sex with the intern, Charley. She fears that Christmas knows what was happening and might tell on her. Once again, as with Hines and the circus worker, she has no way of knowing his racial genealogy, for he was found on the steps of the orphanage. Nevertheless, she tells Hines, "Well. You don't have to tell me. I know, anyway. I've known it all the time that he's part nigger" (129). If she reveals to the matron of the orphanage that Christmas is black, he will have to be sent away to the "nigger" orphanage and her secret will be safe. " 'All I need to do is to make the madam believe,' she thought. And then she thought *He will look just like a pea in a pan full of coffee beans"* (130, Faulkner's italics). Christmas becomes racialized as black because this racialization will obfuscate the dietitian's own guilt.

Lena's runaway lover and Joe Christmas's roommate and business partner, Lucas Burch/Joe Brown, invokes Christmas's blackness in the same way. Christmas's racial constitution does not bother Brown until the sheriff questions him about the murder of Joanna Burden and the fire that destroys her house. As the sheriff begins to trip Brown up by pointing out the inconsistencies in his story, Brown gets desperate and defers his own complicity by calling Christmas a "nigger." As Bunch relates the story to Hightower: "they said it was like he had been saving what he told them next for just such a time as this. Like he had knowed that if it come to a pinch, this would save him" (97). In fact, it was not so much that Brown saved what he told them for when he was in a bind, it simply was not pertinent until then. But when the sheriff gets him into a rhetorical trap, Brown pouts, " 'That's right. . . . Go on. Accuse me. Accuse the white man that's trying to help you with what he knows. Accuse the white man and let the nigger go free.' " The evocation of "nigger" does not need any evidence, for suddenly "It's like [Brown] knew he had them then. Like nothing they could believe he had done would be as bad as what he could tell that somebody else had done" (97–98). The sheriff and the marshal need no proof whatever of Brown's accusation. " 'A nigger,' the marshal said. 'I always thought there was something funny about that fellow.' " And the sheriff says to Brown, who he knows is a whiskey dealer and a con artist, " 'I believe you are telling the truth at last' " (99).

Just as this community believes an acknowledged madman, they also believe a known liar. As Thadious Davis points out, "The nigger's lust for the white woman and the white man's heroism in thwarting that satanic sexual drive are enduring myths that surface as soon as Joe Brown informs the sheriff that Christmas is black."[3] The stereotypes and myths are so deeply in place, so "naturalized," that as soon as the townspeople find a white woman murdered, they "believed aloud that it was an anonymous negro crime committed not by a negro but by Negro" (*LIA* 288). Since this is a "Negro" crime, any person committing it could be categorized "negro," regardless of biology and/or skin color.

The implication of these examples is that Christmas's racialization is cultural, not biological or natural. His white body is materialized into black by what other characters have called him, rather than by his physical and biological self. Thadious Davis asserts that "Faulkner dramatizes his conception that a social, not a biological, definition of Negro underpins Southern thought," and Cleanth Brooks concurs that "the biological matter is quite irrelevant."[4] This underscores what Butler says about the materialization of the body within culture. The labels that are given to the body have less to do with the material on which they are based than on the exclusions that they form. In other words, a body is categorized within culture as male or female, black or white, not because skin color or genitalia are inherently important physiological features, but because Western culture places significance on those body parts in the service of specific ideological relations of power. Although gender does not work in exactly the same way as race, the ways that Hines, Brown, and the dietitian are able to discursively inscribe Christmas as black reveal that race is a social construction rather than an indisputable material given, even though it simultaneously reifies white racial domination.

How Christmas responds to this materialization in the novel has more significant implications concerning the social construction of race and gender because it suggests the capacity for human agency even within these constructions. Doc Hines's original (and originary) utterance that Christmas is "a nigger" is a performative: "that discursive practice that enacts or produces that which it names."[5] Butler uses the example of the creation story in Genesis in which God pronounces "Let there be light" and light is produced by the utterance (13). She goes on to explain that individual humans do not possess quite the same productive power over their own bodies. Rather, they must constantly reiterate and re"cite" the pronouncements of a cultural authority, one who does have this productive power. Thus, when a subject invokes a racial or gender identity, it is not so much performative as it is "citational"; it cites the cultural authority who originally categorized the subject's body in a given way.

Butler rethinks performativity as "citationality" in *Bodies that Matter* in order to make a distinction between performativity and performance. The key difference between the two rests in the issue of agency. Performativity as citationality suggests that a human subject reiterates an identity, but does not originally produce that identity. The subject has some agency in how to "perform" the roles that such an identity requires. But a subject does not have agency in choosing either the identity category itself (it is already inscribed upon the subject by the regulatory system) or acceptable behaviors available to such a category. A subject may choose to perform in a way that is unacceptable given his/her categorization, but thereby abjects him/herself from society. Thus performativity/citationality is not tantamount to a complete lack of agency, although agency is significantly limited. Agency, of course, is the issue that "getting around" is getting at. Can a "body" "get around" cultural categorization?

While Joe Christmas does not originally produce his black identity, he reiterates this inscription and thus continually reproduces that black identity. Because his skin is white, Christmas "performs" as white in order to "get around" the limitations imposed upon a black body. Donald M. Kartiganer and Thadious Davis posit that Christmas's dilemma is that he does not know his racial identity. Kartiganer believes that Christmas "drives incessantly toward identity"; Davis reads "Joe's problem" as "one of personal identity" and finds that "Faulkner attempts to make Joe's tragedy his not knowing."[6] However, an application of Butler's definition of citationality and performance reveals that Christmas does have an identity. He clearly self-identifies as black. His dilemma is that he loathes this identification. The product of a white supremacist society, he sees his own blackness as repulsive, especially since that blackness is associated with sin, illegitimacy, and criminality. Consequently, he "passes" as white publicly throughout the novel, yet continually reiterates his black identity at key private moments. A close reading of these private moments offers evidence of his self-identification and consequent self-loathing.

Perhaps the earliest instance in which Christmas iterates his identity is with the white prostitute, Bobbie Allen. Although "he had been her lover for a month" (195), one night they begin to talk to each other about their bodies for the first time. They converse "not about where she had come from and what she had even done, but about her body as if no one had ever done this before, with her or with anyone else" (195–96). The discussion of her body and the "secret bodily functions" that make her a woman leads Christmas to reveal to her the secret of his body, his blackness. Not wanting to state it aloud to her, he tries to get her to guess what is "different" about him. When she refuses and candidly asks, "What are you?," he does not answer right away. But, "It was not as if he were tantalising her. It was as if he just had not thought to speak on." He wants her to know; he encourages her to guess, but it had not occurred to him that he would have to speak it himself. The reason that he does not want to verbalize his race is that the speaking has the effect of reinscribing that racial identity. When she persists, he answers quite factually with the direct statement, "I got some nigger blood in me." Her response to this at first is silence: "Then she lay perfectly still, with a different stillness." But then she asks him to repeat it. He repeats it with a difference, softening the direct "I got" of his earlier statement, by saying "*I think* I got some nigger blood in me" (196, my emphasis). At last, he admits, "I dont know. I believe I have" (197). Christmas reiterates his racial identity three times in this passage, each time with a difference. While on the surface, each iteration seems less certain than the previous, because they get continuously less factual and straightforward, they actually become more intense. The movement from "I got" to "I think" to "I believe" echoes the passage that opens chapter 6 (and is repeated elsewhere in the novel): "Memory believes before knowing remembers. Believes longer than recollects, longer than knowing even wonders. Knows remembers believes." (119). Believing, although not based on sensory or cognitive fact (like knowing), is somehow stronger than

knowing; it is "longer than knowing even wonders." "Knowing" or
not knowing what he is is not Christmas's conflict. It is what he
"believes" he is that causes him such turmoil. He "believes" that
he is black, yet he "knows" that to be black is to be illegitimate,
evil, and abject. Bobbie reinforces this knowledge when she refuses to believe what he has just confided in her, telling him
"You're lying" (197). Her "believing" would mean the end of their
relationship.

When Christmas's relationship with Bobbie does come to its
violent end, he continues to reiterate his racial identity. When he
sets out on the "street which was to run for fifteen years" (223), he
is setting out to "get around" his racialized body but also to reaf-
firm his conviction of white superiority. Thus he publicly passes as
white as he "gets around" the country, yet he reiterates his blackness in order to "get around" sexually. He performs as a white
man in order to be granted the freedom to travel. He consciously
dresses in the "clothes (even when soiled and worn) of a city man"
rather than the overalls and clodhopper shoes of the "pickaninny."
And yet Christmas continues to reiterate his blackness. He recites
this identity in some cases in order to "get around" with women:
"he bedded with the women and paid them when he had the
money, and when he did not have it he bedded with them anyway
and told them he was a negro" (224). On first read, this might
suggest that he is "passing" as black just to get sex without paying
rather than citing a black identity. However, he is still going
through the motions of being white. He is dressed like a white
man and is visiting the whorehouse of a white man. But he *says*
that he is black. It is worth noting that Christmas only verbalizes
or iterates a black identity. He never verbally states that he is
white in the way that he repeatedly tells women that he is a negro.
Christmas's evoking of his blackness to the women he beds not
only allows him to obtain sex for free, but it also reaffirms his
conviction that white is superior to black. He knows that claiming
he is black will produce outrage and the outrage is what allows
him to "get around" payment. In fact, when the woman in Detroit
is not outraged, Christmas almost kills her. It is something that

completely disrupts his hierarchical view of white over black to such an extent that "[he] was sick after that. He did not know until then that there were white women who would take a man with a black skin. He stayed sick for two years" (225). Although he tries to live with Negroes after this incident, "shunning white people," he cannot "expel from himself the white blood and the white thinking and being"—that is, the white notion that blacks are inferior. He cannot overcome his abhorrence: "His whole being [would] writhe and strain with physical outrage and spiritual denial" (226).

His materialization as black and his loathing of his black identity crystalizes in his next and final erotic entanglement, his relationship with Joanna Burden. After they have been lovers for over a year, Joe realizes one day that "she had never invited him inside the house proper" (234). He recalls as well that "[h]e had never been further than the kitchen, which he had already entered of his own accord," and that "when he entered the house at night it was as he had entered it that first night." These realizations make him feel "like a thief, a robber, even while he mounted to the bedroom where she waited." He observes that "[e]ven after a year it was as though he entered by stealth to despoil her virginity each time anew" (234). That initial realization snowballs and Joe begins to perceive all the events of the preceding year as racializing him. He "believes" that the way he enters the house ("by stealth," "like a thief") and even his sexual relations with Joanna have been manipulated to make him play the part of the "nigger." In his outrage at the perceived insult, he rapes Joanna, thinking "I'll show the bitch" (236). But rather than punishing her for the affront, the rape only makes him "blacker" and Joanna more the white, Southern lady. At this point, Joe believes that even the food she sets out for him is racializing. "He went directly to the table where she set out his food. He did not need to see. His hands saw; the dishes were still a little warm, thinking *Set out for the nigger. For the nigger*" (237–38). He throws the dishes one by one over his shoulder, listening to them crash, thinking, *"This is fun. Why didn't I think of this before?"* and "Woman's muck" (238).

The next day, he takes the job at the planing mill. The job provides him with enough money to eat in town, rather than the "nigger" food that Joanna left for him. He goes the three days until payday without eating in order to avoid the "nigger" food at Joanna's. Although the planing mill is two miles away, he walks those miles back to the cabin to change clothes before returning two miles back to town to eat. He changes into "the white shirt and the dark creased trousers before walking the two miles back to town to eat, as if he were ashamed of the overalls" (239). The overalls seem racializing to Joe, as well. Perhaps he associates them with the clothing of the "pickaninny." He seems to associate cheap clothing or work clothes with blackness. When he is in Freedmantown, the black section of Jefferson, he could "smell negro; he could smell cheap cloth and sweat" (117). Whatever the reason for the association, he is clearly ashamed of the overalls, or if not ashamed "very likely he could no more have said what it was than he could have said that it was not shame" (239). Christmas travels four miles each day to be sure he dressed in "white" clothes when he is in public. He is clearly performing or "passing" as white.

While Joanna is aware that Joe believes that he is black and she herself firmly believes in a racial hierarchy (253), she does not realize the extent of his self-hatred—that he despises this blackness.[7] Later, in the third phase of their relationship, when she wants him to attend a black law school and then take over her business affairs, he reveals his contempt for Negroes. When she first explains her plans to him, he listens with "mounting rage and amazement" (268). It is later evident that he is furious because her scheme depends on his publicly admitting that he is black. Joanna tells him that she can get him a free education in any one of the Negro schools she consults for. Joe's response is "A *nigger* school. *Me*" (276, italics mine). She then will arrange for him to study law with her black lawyer in Memphis. To which Joe responds, "And then learn law in the office of a *nigger* lawyer." She restates that in return, she will turn over all her business and all her money to him. But he can only incredulously reply, "But a *nigger* college, a *nigger* lawyer." He is not averse to going to school or learning law, but to being constructed as a black man.

If the mere association with negroes was enough to repel him, what Joanna then proposes outrages him. She asks him to "Tell them." This public confession seems to be what Joe reacts most strongly against, saying "Tell niggers that I am a nigger too?" (277). Although he has continually reiterated his black identity throughout the novel, he has never done it publicly. He has only admitted it in private and usually only to women (Joe Brown is the only exception). His outrage is evident in his cruel response to her; he degrades her body: "You're old. I never noticed that before. An old woman. . . . You just got old and it happened to you and now you are not any good anymore" (277).

Christmas does literally get around by "passing" as white. He is able to travel all over the country by dressing, speaking, and behaving as a white man. He is also able to "get around" sexually without having to pay for it, by misbehaving. He invokes his blackness to get thrown out of the whorehouse. But does Christmas ever get beyond "passing"? Does he ever get around what he believes his body to be? "Passing" allows him to get around some of the constraints imposed upon a black body, but it does not disrupt the racial hierarchy. It reifies white superiority. It is not until the end of the novel that Christmas realizes his complicity in racism. He realizes that he has only endured his body and the racial constructions and stereotypes which that body symbolizes. He has not gotten around them or prevailed over them.

In a complex and intricate—even fractal—pattern, Joe's fifteen-year travel circumscribes his seven-day evasion of the Jefferson sheriff and his dogs. While he is successful in evading the law for seven days, the regulatory law itself remains intact, even if Christmas does momentarily escape it. He realizes at last, after he has "lurked and crept among its [the country's] secret places," the effects that the regulatory law has had on his body. He comes to understand that "his physical shape and his thought had been molded by its compulsions without his learning anything about its actual shape and feel" (338). He did not experience his own body.

Rather, he acted out the roles prescribed for a white body when he "believes" his own body to be black, a body that is loathsome, uninhabitable, and abject to him. The peace that he gets from this realization liberates him from his body so that he "feels dry and light," thinking, "I dont have to bother about having to eat anymore. . . . That's what it is." He is freed from attending to his body: literally, his bodily needs, and symbolically the cultural inscriptions that his body has had to bear. As a result, he becomes almost disembodied, "He is not sleepy or hungry or even tired. He is somewhere between and among them, suspended, swaying to the motion of the wagon without thought, without feeling. He has lost account of time and distance" (339). At this point, the "negro" shoes that he is wearing, instead of being a means of evading the law, become a performative gesture of his black identity. For suddenly the "the black shoes smelling of negro" begin to "mark on his ankles the gauge definite and ineradicable of the black tide creeping up his legs, moving from his feet upward as death moves" (339).

While his acceptance momentarily brings him peace, he recognizes that the law is still intact. He realizes, as well, that all of his "getting around" has only helped to weave the restrictive web which binds him. This web of inscription, reinscription, and circumscription woven by the reiteration and citation of cultural norms is manifest in the following passage:

> he is entering it again, the street which ran for thirty years. It had been a paved street, where going should be fast. It had made a circle and he is still inside of it. Though during the last seven days he has had no paved street, yet he has travelled further than in all the thirty years before. And yet he is still inside the circle. "And yet I have been further in these seven days than in all the thirty years," he thinks. "But I have never got outside that circle. I have never broken out of the ring of what I have already done and cannot ever undo." (339)

The constitutive effects of his acts, gestures, and words over the last thirty years have continually circumscribed his body, binding him in a web of discursive inscriptions which he has been unable to escape. He has gotten around within these inscriptions on that "paved road" (paved because it is a man-made construction), but he has "never broken out" of their bind. His performances as white, as masculine, and even as heterosexual have only reified white supremacy, patriarchy, and compulsory heterosexuality.

Although he cannot ever undo what he has already done to his own body and what he has done to reconstitute the regulatory norms which circumscribe it, he realizes that he can and must break "out of the ring." He does this by walking straight into the law, by deliberately getting captured and then breaking out again. The consequence is the death of his own body at the hands of the law that governs it.[8] Only then is he freed from his body and that circumscriptive law. Just before he dies he "looked up at them with peaceful and unfathomable and unbearable eyes. Then his face, body, all, seemed to collapse, to fall in upon itself" (464–65). All the constructions imposed upon his body collapse. He "gets through" rather than just "gets around." This "getting through" is narrated by the anonymous communal voice and described as "from out the slashed garments about his hips and loins the pent black blood seemed to rush like a released breath" (465). His blackness erupts through the white man's garments and his white skin; it rushes "out of his pale body like the rush of sparks from a rising rocket" and is no longer contained by whiteness. He breaks through the boundaries of cultural categorization, disrupting those very boundaries by revealing their arbitrary nature.

It is these acts, completed after he emerges from the woods, that are subversive. His deliberate capture is disruptive to the citizens of Jefferson because as they continuously repeat, "[he] never acted like either a nigger or a white man. That was it. That was what made the folks so mad" (350). Christmas just walks into town, gets a shave and haircut and purchases some new clothes. The town is outraged: "For him to be a murderer and all dressed up and walking the town like he dared them to touch him, when he ought to have been skulking or hiding in the woods, muddy and dirty and running. It was like he never even knew he was a murderer, let alone a nigger too" (350). Even Gavin Stevens, the district attorney—the town authority on The Law—cannot adequately define or fix what drove Christmas to his capture, escape, and death. While he attempts to ascribe some of Joe's actions to his "black blood" and others to his "white blood," he succeeds in proving the exact opposite of what he intends to prove, namely that no behavior is the causal effect of a biological determinant. Contrary to his intent, Stevens's sophistry exposes blackness as a social construction and heightens the disruptive effects of Joe's inexplicable behavior. Christmas finally succeeds and "rise[s] soaring into their memories forever and ever. . . . musing, quiet, steadfast . . . of itself alone serene, of itself alone triumphant" (465).

Obviously, the death of the body is not a satisfactory solution for escaping the cultural constraints on the body. Furthermore, what does all this have to do with Lena Grove? Although Joe's and Lena's paths draw near each other, they never actually cross. But Cleanth Brooks has observed, "their very likenesses stress their basic differences" (55). The key likeness for this comparison is their wanderings: how Lena and Joe "get around" with their bodies and thus get around those bodies themselves. Christmas cannot get around what his culture has led him to "believe" about his body—that it is indelibly marked with the blackness of "bitchery and abomination." Nor can he get around what this means to him and to that culture that shaped and materialized him. He can only escape cultural inscription if he can escape his body; he can only escape his body by destroying it. While Christmas does disrupt the restrictive order, he does not live to enjoy the effects of that disruption.

Lena offers a much more affirmative means of circumventing cultural categorization. She gets around from Alabama to Mississippi and then to Tennessee without provoking either the physical or psychological violence that attends Joe Christmas. She does this by properly performing the roles prescribed to her gendered body. Paradoxically, her repetitious performances of those roles—roles that are constructed to confine women—are the vehicle for her travel. This is because her performances parody those proscriptive roles and thereby reveal that they are cultural constructions. Establishing that her behavior is consciously performed (even if it is not intentionally parodic), I will discuss how those performances are parodic. They subvert the rigid codes which aim to confine the gendered body. While both Lena and Joe are subversive in their own way, I find that Lena is actually the one "alone, serene, triumphant" by the novel's close; she is the one who "gets around" her body.

The cultural construction of women in *Light in August*, specifically mothers and mothers-to-be, dictates that they must be contained within the sphere of the home under the control of a father, husband, brother, uncle, or some other male. The biological role of women in procreation is used within patriarchy to shore up the "domestication" of women, abjecting them from the public realm of political, economic, and social power. The construction of mothers as biologically unsuited for participation in the public realm simultaneously constructs them as helplessly dependent on men. While this forges the hegemonic position of men in patriarchy, at the same time, the construction makes men responsible for looking after women. Lena's "getting around" outside the domestic realm threatens this relation of power. It is in the interest of patriarchy, of the "menfolks," that she finds her man and a home.

An unwed pregnant woman outside the confines of a male-controlled household, in the 1930s and in the South, Lena Grove is clearly an abject body. Nevertheless, she succeeds in getting around the country with no money, no food, and no transportation by using this very body. Unable to hide her advanced pregnancy, Lena cannot "pass" as unpregnant in the way that Joe Christmas "passes" as white. Instead she plays it up by demurely lying that she is married and by pretending that she is looking for her husband. She realizes that her lie will not be believed because as Armstid points out right away, " 'folks can look at a strange young gal walking the road in your shape and know that her husband has left her' " (13). She also knows, however, that she must lie to look as if she were concerned about her unwed state. The road she sets out on is "peopled with kind and nameless faces and voices" (7) who reach out and help her, because the man who is responsible for her has abandoned her. She is cared for because she appears to comply with the Law of the Father in stating that she's looking for Burch. In other words, if she were not actively looking for the guy who got her "in trouble," she would not have gotten a free ride; she would not be "getting around." Intuiting this, Lena pretends that she aims to find Burch.

Lena is able to manipulate the restrictive construction of women/mothers to her interests. Rather than confining her to the home, she uses the construction as a vehicle for "getting around." Once she sets out on that road, she no longer needs a man to care for her. The community reaches out to help her instead. As Brooks points out, "[e]ven the women who look upon her swollen body with evident disapproval press their small store of coins upon her" (55). The furniture dealer at the end of the novel recognizes that Lena is not really looking for Burch. He postulates to his wife:

> I think she was just travelling. I dont think she had any idea of finding whoever it was she was following. I dont think she had ever aimed to, only she hadn't told him [Bunch] yet. I reckon this was the first time she had ever been further away from home than she could walk back before sundown in her life. And that she had got along all right this far, with folks taking good care of her. And so I think she had just made up her mind to travel a little further and see as much as she could, since I reckon she knew that when she settled down this time, it would likely be for the rest of her life. (506)

It is her "performing" as if she were looking for Burch that gets her around.

There is textual evidence that Lena's looking for Burch is a performance. As she enters Armstid's kitchen for breakfast, her face is "fixed in an expression immanent with smiling, with speech, with prepared speech" (22). The "facts" that she tells the Armstids are rehearsed as if scripted for a performance. When Armstid drops her off at Varner's store to catch a ride to Jefferson, she recites her lines again, "not even waiting for them to ask her about it before she begins to tell. Telling them of her own accord about that durn fellow like she never had nothing particular to either hide or tell" (24–25). From the point of view of those "menfolks" who aid and protect Lena, Burch is a "durn fellow," because he abdicates his responsibility to Lena and his control over her as well. Lena's repetitive telling of the story as if she had "nothing particular to either hide nor tell" is unpleasant and threatening to those men.

The way that she is described as telling the story is especially indicative of its "performed" nature: "Lena tells her story again, *with that patient and transparent recapitulation of a lying child*, the squatting overalled men listening quietly" (25, italics mine). Acting childlike makes her seem even more helpless and dependent than her pregnancy does. The story is her ticket to Jefferson, and when she gets there, it buys her a few nights in the cabin behind the now-burned Burden house. As the deputy tells the sheriff after investigating her presence in the cabin, she "begun telling me almost before I got inside the cabin, like it was a speech. Like she had done got used to telling it, done got into the habit" (319). It is a rehearsed and oft repeated "speech" which has become so familiar as to be a "habit" because it is effective; it works. It is how she is "getting around."

Telling her story is not the only way that Lena performs on her journey. There is other behavior indicative of her performance, particularly the way that she eats. The way that she makes sure she "et polite. . . . Like a lady I et" (26). While her polite and genteel behavior is sincere, it is deliberately performed. Armstid even notices that her appetite is "corrupted" with a "quality of polite and almost finicking restraint" (23). She is not eating merely to satisfy her appetite. She is restraining in order to seem a lady. She minds her manners and observes the proper protocol in gratitude to the charity she receives. She plays the part of the gracious "lady travelling" (26); she is not out to take advantage of folks' "kindness." She is, however, intentionally performing. Thadious Davis, writing in 1982, sees the theatricality in Lena's actions, calling her both "a natural actress" (153) and "an actress who plays a self-created role" (149). Despite calling her role "self-created," Davis seems to recognize that it is not, affirming that in "a system of values that emanates from rigid social and cultural mandates," her "adherence to types and to the system assures Lena of acceptance, or at least charitable tolerance" (149). In other words, Lena "gets around" because she "plays out her role, while Joe refuses to act out the part assigned to him" (Davis 149). Joe Christmas does not repeat with a difference, since he does not "repeat" anything at all; he does not play out the roles assigned to him. Lena Grove does play out the roles which regulate her. She plays them out with significant differences.

Although Lena acts properly in order to elicit community support and to "get around," she is disruptive nevertheless. Her performances, while they appear or pass as proper, are often in (f)act parodic. While Carolyn Porter and Michael Millgate have called Lena Grove an "Earth goddess" and have labelled her "mythic," she parodies this archetype.[9] She is grounded firmly in the physical, material world, not the metaphysical or mythic. Although Porter asserts that Lena belongs to the "natural procreative realm" of the archetypal mother, given the materiality with which Faulkner describes her body, Lena seems rather to parody that realm. The archetypal earth mother is an idealization of fertility, not a celebration of the mother's body. As Diane Roberts points out, the Southern version of this idealization, the plantation mother, has the "classical" body, defined by Bakhtin as "finished, completed, strictly limited. . . . All orifices of the body are closed." While the plantation mother is expected to reproduce heirs, "the verbal norms of the official and literary language of the canon, prohibit all that is linked with fecundation, pregnancy, childbirth" in association with this mother.[10] Her body and its biological functions are not spoken about. She is above it. Her productivity is celebrated, but not her body or physical reality. Lena Grove is neither a plantation mother nor a classical body. She is persistently described as material, with mass and weightiness, not exalted fecundity. Lena is "heavybodied" (52) and "swolebellied" (101). When Bunch first meets her, he sees her "swollen body, her heavy loins, the reddust upon the man's heavy shoes upon her feet" (50). Both the weightiness of her body and the heavy shoes with their layer of earthy dust ground her in the physical, material world. Lena Grove is not the stuff of ethereal fertility myth.

If her swollen and heavy body is not a parody of the mythic earth goddess, the way that she eats certainly is. After all, do earth goddesses eat sardines? Do they have to eat at all? Surely they break bread now and then, but do they *have* to eat? And do they ever eat with "tranquil and hearty decorum" (23) as Lena does at the Armstids' table and at Mrs. Beard's where she "ate heartily again, with that grave and hearty decorum" (86)? Surely if earth goddesses do have to eat, they do not have to pause and contemplate whether to eat or not to eat. Sitting on the steps at Varner's— while the men think she is thinking about her man—Lena "is waging a mild battle with that providential caution of the old earth" (27); she is trying to decide whether to save her money or buy a snack since she ate so daintily at breakfast with Armstid.

Supposing an earth goddess were to get hungry and be faced with the dilemma of eating now or saving her money for later, would she buy sardines? Earth goddesses are associated with a bountiful harvest, with hearty grains, luscious fruits, and fresh vegetables. Would an earth goddess have to purchase food in a store and would her selection be smelly, tinned fish? Finally would she "[eat] slowly, steadily, sucking the rich sardine oil from her fingers with slow and complete relish" (29)? I think not. Lena is no earth goddess. Nevertheless, the evocation of the pagan, which Millgate associates with the name "Grove," is intended. However, Lena is not intended to *be* an earth goddess; she parodies earth goddess.

Reading a pregnant woman as "mythic" is certainly a typical critical move; it is the stereotypical and biologically reductionist reading of a pregnant body in literature. To say that Lena Grove is the procreative goddess of myth reduces her to the "figural functions" which, as Julia Kristeva, Judith Butler, and many other feminists point out, have been ascribed to women since time immemorial. This view is voiced in the novel by Hightower, who describes Joanna as a "[p]oor, barren woman." She is pitied because she was "barren" (406). In contrast, he associates Lena's pregnancy with "luck" (406) and good fortune. Clearly, to Lena the pregnancy is not lucky. She says to herself when she discovers the pregnancy, "That's just my luck" (6). Indeed, pregnancy and childrearing are lucky for men such as Hightower; their bodies participate in the pleasurable functions of the reproductive process, but, as Lucas Burch demonstrates, they are exempt from the pain and responsibility. While this matter is biological, the celebration of motherhood as "lucky," always fortunate, and the stigmatization of barrenness as unfortunate are cultural constructions. It is an idealization that is biologically reductionist, hypostasizing women, fixing and containing them in the domestic realm and prohibiting other possibilities for fulfillment.

It is this construction that Brooks reifies when, speculating on Joanna Burden's "throes of nymphomania" (*LIA* 259) in the second phase of her relationship with Joe, explains that her "needs and desires are there, and when they are awakened too late for fulfillment in children and a home, something terrible happens to her" (57). Diane Roberts maintains that "Southern culture wants to 'solve' the female body by declaring it dangerous or anomalous unless defined by a man or a child" (193). That Lena escapes this hypostasization despite her pregnancy is truly incredible. It is why Lena is so surprised and pleased that her "body does get around." Yet critics continue to "solve" her body by defining it in relation to her child, reading Lena as the glorified baby machine ameliorated by the nomer "earth goddess." If critics such as Carolyn Porter are "not content with concluding" at Lena's "single metaphysical profundity" (64)—that a body does get around—it is perhaps that its profundity has gone unexamined in the body of criticism about Lena Grove.

Lena's body venturing out of her brother's home, across the state of Alabama, and into Mississippi is indeed profound because it is very disruptive. Literally, she has broken out of the patriarchal control represented by her brother's house by stealing out of the window at night. Although, when she leaves the house for good, she could have "departed by the door, by daylight. Nobody would have stopped her" (6), even her initial disruption of her brother's control was still out the window in the night. She upsets the patriarchal control of female sexuality the first time she slips out to meet Lucas Burch and every time thereafter. The lean-to room in which she sleeps with her three nephews does not contain or fix her; she breaks through and "gets around."

Merely reaching Mississippi, when she should have been contained in the lean-to room in Alabama, is disruptive to Armstid. He is astonished that she has been allowed to travel "all the way here, afoot, by yourself, hunting for him?" (12). And when she answers that she has managed because "[f]olks have been kind . . . right kind" (12), Armstid questions, "Womenfolks too?" He knows that "womenfolks are likely to be good without being very kind." He knows that her "getting around" will be especially disruptive to other women.

Mrs. Armstid is certainly upset by her presence. Lillian Smith claims that "the majority of southern women convinced themselves that God ordained that they be deprived of pleasure."[11] Mrs. Armstid has clearly surrendered to this belief. The freedom with which Lena moves and her unabashed enjoyment of that freedom is a slap in the face of this woman who obeyed the law and "tied the knot" with—and her body to—a man. Mrs. Armstid can hardly stand to look at Lena. Early in their encounter "Mrs. Armstid does not look around. She clashes the stove lid savagely." Then a bit later, she still "does not look around either. She is still busy at the stove. It appears to require an amount of attention out of all proportion to the savage finality with which she built the fire" (17). The double use of "savage" and her refusal to look at Lena betray the agitation that Lena causes her. The next day, Mrs. Armstid cannot even face Lena at breakfast. Her anger is less at Lena herself than at the cultural constructions, particularly the gender roles, that Lucas's desertion and Lena's unmarried and pregnant state threaten. Mrs. Armstid has lived a hard life being an "honest woman." She is described as a "gray woman with a cold, harsh, irascible face, who bore five children in six years and raised them to man- and womanhood" (15). Marriage and childbirth have taken the warmth, the humor, and the color out of her life. Lena's "pleasantfaced" and free presence in her house is an outrage to the life she has spent homebound and childrearing. She faces Armstid, "the gray woman not plump and not thin, manhard, workhard, in

a serviceable gray garment worn savage and brusque, her hands
on her hips, her face like those of generals who have been defeated
in battle" (16), and curses him and his kind. " 'You men' " she
fumes, and repeats it again, " 'You men. . . . You durn men' " (16).

The musings of Armstid himself reveal not only how disruptive
she is to women, but to men as well:

> . . . that's the woman of it. Her own self one of the first ones to cut the
> ground from under a sister woman, she'll walk the public country her-
> self without shame because she knows that folks, menfolks, will take
> care of her. She dont care nothing about womenfolks. It wasn't any
> woman that got her into what she dont even call trouble. Yes, sir. You
> just let one of them get married or get into trouble without being
> married, and right then and there is where she secedes from the
> woman race and species and spends the rest of her life trying to get
> joined up with the man race. That's why they dip snuff and smoke and
> want to vote. (14–15)

Armstid's bitter musings are misogynist myths. It is quite true that
no "woman got her into what she dont even call trouble," and yet
he blames Lena, the woman, for her plight anyway. What is ironic
about his thoughts is that Lena is neither trying to "get joined up
with the man race" nor performing the gendered behaviors which
he lists: "dip snuff and smoke and want to vote." She is simply
enjoying the liberation of leaving the house. Her escape from this
confinement does "cut the ground from under a sister woman,"
but Lena does not seem to intend it that way. She is subversive
nonetheless; she reveals to both Armstid and his wife that a female
body can "get around." Lena is "walk[ing] the public country herself without shame," not confined in the gendered domestic
sphere. Her refusal to be ashamed is disruptive.

The final chapter of *Light in August* offers even further evidence
of Lena's disruptive effects. In this chapter, the story of Lena's
comic upsetting of traditional gender roles is retold by a furniture
dealer to his wife while they are in bed. While many critics have
been puzzled by Faulkner's introduction of a new narrator for this
chapter, I would like to suggest that the furniture dealer tells the
story in order to reveal the reverberative effects of Lena's subver-

sion of gender roles. Because Lena's relationship with Bunch is so troublesome, the furniture dealer is compelled to repeat the story to his wife. His repeating of the story opens up the possibility that she has prompted others to similar retellings. The retelling illustrates that Lena's humorous "gender bending" reverberates across a much wider audience than just those with whom she comes into contact. These repetitious retellings expose the constructedness of sex and gender categories and so have the potential to break down their rigid boundaries. Both the event which the furniture dealer narrates and the way in which he narrates it have this deconstructive and reverberative effect.

The event that the furniture dealer reiterates is Byron getting himself "desperated up" to make a pass at Lena. Lena and Byron have been riding with the furniture dealer for the day. At night they camp off the road and in the woods. Lena is in the truck sleeping, the furniture dealer is by the fire pretending to sleep when Byron climbs into the truck to make his move. There are a few seconds of silence until Lena wakes up. Then, as the furniture dealer tells it:

> I heard one kind of astonished sound she made when she woke up, like she was just surprised and then a little put out without being scared at all, and she says, not loud neither: "Why, Mr. Bunch. Aint you ashamed. You might have woke the baby, too." Then he come out the back door of the truck. Not fast, and not climbing down on his legs at all. I be dog if I dont believe she picked him up and set him back outside on the ground like she would have that baby if it had been about six years old. (503)

The deconstructive play of gender and sexuality in this passage is hilarious. Lena takes on the role of a reprimanding mother, reducing Byron to a mischievous little boy. She completely frustrates his desire with almost manlike physical strength and lack of fear. She refuses to be passive and accepting; she rejects the role of the vessel that "unless 'filled' by the masculine, contains only empty—meaningless—space" (Roberts 193).

The furniture dealer riddles his story with sexual banter and innuendo, so that its repetition is subversive as well. His scandalized wife chides, "Aint you shamed? . . . Talking that way before a lady." Faulkner himself humorously climbs into their marriage bed at this point and tells the reader, "They are talking in the dark." Layers of gender and sexual constructions are deconstructed by such a narrative configuration. The furniture dealer retelling a story that exposes gender as construction using "dirty" language, his wife admonishing him for such impropriety in front of a Southern "lady," and Faulkner suspending the dealer's narration to tell us that they are in the dark expose some of the constructions of woman that *Light in August* explores: the mother, the whore, and the lady. They are in bed and in the dark, so he is not "in front of" a lady or in public view. They have just had mutually enjoyable sex so his tale of someone else in pursuit of such pleasure cannot really be an affront. The story itself shows that Byron was wrong in assuming that Lena's lost virginity meant that she was open to advances. It also reveals that mothers need not be passive and self-sacrificing; it is not "ordained that they be deprived of pleasure" (Smith 137).

Finally, to reiterate one more time the questions raised about getting around at the beginning of this essay, how and to what extent is a "body" able to "get around," despite the limitations imposed upon it by cultural categorizations? Can a body get around these very restrictions or at least get around within them? Clearly both Lena Grove and Joe Christmas get around the restrictions imposed on their gendered or racialized bodies. Both Grove and Christmas to an extent disrupt the regulatory systems which racialize or gender their bodies as well. But Christmas destroys himself in the process of getting through that regulatory law. He is only freed from it by getting out of the body itself, by death, by destruction.

Lena Grove, in the very process of getting around, disrupts the system and breaks through it. Her complete rapture at breaking out of traditional gender roles, her humorous twisting of those roles in her relations with Byron Bunch, and her utter content with just being on the road all suggest that Lena has "gotten out of the ring" of signification and regulatory circumscription which bound Christmas. The furniture dealer's humorous retelling of Lena's story further suggests that Lena has disruptive reverberations that reach much farther than those whose lives actually cross hers.

Granted, Joe Christmas's story is much more complex. While Lena's body bears the mark of only gender, Joe's body is marked by race, gender, and possibly an irresolute sexuality. These marks signify violence and exclusion. Furthermore, Joe "believes" the marks mean damnation. While Lena's strand is the positive counterpoint to Joe's destructive narrative, one reason for her success is that her situation is much simpler. Her success seems related to "belief," or rather, lack of belief. Lena does acknowledge the cultural constructions which are imposed upon her body, but she does not "believe" in them in the way that Christmas does. Therefore, her behavior does not bind her body in the inscriptions those behaviors produce; her actions are not generative; they are parodic. Since Christmas does put faith in or "believe" that the values placed on his bodily inscriptions, his actions affirm those hierarchical positions; his confessions of blackness produce outrage and violence.

The more general implications of Lena's success in contrast to Joe's failure come back to the issue of agency, the role of the subject in constituting his/her own body. While subjects do not choose their race, sex, or gender or the behavior that is assigned to those bodily categorizations, subjects can choose what to do with those categories, those behaviors. One *can* misbehave—as Joe does to get thrown out of the whorehouse—or one can overbehave—as Joanna does as Woman in Love. Both are viable ways to liberate the body from cultural constraints and begin to break down and resignify those categories. The destruction of the body or the more radical destruction of all categorization itself are alternative paths, but while the former is a dead-end street, the latter produces unmapped, even unnavigable terrain. As Butler points out, categorization is necessary to even think about bodies at all. Travelling a paved road—that is, navigating cultural constructions—does not necessarily mean that one participates in those constructions. Lena travels that road without "paying the toll." It is the well-travelled road that gets cracks and potholes. Cracks and holes get bigger as they are repetitiously renavigated. But if all roads were obliterated, how would we "get around" at all? And how would we know whether or not we were getting anywhere or just going in circles as Christmas did? Indeed, if it were not for the road, Lena would not "get around." The story of her disruptiveness would not reverberate down the road either. As indicated in the character of Joe Christmas, navigating those spaces where race, gender, and sexuality intersect is much more complicated than circumnavigating gender constructions only. But Lena's story, and Faulkner's point in countering Joe's with hers, suggests that circumnavigation is possible; resourceful people can navigate cultural constraints. If a body does not merely surrender to cultural victimization, then it can and does "get around."

NOTES

1. *Light in August*, the corrected text, ed. Noel Polk (New York: Vintage International Edition, 1990), 30 and 507. All further references to *Light in August* are to this edition and will be cited parenthetically in the text and abbreviated *LIA*.

2. Judith Butler, *Bodies that Matter: On the Discursive Limits of Sex* (New York: Routledge, 1993). "Citation" refers to the "citing" of cultural authority when one claims an identity. For example, one is a "girl" because culture categorizes certain anatomical parts as "girl" parts and classifies a body as "girl" based on an identification of those parts. When a subject claims "I am a girl," she is "citing" that authority which categorized her anatomy as "girl." These identity categories must constantly be "reiterated" because they are not stable or fixed. A subject must continually "cite" his or her identity, continually reinscribing and fixing that instability.

3. Thadious M. Davis, *Faulkner's Negro: Art and the Southern Context* (Baton Rouge: Louisiana State University Press, 1983), 65.

4. Davis, 131; Cleanth Brooks, *William Faulkner: The Yoknapatawpha Country* (New Haven: Yale University Press, 1963), 51.

5. Butler, 13.

6. Donald M. Kartiganer, "The Meaning of Form in Faulkner's *Light in August*," in *Faulkner's "Light in August": Modern Critical Interpretations*, ed. Harold Bloom (New York: Chelsea House, 1988), 15; Davis, 170.

7. Joe tells Joanna that he "dont know" that he is a "nigger" but that he "believes" he is in chapter 11. This is not the first time that he has revealed this belief to her. He follows his statement with: "Like I told you before" (254).

Joanna does not despise Joe's blackness, but she believes in a racial hierarchy. She has been taught that "negroes" are the curse and the burden of white men and women and that she cannot escape from this burden. Rather she must "struggle, rise. But in order to rise [she] must raise the shadow with [her]. But [she] can never lift it to [her] level" (*LIA* 253). Consequently, she feels she must try to get Joe to improve himself through education and employment, "to raise the shadow," even though "raising the shadow" keeps the hierarchy intact.

8. His escape to Hightower's house and subsequent death are described "as though he had set out and made his plans to passively commit suicide" (*LIA* 443).

9. Michael Millgate. *The Achievement of William Faulkner* (New York: Random House, 1966) and Carolyn Porter, "The Reified Reader: *Light in August*," in *Faulkner's "Light in August": Modern Critical Interpretations*, ed. Harold Bloom (New York: Chelsea House, 1988).

10. Diane Roberts, *Faulkner and Southern Womanhood* (Athens: University of Georgia Press, 1994); quotations are from Mikhail Bakhtin, *Rabelais and His World* (Bloomington: Indiana University Press, 1984), 320.

11. Lillian Smith, *Killers of the Dream* (New York: Norton, 1948), 137.

Thomas Sutpen's Marriage to the Dark Body of the Land

LOUISE WESTLING

A strange bedroom scene frames the tentative, patched-together narrative of *Absalom, Absalom!* This novel is one that many have described as obsessively focused on forbidden passions, thwarted courtships, and failed marriages. Yet much of the reconstruction of these doomed courtships and marriages occurs in the unlikely setting of the college room of two inexperienced young men. Quentin and Shreve could hardly be in a more different place than the one they are talking about. Their Harvard room is surrounded by the iron snowy cold and darkness of a New England winter night. Faulkner draws this place in stark contrast to the languid, late summer heat of Mississippi, its heavy air ripe with the fragrance of wisteria. The boys are talking about dark matters—the curse of the South, its taboos and secret crimes. And as Thadious Davis noticed a good many years ago, "a black presence dominates this work as it does perhaps no other Faulkner novel," even though there are really no major African American characters.[1] Perhaps that black presence is the reason Faulkner's repeated emphasis on the pink flesh of Shreve's naked torso is so striking. First we see his "blond square hand red and raw with cold" and then "the smooth cupid-fleshed forearm and hand," of a body "naked to the waist" in preparation for his deep-breathing exercises in the "warm and rosy orifice" of their window above the quad. Faulkner wants us to know that anyone walking into the room would take Shreve's seated form to be stark naked. Shreve seems "a baroque effigy created out of [pink] colored cake dough."[2]

What is all this about? Why so much attention to this overgrown Canadian cherub with the pink and gleaming flesh? Shreve's body is insistently offered as spectacle accompanying a reciprocal process that Faulkner at one point calls a "happy marriage of speaking and hearing" in which it does not matter which one—Shreve or Quentin—does the talking (316). This "marriage" functions to decipher the relationships of intertwined pairs and trios of women and men in a fever of choked passion. Excellent previous studies by such critics as John Irwin and Eric Sundquist have explored the convoluted sexual magnetisms that seem to dominate the novel. But I would argue that these courtship themes are really only a diversionary tactic to deflect attention from the real passion of *Absalom, Absalom!* that Shreve's naked pink flesh defines. That is the obsession with dark bodies that stand for the wild energies and dark volcanic body of the earth. In shaping the story of Sutpen's bond with his slaves and the frontier landscape, Faulkner echoes the oldest epic known—the story of Sumerian king Gilgamesh whose alliance with the wild man Enkidu makes possible the conquest of another, far earlier, wilderness landscape.[3] If we look closely at the relation of Sutpen to his slaves and the dark landscape, we will discover how Faulkner was groping in *Absalom, Absalom!* to unravel not only a peculiarly Southern problem of identity but an American one that implicates the entire European colonial project in the New World. Furthermore, against a deep literary history going back to the *The Epic of Gilgamesh*, the American case reveals a very long and troubling habit of gendered antagonism to the natural world as it is figured in the landscape.

Faulkner clearly demonstrates the connection between the slaves and the land in the Haiti sections and again in General Compson's account of the construction of Sutpen's Mississippi plantation.[4] Sutpen made the mistake, according to Quentin's grandfather, of assuming that "the earth was kind and gentle"— the safe, comforting mother it had seemed in his Virginia mountain childhood. But Haiti taught him that it was actually a dark volcanic body whose "heart" and vital energies were expressed in the chanting and drums of slaves who still lived close to its primal power

(251). Sutpen's real marriage is to the primitive landscapes of Haiti and Mississippi. From their fecund soil he draws his strength, and through violent physical conjunctions with their avatars, the "wild niggers" he took with him from Haiti to Mississippi, he repeatedly restages the union that produces his wealth and power. When he separates himself from this source, his empire self-destructs. With *Absalom, Absalom!* Faulkner is writing his way towards an understanding of white America's relationship to the landscape of the New World that he most fully realizes later, in *Go Down, Moses*. In Faulkner's mind, white men's crimes against the land are paralleled by, and implicated in, crimes against dark-skinned people.

Quentin and Shreve's unstable synthesis of previous stories —most of them created by other talking pairs of men who make up Quentin's paternal legacy (Thomas Sutpen and General Compson, General Compson and his son Jason, and Jason and his son Quentin)—is stitched together into a defense against Rosa Coldfield's challenge to the heroic fable of the Lost Cause. Quentin uses his father and Shreve as allies against Miss Rosa's charges, and the bedroom scene at Harvard is meant to substitute for the inverted courtship of the novel's opening scene in which Quentin must pay attendance to the aged, embattled spinster who burdens him with the horrors of the Sutpen past, and through it the past of the entire South. In spite of their resistance, however, the men's stories ultimately confirm Rosa Coldfield's; even General Compson supports her assertion of the savagery of Sutpen and his "wild" slaves, the hellish associations that hover about them, and their essential connections with the swampy muck of the frontier landscape. In spite of their differences, all the narrators are fascinated by the primal scene of Thomas Sutpen's naked body grappling with the naked body of a slave in the ritual combats that are the most passionate conjunctions of the novel. Such a battle in Sutpen's barn is the finale of Miss Rosa's introduction to Sutpen's story. It caps the demonic images that she unfurls in her dark and airless room throughout the first chapter, and it stands as prelude to the mystery the novel will seek to unravel.

Miss Rosa says later that *"there is something in the touch of flesh with flesh which abrogates, cuts sharp and straight across the devious intricate channels of decorous ordering, which enemies as well as lovers know because it makes them both . . . . let flesh touch with flesh, and watch the fall of all the eggshell shibboleth of caste and color too"* (139). This is a claim for essential embodied humanity which touch affirms and Thomas Sutpen enacts when he wrestles with his slaves, but that violent combat is also Sutpen's way of denying by domination the very bond that makes him whole. To understand how profoundly Sutpen's slaves are at once his black-skinned enemies and his necessary brothers and allies, we must look closely at what General Compson told Quentin's father about the "furnace" experience in Haiti that gave Sutpen's face the appearance of pottery fired in hell. We remember that General Compson defines Haiti as "a theater for violence and injustice and bloodshed and all the satanic lusts of human greed and cruelty." He sees it as a halfway point between the cold civilization of white Europe and the dark, inscrutable jungle of Africa, and so it is the right place for those extremes to meet. The same implicit opposition functions in the framing scene, with the cold Harvard room defining civilization while its inhabitants obsessively recreate the swampy darkness of frontier Mississippi. Readers should notice, though Shreve and Quentin may not, that the satanic lusts of greed and cruelty General Compson mentions were exercised by supposedly civilized white men who tore the Africans from their homes and forced them to shed their blood on the Caribbean island. The slaves have manured the soil of Haiti with their "black blood" (250–51) so that they seem to have become part of it. Thus Faulkner lays the basis for his claim that their chants and throbbing drums are the voice of the volcanic earth itself.

Quentin's grandfather had sat on a log in the darkness of the Mississippi wilderness on the night when Thomas Sutpen told his Haitian story. Illuminated only by the flickering torches held by Sutpen's slaves, this setting recalls the Haitian crisis to Sutpen's mind because it is a similarly hot and primitive scene (246). Faulkner underlines the analogy between Haiti and the Mississippi wilderness by having Quentin precede the description of Sutpen's

confrontation of the attacking Haitian slaves with a reminder of
his later habit of single combat: "[Sutpen is] the man Grandfather
himself had seen fight naked chest to chest with one of his wild
niggers by the light of the camp fire while his house was building
and who still fought with them by lantern light in the stable after
he had got at last that wife who would be adjunctive to the for-
warding of that design he had in mind" (253). The placement of
this reference to the wrestling clearly links it to the original Haitian battle and "satanic" compact with the dark earth which Sutpen had fled by coming to the Mississippi frontier. Its implications
trouble General Compson.

He must sense an essential kinship between Thomas Sutpen
and the Africans. It is marked on Sutpen's body by scars from the
original confrontation by which he had subdued them, and
through them, the earth whose riches gave him access to authority
and position. Quentin speculates that Sutpen was able to walk out
into the night and conquer the Haitian rebels because his was a
body with "white arms and legs shaped like theirs and from which
blood could be made to spurt and flow as it could from theirs and
containing an indomitable spirit which *should* have come from the
same primary fire which theirs came from *but which could not
have, could not possibly have*" (my emphasis, 254). Quentin cannot
allow this possibility, because he is trying to accept Thomas Sutpen as a gentleman like his grandfather. In the cultural economy
of white aristocracy, nobility must be defined in opposition to the
wild landscape, primal nature, and the animals and people who
are part of it. But we as readers know that Sutpen grew up in an
American wilderness hardly less primitive than Africa. There is no
reason Sutpen's spirit could not have derived from the same "primary fire" of savage landscape. And Faulkner has already under-
mined the pretensions of "civilized" white men by implying that
the real savagery of the Caribbean colonial theater was enacted by
their own kind.

Because the planter aristocracy's myth of racial purity had to be
maintained, the triumph which young Thomas Sutpen had wrung
from Haiti's volcanic earth was tainted by his new wife's "Negro

blood." However, according to the coding we have just seen inadvertently or unconsciously defined by Quentin's version of General Compson's narrative, miscegenation is the sign of Sutpen's relation to the landscape and the slaves. Sutpen does not realize this, of course, and so he abruptly cancels his Haitian life and goes to Mississippi to begin again, but not without taking a group of "wild niggers," his accomplices in that primitive bonding, along with him. Rosa Coldfield noticed their kinship at the age of three when she glimpsed the terrifying approach of the Sutpen carriage in whose front seat were "the face and teeth of the wild negro who was driving," and Sutpen, "his face exactly like the negro's save for the teeth" doubtless hidden by his beard (23).

The degree of kinship between the plantation owner and his slaves is more fully developed in General Compson's description of the building of Sutpen's Hundred, as it filters down to Quentin through his father's commentary on Rosa Coldfield's version of events. Though his language is more restrained than Miss Rosa's, Jason Compson's recreation of events supports her account of the violence of Sutpen's engagement with the virgin bottom land. It is a process of submersion, physical union, and an almost erotic struggle with the substance of the wilderness earth. Sutpen's Haitian slaves are animalized in this account, just as they are in Miss Rosa's. The wagon in which they arrive is said to be "a black tunnel filled with still eyeballs and his smelling like a wolfden," they are sent by Sutpen to hunt in the swamp like a pack of hounds, and one is described as sleeping in the mud like an alligator and only narrowly prevented from killing an unsuspecting coon hunter who stumbles upon him by accident. Sutpen, like all his slaves, is stark naked beneath a coating of "croaching and pervading mud," and he looks exactly like them except for his eyes and beard (35–37). In physical fusion with the wild earth, they are all the same muddy color. Because of this kinship, Sutpen "never raised his voice at them, [but] instead he led them, caught them at the psychological instant by example" (37). Later, after he has completed his house and furnished it and withdrawn himself from his savage source, he continues to reestablish contact through the naked wrestling matches in the barn. His essential animal strength is reasserted in Miss Rosa's claim that what her sister saw in the barn was two beasts naked to the waist, a white one and a black one "gouging at one another's eyes as if they should not only have been the same color, but should have been covered with fur too" (29).

As in the earlier case of his Haitian adventure, Sutpen's bargain with the Mississippi earth is signaled by miscegenation, but this time resulting from a deliberate connection with a slave woman. Clytie and Charles Bon, the two mixed-blood children of these unions, are Thomas Sutpen's real children. They alone survive the collapse of his dynasty, in the sense that Clytie controls the household up to the point of its fiery end, and Charles's idiot grandson is the only living Sutpen at the end of the novel. It is also worthy of notice that until the end of his life, Thomas Sutpen rides a black stallion, performing as a sort of centaur image for his real alliances.[5]

In spite of his own anguished ambivalence about these relationships, Faulkner intends us to see that Thomas Sutpen's fatal innocence is really a willed ignorance of human responsibility that stands for that of the whole South. As Eric Sundquist puts it, "The ratio between fortune and cost is the haunting depth and complex immediacy, the potent nostalgia and the troubling contemporary relevance, of Faulkner's fiction, whose own design, like that of Lincoln, struggles yet with a 'flaw' insistently fratricidal. The long act of retrospection—delaying, postponing, meeting only indirectly its critical question—that Faulkner undertakes in *Absalom, Absalom!* and *Go Down, Moses* is one that brings the twentieth and nineteenth centuries together in fiction and in fact, inevitably entangling white and black, curse and revenge, promise and betrayal."[6]

But there is something gravely wrong with the implicit line of reasoning Faulkner traces as he continues to explore the complexities of race, gender, and American history that he had initially confronted in *Light in August*. Toni Morrison is a writer who is Faulkner's heir in many ways, and who has taken up these same problems from the other side. Most obviously, in *Beloved* she treats the experience of slavery and its aftermath, engaging both the African American narrative tradition of the slave narrative and the powerful tropes fixed in the national imagination by Stowe's *Uncle Tom's Cabin*. A character in *Beloved* puts his finger upon the habit at the heart of the tradition in which Faulkner writes.

> Whitepeople believed that whatever the manners, under every dark skin was a jungle. Swift unnavigable waters, swinging screaming baboons, sleeping snakes, red gums ready for their sweet white blood. . . . But it wasn't the jungle blacks brought with them to this place from the other (livable) place. It was the jungle whitefolks planted in them.[7]

This is not far from the jungle planted by the narrators of *Absalom, Absalom!* in Sutpen's slaves. Morrison comments directly on *Absalom, Absalom!* in *Playing in the Dark*, her meditation on the "white" imagination that has defined American literature. In considering the semiotic games by which white Americans have used dark-skinned Others to construct their ideas of power and independence, Morrison calls our attention to a planter named William Dunbar, who actually lived on the Mississippi frontier and was hauntingly similar to Thomas Sutpen. This man had a far more "civilized" upbringing than Sutpen, because he grew up as an Enlightenment gentleman in Edinburgh and London. However, he shed his inhibitions on the frontier when he appeared with a battalion of Caribbean slaves and began to build his plantation. His diary for July of 1776 does not comment on the colonial movement towards independence from England but instead records punishments of 500 lashes each on three different occasions to slaves who had tried to escape from him. Thinking about the paradoxical freedom that this Southern American success story dramatizes, Morrison finds Dunbar an especially revealing example of how "Africanism, deployed as rawness and savagery . . . provided the staging ground and arena for the elaboration of the quintessential American identity." Morrison's analysis of Dunbar's heroic individualism is especially pertinent to an understanding of what is wrong with Faulkner's connection of dark bodies to animal energies and the wildness of the frontier landscape:

Autonomy is freedom and translates into the much championed and revered "individualism"; newness translates into "innocence"; distinctiveness becomes difference and the erection of strategies for maintaining it; authority and absolute power become a romantic, conquering, "heroism," virility, and the problematics of wielding absolute power over the lives of others. All the rest are made possible by this last, it would seem—absolute power called forth and payed against and within a natural and mental landscape conceived of as a "raw, half-savage world."

There is a guilty undercurrent moving beneath these standard heroic qualities, as Morrison suggests by her emphasis on Dunbar's punishments of his slaves. She probes it by raising broad questions we should apply to Thomas Sutpen and his defenders: "What are Americans always so insistently innocent of? Different from?"[8]

General Compson, Jason Compson, Quentin, and even Shreve need to see Thomas Sutpen as innocent and heroic, because he is the kind of man who won the frontier and accomplished the Manifest Destiny of the nation. But Thomas Sutpen is neither innocent nor heroic. Faulkner has written *Absalom, Absalom!* in such a way that we must see his insensitivity toward his first wife and son, Charles, toward Ellen and Rosa Coldfield, toward Wash Jones's granddaughter Milly, and toward his slaves. In the accounting language of chapter 8, Faulkner makes it clear that for Sutpen these people are merely ciphers on a mental balance sheet, instrumental to his design but as expendable or replaceable as livestock. Deeply related to these failures to acknowledge individual human kinship is the failure to accept responsibility for the landscape which is intimately linked to the human community. The landscape is at the heart of a gendered symbolic economy that shapes the elaboration of Yoknapatawpha County in all of Faulkner's books. The land is always female, always associated with dark powers and repulsive, mucky substances that André Bleikasten has anatomized: "The revulsion from thick liquidity is first and foremost a revulsion from the female body, which is phantasmically conceived as soft, fluid, formless matter threatening engulfment and as 'matter out of place,' as dirt. Dirt is earth; earth, fecund and foul, is woman.

Dirt is filth, and all filth comes down to 'womanfilth,' as Doc Hines puts it, the 'periodical filth' of menstrual blood, which for Christmas as for other Faulkner males is the visible trace of woman's 'curse,' the unmistakable sign of her fallen and soiled condition. The 'thick still black pool' is indeed 'more than water': a metaphor of female blood, a metonymy of female flesh."[9] What is unusual about *Absalom, Absalom!* is Sutpen's complete immersion in this dark element during the creation phase of his design in Mississippi, and the way it clings to him thereafter. For Quentin of *The Sound and the Fury* immersion had been fatal, and Joe Christmas of *Light in August* could barely breathe after his descent into the "thick black pit" and horrifying "lightless hot wet primogenitive Female" space of Freedman Town.[10] But by the time he wrote *Absalom, Absalom!*, Faulkner was able to accept a necessary engagement with the body of the earth. In *Go Down, Moses* he went even further towards a calm integration into this elemental physical realm for Ike McCaslin. As we have seen, however, the semiotic coding underlying this progressive understanding requires that African Americans, and indeed any dark-skinned people such as Indians, must be defined as extensions of a primal, essentially "female" reality. The traditional hero needs to subordinate these Others in order to shape and verify himself.

So let us return to Toni Morrison's questions. What are Americans so insistently innocent of? *Absalom, Absalom!* is an effort to expose the bankruptcy of their claims to be innocent of violating the most sacred communal bonds as well as the sacred body of the land. What are they different from? Morrison takes William Dunbar and his fictional counterpart Thomas Sutpen to be portraits "of the process by which the American as new, white, and male was constituted" (43). These Americans are different from people with dark skins and they are different, of course, from all women. An often desperate insistence on such difference pervades all of Faulkner's fiction and is centrally implicated in white men's crimes against women and land. Karl Zink has suggested that "the male's ambiguous fear and hatred and love of woman [in Faulkner's fiction] must be explained in terms of his fear and hatred and love of the old Earth itself, to which Woman is so disturbingly related."[11]

As I suggested at the beginning of this discusion, such an attitude is neither unique to Faulkner nor to Americans. It lies at the heart of the earliest epic, producing the heroism and tragedy of Gilgamesh in a vision of male bonding as a violent alternative to cooperation with women. Gilgamesh's alliance with Enkidu realizes its fullest intensity in catastrophic attack on wild nature and its presumed feminine sources. At the beginning of the standard Babylonian form of the epic, the semidivine hero Gilgamesh has the terrible beauty and strength of a wild bull, but his arrogance and voracious appetities ravage the city of Uruk. Gods must intervene to save the city from the rampage of this young king who ought to be its guardian.

In a curious doubling technique, a distraction is created for Gilgamesh in the form of a wild man whose hairy appearance seems to match Gilgamesh's disorderly, uncivilized behavior. When he is first created, however, Enkidu is innocent of humankind and dwells peacefully with wild animals. His life in the wilderness prefigures the monster Humbaba who guards the wild cedar forest sacred to Ishtar. To prepare him for his destined relationship with Gilgamesh, Enkidu is robbed of his natural innocence by a "harlot" brought from the temple of the goddess to humanize him. Then he is ready to go to Uruk and challenge Gilgamesh.

Enkidu replaces women as the object of Gilgamesh's attention; even before he arrives in the city, Gilgamesh dreams of a meteor and a magic axe, both of which attract him "like the love of a woman." Gilgamesh's mother Ninsun explains that both represent a strong companion who is on his way to Uruk. She says, "You will love him as a woman and he will never forsake you."[12] On his arrival in the city, Enkidu blocks Gilgamesh from performing the ritual marriage to Ishtar (Sumerian Inanna), goddess of love and war. Annually Sumerian and Babylonian kings joined with a priestess representing Inanna or Ishtar in the performance of the ritual marriage found in most archaic cultures of the Mesopotamian/ Mediterranean world. This is the ceremony invoked in Sumerian courtship hymns to Inanna in which the goddess's body is identified with the "high field" and "wet ground" that brings forth grain and plants for her servants. The priestesses who served the goddess (and these include, presumably, the one who seduces Enkidu) engaged in a sacred sexuality that was necessary to stimulate the landscape's fertility and vitalize the human community each year. Ordinary human procreation was understood to be similarly sacred.[13] Yet the epic sets the fertility ritual in a negative context and locks the king in violent combat with the Doppelganger Enkidu instead of allowing him to continue his service to the goddess. Grappling together like bulls, the two smash the doors of the goddess's temple, The House of Marriage where the priestess awaits him. When Gilgamesh finally throws the challenger, the two embrace and become inseparable companions. The male bond replaces Gilgamesh's connection with female fertility, and it is the basis for the series of heroic adventures which define his stature. Clearly Enkidu is a consort who replaces the wife in the narrative; when he dies Gilgamesh covers his body with a veil, "as one veils the bride" (95).

The replacement of male-female conjunction by a masculine alliance in this ancient story is important as a corollary to the replacement of reverence for the natural landscape by violent conquest and destruction. Both represent what I believe to be the supplanting of one cultural system by another—a neolithic agricultural system of belief focused on reverence for the landscape and its supposedly feminine powers on the one hand, and a masculine heroic code antagonistic to the natural world on the other.

There are versions of *The Epic of Gilgamesh* from many cultures, representing at least 1,500 years of continuous literary transmission, to say nothing of the long oral traditions that must have preceded it. Thus we can see the evolution and elaboration of the epic from Sumer to the Hittite Kingdom and Babylon. In the earliest versions from ancient Sumer—clay tablets about 4,000 years old—the major parent of Gilgamesh and his companions is the mother, but by the time of the late Babylonian texts 1,500 years later, the father has replaced her in importance. The one interesting exception is Gilgamesh, who goes to his mother for advice and whose father is barely mentioned. Even though a number of such apparent remnants of the older system remain in the later epic, the major force of the hero's energies is spent attacking the natural phenomena associated with the goddess Inanna/Ishtar. Gilgamesh's ambition to set up his name in the land is realized by the cutting down of the sacred forest, the killing of its wild guardian Humbaba, and the murder shortly afterward of the Bull of Heaven sacred to Ishtar. One irony here is the frequent early associations of Gilgamesh and Enkidu with wild bulls. But there is a more important, tragic indication that in attacking the forest and its protectors Gilgamesh is attacking the sources of his own strength. That is the sudden illness and death of his primitive double and beloved companion Enkidu.

This story has many more direct links to *Go Down, Moses*, as I have explained elsewhere,[14] but for *Absalom, Absalom!* it does provide an important sense of the ancient provenance and cultural associations of Thomas Sutpen's relationship to his slaves and to the primordial landscapes of Haiti and the Mississippi wilderness. Sutpen, like Gilgamesh, is a hero fiercely determined to establish his name in the land. His allies in this enterprise are "wild" men with whom he wrestles in a violent but profound bonding ritual. The close relation of his slaves to the landscape and to wildness is marked by skin color rather than by the body hair that shows Enkidu's associations, but the general dynamic is similar. The parallels more or less end here, but the epic is important in demonstrating the long narrative tradition of masculine alliances opposed to nature and woman.[15]

Harold Bloom has called Thomas Sutpen "a blind will in a cognitive vacuum,"[16] but in fact he is quite the opposite when seen against the background of a deep literary history which I have not space here to adequately survey. I have tried to suggest by looking at *The Epic of Gilgamesh* what that deep history reveals, but other archaic works such as Hesiod's *Theogony*, the Homeric Hymns, and Euripides's *Bacchae* also yield instructive evidence.[17] Quentin's father claims, "Years ago we in the South made our women

into ladies. Then the War came and made the ladies into ghosts"
(12). Aside from the question of which Southern women he has in
mind (poor ones? black ones?), what must be remembered is that
the planter class was not very interested in thinking of them as full
human beings. Mary Chesnut was right when she said that men of
her class lived like the patriarchs of old, with their chattels (including women and slaves) completely in thrall to their desires.[18] Harriet Jacobs's *Incidents in the Life of a Slave Girl* provides a detailed
inside view of how these desires often found expression.[19] Miscegenation was the most obviously damning result, as Faulkner designed *Absalom, Absalom!* to reveal. But he also understood that
the deeper, far more ancient crime was the attack upon the earth.
He told his editor Hal Smith that the theme of the novel "is a man
who outraged the land, and the land then turned and destroyed
the man's family."[20] Sutpen's betrayals of women, children, and
slaves are only the surface signals of the deeper one—the betrayal
of his marriage to the land. As long as the ritual simulation of this
marriage is regularly restaged in violent grappling contests with
the dark bodies of his slaves, Thomas Sutpen can, like Antaeus,
continue to draw strength from his source. But when he withdraws
into "white" gentility and denies his connections with these men,
and when he refuses to acknowledge the son who represents his
most profound experience of the volcanic earth and his primal
contest with dark bodies, he brings his doom.

To create the frame for his strange courtship narrative, Faulkner
inserted Shreve's pink, cherubic body into the space of the white
Southern woman marked but not adequately supplied by Rosa
Coldfield, whose body is as cold and sterile as the battered landscape that could have blossomed with proper care. Although
Shreve takes Miss Rosa's place as Quentin's interlocutor, he is not
a satisfactory complement to Quentin either, for all the authorial
teasing about their erotic situation in a cozy bedroom, looking at
each other "almost as a youth and a very young girl might out of
virginity itself" (299). The two young men may have a common
connection to the landscape of North America that he says links
them "after a fashion in a sort of geographical transubstantiation

by that Continental Trough, that River which runs not only through the physical land of which it is the geologic umbilical, not only runs through the spiritual lives of the beings within its scope, but is very Environment itself which laughs at degrees of latitude and temperature" (258). With this baroque evocation of the Mississippi River, Faulkner is trying to identify these pink bodies with the whole landscape of North America. He wants to substitute them for the dark bodies and their violent conjunctions in Haiti and the virgin Mississippi swamp. This will allow him to broaden the marriage of men and land to include not only the North and South of the United States but all of Canada as well. But Quentin and Shreve are only two distant voyeurs fixated on the bodies of Sutpen and his slaves in the tableau of their ritual combat. They are two pink bodies whose frailty and softness shapes by contrast the heroic masculinity of Thomas Sutpen and his "wild niggers." What Faulkner seems to be attempting with Quentin and Shreve's "happy marriage of speaking and hearing" is a Platonic marriage of words that he cannot really believe. In the sense of Diotima's description of the transcendent lovers of Plato's *Symposium,* they concentrate their attention first on the physical conjunction of Sutpen and his slaves, but then trade, join, and share words as they strain toward the "Truth" behind those bodies, in order to become "free of flesh" like the ghosts they conjure. This should be a purer union of males than the gross bestial embrace of Thomas Sutpen and his slaves, but the promised elevation (transcendence) cannot occur. They remain embodied, living humans who must cover their flesh in the rapidly cooling and then icy bedroom. Quentin's violent shaking beneath the covers of his bed at the end signals both the fact of his physical involvement in the natural world and his tormented understanding that he and Shreve must admit their complicity with Thomas Sutpen. They are William Faulkner's surrogates for a halting, delayed, coyly postponed, oblique, but also obsessive and passionate unraveling of the taboo of miscegenation and its devastating effect on the mind of the South. What is deeply unfortunate about *Absalom, Absalom!* is that Faulkner had to play in the dark so intensely in order to achieve his end, picturing dark-

skinned people and women as inevitably close to animals, associated with matter, body, and the horror of undifferentiated merging
with nature. Of course he is not alone in his reliance on these
.tropes. His excesses and contradictions help to signal what is
wrong with them. He was writing his way toward an ever clearer
understanding of the full burden of American history, including
the recognition of the full humanity of African Americans, Indians,
and women, as well as a return to reverence for the land so badly
abused in the past four hundred years. If Isaac McCaslin cannot
rise to welcome his young cousin and her baby at the end of "Delta
Autumn," and if his thoughts are bitterly racist and anti-Semitic,
Faulkner nevertheless sets them in a context that condemns Ike's
passivity and his meanness of spirit. *Absalom, Absalom!* is the beginning of a painful, often confused exploration into the past,
which leads to Ike McCaslin and moves him very far towards expi-
ation and justice for people and their natural world. It is up to
us to take further steps to release ourselves from the unfortunate
metaphoric and political habits that have led us astray for even
thousands of years. "It will do no harm to hope," writes Quentin's
father. "So let it be hope" (377).

NOTES

1. Thadious M. Davis, *Faulkner's "Negro": Art and the Southern Context* (Baton Rouge:
Louisiana State University Press, 1983), 180.

2. William Faulkner, *Absalom, Absalom!* (New York: Random House, 1936), 173, 217–
218. All subsequent references are to this edition.

3. Faulkner could have known *The Epic of Gilgamesh*, which was available in Campbell
Thompson's English hexameter translation published in 1928 and 1930. See N. K. Sandars,
introduction to *The Epic of Gilgamesh*, trans. N. K. Sandars, revised edition (London: Penguin, 1972), 50–51.

4. Thadious Davis suggests this link, 190–91.

5. Such a connection is implied when Mr. Compson likens the interbreeding of wild
and tame blacks to the breeding of Sutpen's black stallion with tamer horseflesh, as well as
the mingling of his own ruthless blood with that of the tame Coldfield family (85).

6. Eric Sundquist, *Faulkner: The House Divided* (Baltimore: Johns Hopkins University
Press, 1983), 129.

7. Toni Morrison, *Beloved* (New York: Knopf, 1987), 198.

8. Morrison, *Playing in the Dark* (New York: Random House, 1993), 44–45.

9. André Bleikasten, *The Ink of Melancholy: Faulkner's Novels from "The Sound and
the Fury" to "Light in August"* (Bloomington: Indiana University Press, 1990), 290.

10. Faulkner, *Light in August* (New York: Random House, 1932), 99–100.

11. Karl E. Zink, "Faulkner's Garden: Woman and the Immemorial Earth," *Modern Fiction Studies* 2 (1956): 149.

12. *The Epic of Gilgamesh*, 66.

13. See Diane Wolkstein and Samuel Noah Kramer, *Inanna, Queen of Heaven and Earth: Her Stories and Hymns from Sumer* (New York: Harper, 1983), 124–25; Jane Ellen Harrison, *Prolegomena to the Study of Greek Religion*, 1907 (London: Merlin, 1962), 534–51; Walter Burkert, *Greek Religion*, trans. John Raffan (Cambridge: Harvard University Press, 1985), 108–9; Gerda Lerner, *The Creation of Patriarchy* (New York: Oxford, 1986), 126–27; and Page DuBois, *Sowing the Body: Psychoanalysis and Ancient Representations of Women* (Chicago: University of Chicago Press, 1988), 40–42.

14. *The Green Breast of the New World* (Athens: University of Georgia Press, 1996), 121.

15. Many European mythic and folk traditions continue what I have labeled the older narrative habits in which the hero's forays into wild land or forest are necessary to gaining strength and success. Most of them are positive, however, where *The Epic of Gilgamesh* is not. The old Celtic "Dream of Oengus," the Celtic patterns of renewal in *Sir Gawain and the Green Knight*, and Grimms' stories like "Iron Hans" and "Hans My Hedgehog" are only a few examples of the pattern in which a hero returns to wild sources in a spirit of harmony rather than combat. Faulkner's Ike McCaslin tries to move in this direction in *Go Down, Moses*, but he cannot accept active responsibility for the sins of his fathers or the crimes against the land.

16. Harold Bloom, Introduction to *William Faulkner's "Absalom, Absalom!,"* ed. Harold Bloom (New York: Chelsea House, 1987), 7.

17. See Westling, *The Green Breast of the New World*, 3–53.

18. *Mary Chesnut's Civil War*, ed. C. Vann Woodward (New Haven: Yale University Press, 1981), 29, 168–69, 276.

19. Harriet Jacobs, *Incidents in the Life of a Slave Girl*, ed. Jean Fagan Yellin (Cambridge, Massachusetts: Harvard University Press, 1987).

20. Joseph Blotner, *Faulkner: A Biography*, 1-vol. rev. (New York: Random House, 1984), 327.

Faulkner and the Unnatural

MYRA JEHLEN

Though it is hard to tell from the very sophisticated talk the natural world has inspired in these meetings, nature goes way back also with idiots. The term "a natural," to denote someone mentally deficient, is only a little archaic and, judging by recent movies, may be coming back: *The Rainman, Forrest Gump*, and, even more to the point, the French *The Eighth Day*, winner of many prizes at Cannes 1996. And while American thinking traditionally has cast nature opposite civilization, their complicity goes farther back, to ancient times when the founders of civilization consorted regularly with beasts of field and forest. On a first reading, the episode in *The Hamlet* in which Ike Snopes, the family idiot, has a romance with a cow can appear almost a set piece. Yet on a recent rereading, it suddenly seemed altogether unexpected, possibly ground for a reversal of my earlier understanding, not just of this first Snopes novel, but of the Yoknapatawpha saga in general.

The episode unfolds over sections 2 and 3 of the first chapter of "The Long Summer" but this discussion will focus on the first part. (See Number 1 in accompanying text.) It begins, "As winter became spring and the spring itself advanced . . . ," signaling that we are entering the world of nature. By the end of the first paragraph, a familiar situation is becoming apparent: a character who, for yet unspecified reasons, finds society difficult, escapes into nature where, one morning at dawn, he lies "in the drenched myriad waking life of grasses." (Faulkner may be looking sidelong at Walt Whitman.) Lying in the grass, the unnamed protagonist listens for "her approach," like his, a natural rather than a historical progress: "not . . . after one hour, two hours, three . . . ," there comes a

143

moment when she is simply there. And when that moment has come, her presence consummates the protagonist's unity with nature; "he would hear her and he would lie drenched in the wet grass, serene and one and indivisible in joy." All this is almost banal in its familiarity; and until the long last sentence of the paragraph, a reader has no reason to suspect anything untoward. True, the lover is said to "smell" his approaching beloved; the claim that "the whole mist reeked with her" is unorthodox. But there are precedents like Shakespeare's evocation of his mistress's reeking breath. And since the hands of the mist caressing both establishes a parallel between the lover's "flanks" and his love's "pearled barrel," even an attentive reader may not inquire as to the exact nature of the latter.

Not until the amorous hero is described hearing "the slow planting and the plopping suck of each deliberate cloven mud-spreading hoof" do we realize that this familiar landscape is also very odd. But even now, Faulkner veils the emerging monstrosity with the end of the sentence: the mist, just before filled with panting, plopping, and sucking, is more conclusively (in being at the end of the sentence) "loud with its hymeneal choristers." The cow is "still invisible." Though its inhabitants are a little strange, this is the universe of Nature and Nature's Gods. The cast of *A Midsummer Night's Dream* also features beasts, not to mention the whole body of Greek and Roman classics, which, much to the point, Faulkner evokes in the next sentence with "the bright thin horns of morning." This is nothing more disturbing than a latter-day myth of love in the realm of nature; of natural love in the natural world; of the love of a natural for nature. Moreover, taking Ike's love for a cow as naturally good makes sense in the context of the whole novel where the other Snopeses represent natural evil. With Flem foremost, they are a plague of locusts consuming the agrarian South. Laying waste with their buying and selling, sterile for all their proliferation, they deny natural values even more drastically than slavery and exploitation had earlier. Love is not in the Snopes nature, but Ike is a deformed Snopes. And while his love is also deformed, in that love redeems deformity, it can redeem even its own deformity: Ike's love for his cow is a real love and thus transcendent. The "hymeneal choristers" sing on key, transforming cow love into true love. The once and future rulers of Yoknapatawpha County have blasphemed against Nature, and the ahistorical, unreflective love of the natural, Ike, is a flare of life in a blasted world. His perverse passion is nonetheless truer than the commercial greed that inspires his uncle Flem's marriage to cowlike Eula. The organization of the novel counterpoints the two romances.

But Ike's wondrous love, while recalling those of ancient gods, is also grotesquely misbegotten. Faulkner insists the reader realize that the cow is a cow. The revelation that the beloved approaches on four feet is more shocking for being delayed. Instead of being assimilated at once into pastoral imagery, as it would be were it introduced at the very beginning of the episode, her bovine nature emerges as a distinct and uncompromised fact. Squinting a little to get her animal reality into the sharp focus of fact, we cannot immediately readjust into the soft focus of metaphor. There is a delay, and that delay enacts a gap between nature and pastoral poetics. The reader becomes irrevocably conscious that all this lyricism addresses an idiot and a cow. The paragraph in which the cow first stands wholly revealed is riven by the division between fact and image.

The first two paragraphs concluded with the sounds made by the cow's hooves in the mud, but she has not yet appeared. The sentence opening the third paragraph finally lifts the curtain.

> Then he would see her, the bright thin horns of morning, of sun, would blow the mist away and reveal her, planted, blond, dew-pearled, standing in the parted water of the ford, blowing into the water the thick, warm, heavy, milk-laden breath; and lying in the drenched grasses, his eyes now blind with sun, he would wallow faintly from thigh to thigh, making a faint, thick, hoarse moaning sound.

The unveiling begins with a lyrical fanfare, its rhythms emphasized by the parallel to the first sentence of the preceding paragraph ("Then he would hear her"; "Then he would see her"). Handelian horns of morning blow away the mist "and reveal

her" . . . "planted." A harsh incommensurability divides the suc-
cession from heavenly revelation to thudding autochthony in
"planted"; from epic to comic and even ridiculous, in the sound of
"planted" recalling and sealing the "planting and the plopping
suck of each deliberate mud-spreading hoof." Announced by ce-
lestial horns, "dew-pearled," the cow is no less a four-legged barn
animal; "milk-laden" outranks the high aspiration of "dew-
pearled" (and we have already been advised that these pearls of
dew adorn a "barrel").

Ike, a romantic hero in the beginning of the sentence, falls in
the continuation not just to earth but into the mud. At first he saw,
saw what we saw; later he is "blind with sun," and becomes the
object of the reader's sight, until he sinks still lower, to become an
object of our hearing, "making a faint, thick, hoarse moaning
sound." From the blowing of horns (doubly noble in that the "thin
horns of morning" pun sound with sight), to the unconscious
moanings of a blinded idiot, whose thighs are our last sight, this
progression is set on destroying any idyllic mood.

We were wrong, it seems, to expect that the mythic glory of
Ike's love would transform its brute facts. The cow, fleeing a fire,
stumbles into a ditch from which her lover attempts to rescue her.
(See Number 2 in accompanying text.) The passages describing
the cow's flight and Ike's catastrophic attempt to catch her and
reassure her are microscopically factual. Man and "struggling and
bellowing cow" fall into the ravine, where in her terrified struggle,
the cow—as Faulkner puts it with a delicacy that incarnates the
juxtaposition of fact and fancy—relaxes her bowels on the man.
But at once, the text leaps to the other side of the stage, to the
scene of mythic embellishment, where the cow scrambles away
from Ike, "as though in a blind paroxysm of shame, to escape not
him alone but the very scene of the outragement of privacy where
she had been sprung suddenly upon and without warning from the
dark and betrayed and outraged by her own treacherous biological
inheritance." A bovine body and the soul of a pastoral maiden stare
at one another across an unbridgeable divide.

Before, in the opening passages, a brute and mindless animal existence stood against the high ideals of literary myth; and the former's innocence and truth constituted a claim for compassion and even respect from the latter. Coherence and even cooperation seemed possible between fact and value. But in the incident of the relaxed bowels, instead of a high and potentially tragic drama played out between rustic reality and transcendent ideals, Faulkner writes sentimental parody. The cow, he suggests, is ashamed of her incontinence, and Ike responds in kind: "trying to tell her how this violent violation of her maiden's delicacy is no shame, since such is the very iron imperishable warp of the fabric of love." "But she would not hear." This is hardly surprising; the text has not made clear in what capacity she could hear. Nor, for that matter, as what Ike is speaking. The passage is perfectly readable; comprehensibility is not the issue. We understand it very well. Indeed, in comparison to Faulkner's writing elsewhere, it is exceptionally clear, not only in content but in tone: simply comic.

The problem is that it is also completely disconnected from the characters whose subjective experience it purports to describe. As distinct from articulating the thoughts and feelings of characters who have them but are incapable of their expression (a procedure that enhances their reality), ascribing to characters thoughts and feelings they could not possibly have, drains their reality. In passages like the one evoking the idiot's "down-groping foot descending the ladder to go wait for his love," we feel and see with Ike. But Ike, "trying to tell [the cow] how this violent violation of her maiden's delicacy is no shame," shrivels foolishly, and when, after a slapstick chase, he finally catches up with a "once more maiden meditant, shame-free" cow, the two are a mockery of their earlier selves.

This crisis in Ike's romance is also a crisis in Faulkner's rendering, a crisis whereby the terms of reality and pastoral myth have fallen asunder in mutual parody. The cow fleeing the scene with Ike in hot pursuit is actually going nowhere. So Faulkner stops them, and returns to an enhanced version of his earlier strategy of granting Ike his own identity distinct from his mythic dimension. The cow and Ike come to rest together in a meadow where Jack

Houston, the cow's owner, finds them. Houston's exasperated pity responds to both levels of the story, its idiocy and its poignancy; and before leading his animal back the barn, he tries to restore Ike's humanity by cleaning him up and giving him a fifty-cent piece. The sequence of events in which Ike, left to wander off home, throws away the coin and then attempts to retrieve it, unfolds as the counter to the fall into the ravine. (See Number 3 in accompanying text.) The text ascribes Ike no thought he could not think, while his mental limits are fully evident. The account of his efforts at dressing himself in his washed overalls, of his setting off toward home, of losing and searching for the money, is punctuated by denials of his ability to reason:—"his feet knew the dust of the road . . . though perhaps he himself was unaware of it"—and a litany of "You could not have told if," "He could not have known that."

But these have the opposite effect from that of the attribution to him earlier of complicated thoughts on the shyness of maidens. Here, returning to the stance of the episode's beginning, Faulkner invests Ike with the stuff, if not the means for, a certain grandeur. The passage in which Ike casts down (or just drops) Houston's coin contrasts utterly with the one we have been considering:

> He made no false motion with the hand which held the coin, he had made no motion of any kind, he was standing perfectly still at the moment, yet suddenly his palm was empty. The coin rang dully once on the dusty planks and perhaps glinted once, then vanished, though who to know what motion, infinitesimal and convulsive, of supreme repudiation there might have been, its impulse gone, vanished with the movement, because he even ceased to moan as he stood looking at his empty palm with quiet amazement, turning the hand over to look at the back, even raising and opening the other hand to look into it.

The agnosticism of this description is at each reiteration a mark of respect for the character it describes. Depicting every detail of the event, Faulkner nonetheless refuses omniscience. "Perhaps" the vanishing coin glinted; and especially "who to know what . . . supreme repudiation there might have been." The courtesy of this account lends Ike dignity in equal measure.

In sum, the episode of Ike and the cow begins as an apparently conventional pastoral, but at once reveals a more difficult project, in that its protagonist is no simple and pure rustic. An idiot beset by bestial passion, Ike represents an ultimate abjection. Yet, his kin are worse, and more threatening, while the better sort in Yoknapatawpha—Mrs. Littlejohn, who shelters and feeds the idiot; Houston; and Ratliff, Faulkner's frequent spokesman—are helpless to halt the slide of their world into ruin. The Snopeses embody that ruin, and if redemption or even amelioration were possible in this terrible world, it would begin with Ike, with the humanization of the idiot who is already the closest to being human of any Snopes.

When Faulkner casts Ike in a pastoral myth, therefore, it is not to deny his abjection but, on the contrary, to take its full measure—the measure of its potential good, as against the greater evil of his fellows, and of its degeneracy, as against an undeformed, ideal nature. Hence the duality whose uncertain evolution we have been tracing, the duality whereby Ike and his cow are both divine and subhuman.

The last passage, in which Houston treats Ike with compassion, invests the idiot with both dimensions. And, as if invigorated by this recognition of his better self, Ike now carries out his most complicated action: he kidnaps the cow. With this initiative, he acquires a density of being that promises well for Faulkner's enterprise, which, to repeat, is not to write a pastoral, but rather the history of a world incapable of pastoral ideals. So—rehearsing the basic coordinates set out from the beginning of the episode, Ike is again described knowing nothing of clock time nor of measured distance. He simply keeps moving forward, leading his cow, "toward the pinnacle-keep of evening where morning and afternoon become one." At one with nature's eternal unities, he also deals with specific earthly facts: the cow resists this advance into ideal freedom, pulling back toward the barn where it is time she were milked. After a while, he seems to understand and milks her. The play between fact and mythical ideal—which, by now, we understand to be the deadly struggle of ideal trying to redeem fact—is once more underway, as it was at the beginning of the episode. Recalling that beginning at this new beginning, the text describes Ike again apprehending the cow mainly through her smell: "From the edge of the woods he would look back. She would still be invisible, but he could hear her; it is as though he can see her—the warm breath visible among the tearing roots of grass, the warm reek of the urgent milk a cohered shape amid the fluid and abstract earth." The earth is abstract, but the cow and Ike exist in fact, in flesh; while simultaneously, for the moment, they inhabit an ideal universe.

Then something happens; it happens on the page, as if in the process of writing. Returning from an early morning expedition to steal grain from a nearby barn, all of it described factually, Ike, "carrying the basket awkwardly before him in both arms, leaving in the wet grass a dark fixed wake," "watches the recurrence of that which he discovered for the first time three days ago," something, therefore, that inhabits his understanding as well as the author's. This discovery is that dawn comes up from the earth rather than down from the sky. (See Number 4 in accompanying text.) Who more appropriate than earthbound Ike to make such a discovery?—the more that, while it is no doubt true as an impression, it is also intellectually false.

The text elaborates Ike's discovery into a fantasy of an underworld "Roofed by the woven canopy of blind annealing grass-roots and the roots of trees, dark in the blind dark of time's silt and rich refuse—the constant and unslumbering anonymous worm-glut and the inextricable known bones—Troy's Helen and the nymphs and the snoring mitred bishops, the saviors and the victims and the kings." Anonymous food for worms and lordly bishops lie together in this underworld, from which dawn emerges to glorify even the lowest of Nature's creatures. The vision unfolds extravagantly over the next five or six pages, raising Ike and his love to astonishing heights of rhetoric.

The earth-generated dawn "wakes, up-seeping, attritive in unaccountable creeping channels: first, root; then frond by frond, from whose escaping tips like gas it rises and disseminates and stains the sleep-fast earth with drowsy insect-murmur; then, still upward-seeking, creeps the knitted bark of trunk and limb where, suddenly louder leaf by leaf and dispersive in diffusive sudden speed, melodious with the winged and jeweled throats, it upward bursts and fills night's globed negation with jonquil thunder." Later Ike returns from another foraging expedition, to find the cow, "as he left her, tethered, chewing." (See Number 5 in accompanying text.) But she is no longer just a cow: "Within, the mild enormous moist and pupilless globes he sees himself in twin miniature mirrored by the inscrutable abstraction; one with that which Juno might have looked out with, he watches himself contemplating what those who looked at Juno saw."

A final example. (See Number 6 in accompanying text.) Ike drinks from a spring where "his head interrupts, then replaces as . . . he breaks with drinking the reversed drinking of his drowned and fading image. It is the well of days, the still and insatiable aperture of earth. It holds in tranquil paradox of suspended precipitation dawn, noon, and sunset; yesterday, today, and tomorrow— star-spawn and hieroglyph, the fierce white dying rose, then gradual and invincible speeding up to and into slack-flood's coronal of nympholept noon." Nympholept = "caught by nymphs: one inspired by a violent and unattainable ideal or enthusiasm." All this is projected as the idiot's own meditations. *Ike* is the viewer of the dawn that comes up like "jonquil thunder"; *he* contemplates the sights that amazed Juno's suitors; *he* is the Narcissus of the Yoknapatawpha spring, the drinker at the "well of days" in whose depths he sees all of time "in suspended precipitation" yet forever in motion toward an eternal "nympholept noon."

Only, of course, there is no suggestion that Ike himself senses, let alone understands, any of this. In these passages, in which Faulkner comes close to caricaturing his own style, he also no longer speculates about what his hero knows and does not know, what he could or could not have known, it being evident that the plethora of visions and explanations radiating from him are invisible and inaudible to him. When, toward the close of the section, the text recalls the passage about the underworld cited earlier, the "canopy of the subterrene slumber" upon which Ike walks on his way to a place of sleep, no longer covers an "anonymous worm-glut," but only "Helen and the bishops, the kings and the graceless seraphim." The story of Ike and his love for a cow has become pure myth. "They walk in splendor." The man and the cow who stumbled and kept falling at the beginning of the story, now float off into a universe of gorgeous lyric.

At the very end, the transfigured pair do regain a measure of factual reality, but it is when their reality no longer matters, in the sleep that closes this section of the episode. Here Faulkner carefully observes a real cow who lies down "first the forequarters, then the hinder ones, lowering herself in two distinct stages into the spent ebb of evening, nestling back into the nest-form of sleep, the mammalian attar." But the man and the cow who "lie down together" are each and together pure image.

Hope is implicit in the act itself of writing: Faulkner, describing a degenerate Ike Snopes, ponders a world language is powerless to transform, but which forms itself in the attempt. This combination of hope and despair is expressed through the plot as well. As plot, Ike's bid for freedom is doomed to fly off into pure myth. It is inconceivable that Ike could leave his world, which, despite all the ways the idiot is described living outside society's time and its geography, is entirely circumscribed by them. Under the aegis of time, geography, and physical necessity, Ike takes grain from a nearby barn to feed the cow and leaves a blatant trail; the poor farmer Ike has robbed understands his loss as a final outrageous injustice, following on a lifetime of such. The fugitives are rapidly caught. Any other outcome is literally unimaginable. Faulkner's writing of this doomed escape is thus in itself a doomed escape. Instead of a redeeming pastoral, it turns out that he has been writing the doom of pastoral subsequent upon the doom of natural agrarian life.

Section 3 of "The Long Summer" is the second half of the episode of Ike and the cow. However, they never appear in it, having effectively died in the first half. Now we learn what killed them. The world of predators and ineffectuals of this part of the narrative functions in bitter denial of the pastoral idyll just concluded. We now see the reverse of the myth: Ike's love is a bestial perversion whose spectacle draws leering and paying crowds. The best that the more humane in the community can imagine, given an inhumane context, is to butcher Ike's cow and feed him its flesh to cure him of his passion. This proposition strips fact (flesh or reality) of every larger meaning; its violent literalism kills literature. In language, the two sections of the Ike episode present a dramatic contrast, the lush lyricism of the first versus the grim functionalism of the second. Each offers an explanation for the other's failure to imagine anything of hope or even peace. The first section fails when it slips its hold on life entirely and, thus disengaged, spins off into self-serving excess. The second fails because no one in its universe can imagine literature. There is perhaps more of hope in the first than in the second (which, however, supersedes the first), but the hope lies in writing, which is also the avenue to hope's defeat. There is no good to be found even in the natural world of Yoknapatawpha County, when the best the realm of nature can offer is a perverse and deformed Ike. Value and truth will have to come from the un-naturalness of art. Art is the only possible saving act, but it has to act by telling the facts. The facts are brutal; this is a world in which fact itself has become a brutality and literature is embattled for its life with its subjects. Its traditional ways of investing fact with value—the way of the pastoral for instance—no longer function: fact and meaning, instead of informing, mock one another.

I said at the start that rereading this episode had made me change my view of *The Hamlet* and of the Yoknapatawpha saga as a whole. This is how. I had remembered the Ike episode as proposing that nature provided a core of value in a degenerate world: that nature could inspire one to think pastorally even if the thinking was historically impotent. But nature in Yoknapatawpha is impotent even of inspiration; it lacks not only ethical but esthetic force. Though writing has the power to produce an imagined world with its own value, it too fails, not to change the world (few would expect it to), but to project a persuasive account of something better, which is something literature has sometimes achieved. Faulkner's writing has often been read as elegiac, sorrowing for values and a world doomed but worth remembering for certain abiding truths. In *The Hamlet*, however, his vision is radically disillusioned, devoid of hope, not simply for the future but for the possibility of a moral confrontation of doom. The county's good people, or its better people fail utterly to find in the at least partly transcendent story of Ike and his love for a cow an inspiration to improve matters. It is Ratliff, probably Faulkner's most ethical character, who negotiates the final holocaust of Ike's love.

Faulkner affirmed enduring values in his Nobel Prize speech and critics since have tended to take him at his word. On the evidence of *The Hamlet*, he misrepresented himself in that speech, perhaps out of a sense of social responsibility. For all his commitment to Mississippi and his immersion in Yoknapatawpha County, he seems to have been writing out of alienation. Faulkner may be the darkest of the figures who define this nation's literary tradition, or one of the two darkest, along with Mark Twain. Along with Mark Twain, he may also be one of the country's two most venerated writers. Not Melville, not Hawthorne, not even Emerson, certainly not Henry James, has his status, or his kind of status. For Faulkner is a sort of national Wise Man, the closest to the Poet-Prophet Whitman imagined he might become. There are many reasons for this ascendence, no doubt, but I suggest that his darkness is a central factor. The American cultural tradition is transcendingly optimistic, even when in the short run, defeat and even tragedy abound. Tragedy, for a modern writer, is an optimistic mode, in asserting the possibility of meaningful challenge to the prevailing order of things. There is no tragic confirmation available to Twain's characters, nor to Faulkner's: only failure. Faulkner made literature in the face of failure, or on the way to it. In the story of Ike and the cow, Nature, in fact and fiction, has and is lost; all that remains, as important as it is futile, as futile as it is important, is to write the loss. Faulkner's status in American culture may in part reflect unease with optimism, even in its tragic mode; possibly a suspicion that the nation made sacred by Nature and

Nature's God is and has been all along as brutal and perverse as
any. Shakespeare's sonnet rejects belying "with false compare" a
mistress sufficiently fair in reality. The episode of bestiality in *The
Hamlet* presents a reality beyond the reach of false compare. Writing about it defies both fact and fiction—a doomed defiance, for,
as for Mark Twain at the end of *The Mysterious Stranger*, or *Huck-
leberry Finn*, tragedy does not lie in the novel's events but in the
futility of writing about them.

From "The Long Summer"[1]

1

As winter became spring and the spring itself advanced, he had less
and less of darkness to flee through and from. Soon it was dark only
when he left the barn, backed carefully, with one down-groping foot,
from the harness-room where his quilt-and-straw bed was, and turned
his back on the long rambling loom of the house where last night's
new drummer-faces snored on the pillows of the beds which he had
now learned to make as well as Mrs. Littlejohn could; by April it was
the actual thin depthless suspension of false dawn itself, in which he
could already see and know himself to be an entity solid and cohered
in visibility instead of the uncohered all-sentience of fluid and nerve-
springing terror along and terribly free in the primal sightless inimical-
ity. That was gone now. Now the terror existed only during that moment after the false dawn, that interval's second between it and the
moment which birds and animals know: when the night at last suc-
cumbs to day; and then he would begin to hurry, trot, not to get there
quicker but because he must get back soon, without fear and calmly
now in the growing visibility, the gradation from gray through prim-
rose to the morning's ultimate gold, to the brow of the final hill, to let
himself downward into the creekside mist and lie in the drenched
myriad waking life of grasses and listen for her approach.

Then he would hear her, coming down the creekside in the mist. It
would not be after one hour, two hours, three; the dawn would be
empty, the moment and she would not be, then he would hear her and
he would lie drenched in the wet grass, serene and one and indivisible
in joy, listening to her approach. He would smell her; the whole mist
reeked with her; the same malleate hands of mist which drew along

his prone drenched flanks palped her pearled barrel too and shaped them both somewhere in immediate time, already married. He would not move. He would lie amid the waking instant of earth's teeming minute life, the motionless fronds of water-heavy grasses stooping into the mist before his face in black, fixed curves, along each parabola of which the marching drops held in minute magnification the dawn's rosy miniatures, smelling and even tasting the rich, slow, warm barn-reek milk-reek, the flowing immemorial female, hearing the slow planting and the plopping suck of each deliberate cloven mud-spreading hoof, invisible still in the mist loud with its hymeneal choristers.

Then he would see her; the bright thin horns of morning, of sun, would blow the mist away and reveal her, planted, blond, dew-pearled, standing in the parted water of the ford, blowing into the water the thick, warm, heavy, milk-laden breath; and lying in the drenched grasses, his eyes now blind with sun, he would wallow faintly from thigh to thigh, making a faint, thick, hoarse moaning sound. (182–83)

2

Earth became perpendicular and fled upward—the yawn void without even the meretricious reassurance of graduated steps. He made no sound as the three of them plunged down the crumbling sheer, at the bottom of which the horse rolled to its feet without stopping and galloped on down the ditch and where he, lying beneath the struggling and bellowing cow, received the violent relaxing of her fear-constricted bowels. Overhead, in the down draft of the ravine, the last ragged flame tongued over the lip, tip-curled, and vanished, swirled off into the windless stain of pale smoke on the sunny sky.

At first he couldn't do anything with her at all. She scrambled to her feet, facing him, her head lowered, bellowing. When he moved toward her, she whirled and ran at the crumbling sheer of the slope, scrambling furiously at the vain and shifting sand as though in a blind paroxysm of shame, to escape not him alone but the very scene of the outragement of privacy where she had been sprung suddenly upon and without warning from the dark and betrayed and outraged by her own treacherous biological inheritance, he following again, speaking to her, trying to tell her how this violent violation of her maiden's delicacy is no shame, since such is the very iron imperishable warp of the fabric of love. But she would not hear. (192)

3

He was standing then on a plank bridge over a narrow, shallow, weed-
choked ditch. He made no false motion with the hand which held the
coin, he had made no motion of any kind, he was standing perfectly
still at the moment, yet suddenly his palm was empty. The coin rang
dully once on the dusty planks and perhaps glinted once, then vanished, though who to know what motion, infinitesimal and convulsive,
of supreme repudiation there might have been, its impulse gone, vanished with the movement, because he even ceased to moan as he stood
looking at his empty palm with quiet amazement, turning the hand
over to look at the back, even raising and opening the other hand to
look into it. (196)

4

Now he watches the recurrence of that which he discovered for the
first time three days ago: that dawn, light, is not decanted onto earth
from the sky, but instead is from the earth itself suspired. Roofed by
the woven canopy of blind annealing grass-roots and the roots of trees,
dark in the blind dark of time's silt and rich refuse—the constant and
unslumbering anonymous worm-glut and the inextricable known
bones—Troy's Helen and the nymphs and the snoring mitred bishops,
the saviors and the victims and the kings—it wakes, up-seeping, attritive in uncountable creeping channels; first, root; then frond by frond,
from whose escaping tips like gas it rises and disseminates and stains
the sleep-fast earth with drowsy insect-murmur; then, still upward-
seeking, creeps the knitted bark of trunk and limb where, suddenly
louder leaf by leaf and dispersive in diffusive sudden speed, melodious
with the winged and jeweled throats, it upward bursts and fills night's
globed negation with jonquil thunder. (200)

5

She stands as he left her, tethered, chewing. Within the mild enormous moist and pupilless globes he sees himself in twin miniature
mirrored by the inscrutable abstraction; one with that which Juno
might have looked out with, he watches himself contemplating what
those who looked at Juno saw. (201)

6

Now he can see again. Again his head interrupts, then replaces as once more he breaks with drinking the reversed drinking of his drowned and fading image. It is the well of days, the still and insatiable aperture of earth. It holds in tranquil paradox of suspended precipitation dawn, noon, and sunset; yesterday, today, and tomorrow—starspawn and hieroglyph, the fierce white dying rose, then gradual and invincible speeding up to and into slack-flood's coronal of nympholept noon. (205)

NOTE

1. William Faulkner, *The Hamlet*, The Corrected Text (New York: Vintage International, 1991).

Eula, Linda, and the Death of Nature

DIANE ROBERTS

Faulkner's fictions chart vertiginous instabilities: people's relationships to each other, to their assigned gender, race, class, even to
the earth itself, fall to pieces with the smallest analytical push.
There is one Faulknerian equation we think we know, one that
seems solid: Woman = Nature. Yet this *donnée* of Faulkner criticism from Cleanth Brooks to new feminist readings stops adding
up toward the end of his career.[1]

Before I try to dig up the sod we've all been standing on, I
should reiterate the formula which was a central thesis of Ur-
critics like Brooks, Howe, and Fiedler: the Feminine embodies
the Natural and the Natural figures the Feminine.[2] Here are my
pick-hit examples (I'm sure you have yours): Dewey Dell Bundren
in *As I Lay Dying* saying "I feel like a wet seed wild in the hot,
blind earth"; or Caddy Compson mixed up in her brother's head
with honeysuckle; or the doe in "Delta Autumn," blatantly linked
with the nameless McCaslin-Beauchamp cousin of "mixed" race—
and the lubriciously feminized Delta itself; or the flood which con-
trapuntally illustrates Charlotte Rittenmeyer's powerful bodily
cycles in *The Wild Palms*; or Judith Sutpen, likened in *Absalom,
Absalom!* to a virgin field just waiting to be ploughed and seeded;
or the black stuff the deformed trees ooze in *Light in August* when
Joe Christmas faces the awful truth about menstruation.

The modern world seems rotten, men see women as rotten, and
so the landscape itself reflects this. In *Sanctuary*, the old decorum
has become "a gutted ruin rising gaunt and stark out of a grove
of unpruned cedar trees. It was a landmark, known as the Old
Frenchman Place, built before the Civil War; a plantation house

159

set in the middle of a tract of land; of cotton fields and gardens and lawns long since gone back to jungle" (15). So much of Faulkner's fiction chronicles white men's attempts to contain, regulate, and exploit the land, while they also try to contain, regulate, and exploit female sexuality. Southern culture constructs black women as highly (and overtly) physical, earthy, while it suspects white women of being the same, just papered over with the cult of chastity. Women of both races are seen as organic beings—about the only quality they are allowed to share.

In *The Hamlet* (1940), Eula Varner, too, is a force of nature, part of the flora and fauna of Yoknapatawpha, an overembodiment of fecundity, of mythic plenty, of the very land itself. In both an echo of and answer to the way Judith is figured (by men) in *Absalom, Absalom!* as a field, Eula is "the fine land rich and fecund and foul and eternal and impervious to him who claimed title to it, oblivious" (119). The slide from eroticized landscape to female body is short: the small farmers of the Varner fiefdom live by the fertility of the land—you must get a crop on your fields to live; and life itself, procreation, is another crop. Eula literally represents land: her father owns a great deal of property and she will inherit part of it. In fact, she gets the Old Frenchman Place, the ruined plantation seeded with false stories of buried treasure and clouded by a fragmented history where nature, once at its most ordered, has run amok, and eventually the place where, according to Noel Polk, Mink hides (in a womblike cellar) after killing Flem.[3] The Old Frenchman Place is later (in Yoknapatawpha time) the setting of dispute over another woman's body, an *opposite* body to Eula's: not so agriculturally suggestive. When Tommy, the bootleggers' dogsbody in *Sanctuary*, sees Temple Drake for the first time, he says, looking at her epicene form, "He aint laid no crop by yit, has he?" (43). If Eula was the goddess of the place, her luxuriant spirit is long gone by the time Temple is desecrated there.

Eula in *The Hamlet* is land, but she is also food, "honey in sunlight and bursting grapes." Her eyes are the color of "hothouse grapes," a description associated with highly sexual women in Faulkner most significantly used early on with the "dirty" Belle

Mitchell. Faulkner simply stole it from himself. And Eula is live-stock, the "mammalian female meat" disinclined to move any more than necessary, eating, barely existing, her damp mouth always a little open, a body supporting a system of production which, as Faulkner says, "might as well still have been a foetus" while it "listens in sullen bemusement, with a weary wisdom heired of all mammalian maturity, to the enlargement of her own organs" (90, 89).

She sounds just like a cow. Indeed, she suffers in comparison with a cow in *The Hamlet*; the novel's great pairing is not Eula and Labove, the mad nympholept Ole Miss football star-turned-schoolmaster, or Eula and Hoake McCarron, or (in antithesis) the Venus-Eula netted to the Vulcan-Flem, but a cow described (initially, at least) the way a seventeenth-century pastoral poet would describe a Phyllis or a Clorinda, and a mentally defective Snopes called Ike. Faulkner has linked women and cows before: in *Absalom, Absalom!* Thomas Sutpen's hillfolk sisters are bovine, so are Sarty Snopes's in "Barn Burning." And in *As I Lay Dying*, Dewey Dell has a one-sided but sisterly conversation with a cow: "What you got in you aint nothing to what I got in me" (61).

In *The Hamlet*, Eula is anything but a sentient human being, a voice, a consciousness. Dawn Trouard remarks that she represents "Faulkner's bitterest illustration of the patriarchal subjugation of women in American culture."[4] She is a parody of the silent, still, statuelike white woman: instead of her purity striking strong men dumb with awe (the way Confederate romance writers like Thomas Nelson Page described it), her unconscious sexuality inspires them to bay like dogs. She is a fabliau figure of sexual slapstick, breasts popping out here, buttocks thrusting out there, despite her bourgeois brother Jody's attempt to control her through book-learning and corsets. Like the always-willing white trash women in Erskine Caldwell's fantasies of rural Georgia life from the early thirties, she belongs to the mock-heroic tradition of the libidinous peasantry.[5] We recognize her type in the drawling, underdressed Daisy Maes (and Daisy Dukes) of popular culture, a dirty joke come to life.

Like most women in Faulkner, Eula is "spoken for," that is, someone claims sexual ownership of her, first her father, then her brother, and finally, through the legal fiction of marriage, Flem. Her body, as Joseph Urgo points out, "does not belong to her."[6] Men think they can possess the Earth Goddess of Frenchman's Bend but they are mistaken; recall Labove kneeling at her bench, unable even to molest her, and those drooling local boys trying to outswagger each other until Eula herself (more even than Hoake, her actual lover) beats the tar out of them with the buggy whip handle. When she is found to be pregnant, Hoake clears out, sure: but so do all the local boys, each hoping to be thought the one who "did it," who "took her." But this is mere testosterone-fired fantasy: no one can claim mastery of Eula's Olympian sexuality. The Earth Goddess belongs to the earth and the earth belongs to no man. The prideful illusion of land ownership occupies much of Faulkner's work: the Thomas Sutpens and Ike McCaslins (and later the Flem Snopeses) of the world constantly learn the bitter lesson that land cannot be owned, that, if anything, the land owns *us*.

And yet Faulkner's men persist in this error that they can own land and control women's sexuality. Some of his women characters think this way as well: witness Ike McCaslin's nameless wife who so crudely equates her body with Ike's plantation. Eula is "spoken for" as a woman bartered to Flem Snopes for propriety's and property's sake. She is also a woman spoken for in that she is almost voiceless, described, represented, and circumscribed by men. In becoming the lacuna that paradoxically fills the lives of everyone around her, Eula joins Judith Sutpen, Temple Drake, Lena Grove, the slaves Eunice and Thomasina, and Dewey Dell and Addie Bundren as the supreme invention and *idée fixe* of men's lives, yet whose voice is rarely heard.[7] She is, perhaps, most like Caddy Compson: a hole at the center of the text, the object of obsession with no means to explain herself except the body to which her culture never allows her to give free play. The same is true of *The Town* (1957), though by now the Earth Goddess has moved into Jefferson and acquired a better class of acolyte in Gavin Stevens,

Manfred de Spain, even, to some extent, Ratliff and Chick Mallison, all of whom construct her out of sexual stereotypes that range
from the poignant to the downright idiotic.

The equation woman = land = Nature-with-a-capital "N" begins to fragment in *The Town*, the second installment of the
Snopes trilogy, published seventeen years after *The Hamlet*.
Where the world of *The Hamlet* was a bucolic romp, the milieu of
The Town is bourgeois and repressed—there's hardly any "nature"
at all—no wilderness, little hunting, farms only in the abstract.
Even Frenchman's Bend is talked of (not visited) as if it's another
world. Eula still stops traffic, only now it's not buggies and mules
but cars, and she gets invited to middle-class fêtes like the Cotil-
lion Club Ball: Semiramis has gone suburban.

Indeed, the whole South has gone suburban: the opening images of *The Town* include not the woods, the hills, and the rivers of
Faulkner's familiar rural world, but the water tank, Ratliff's sewing
machines, Manfred de Spain's roadster, the car dealership, and the
power plant. I disagree with critics who say *The Town* and *The
Mansion* have "little to do with actual political issues of the
times."[8] *The Town* (1957) was completed during some crucial years
of the civil rights movement, and *The Mansion* (1959) came out
during some of the first difficult experiments in integration. The
attention to social issues is not overt; *The Town* seems quite un-
concerned with race at all. But there are other tensions, other divi-
sions that arise—somewhat anachronistically. While *The Town*
technically takes place from before the First World War to the
late 1920s or early 1930s, the process Faulkner describes, of the
breakdown of country life, of Snopesian (that is, poor white) migration to the towns, is really more a post–World War II phenomenon. This is even more obvious in *The Mansion*, set in the thirties
and forties but clearly "about" the mid- to late fifties, when the
white South solidified its resistance to threats from within and
without. Beginning in 1948, much of the region signalled its refusal to change by supporting the Dixiecrat Party, which had been
formed to protest Truman's civil rights platform. In Mississippi,
the Dixiecrats polled 87 percent for states' rights candidate Strom

Thurmond.[9] *Intruder in the Dust* obviously reflects these concerns, but so do the novels of the 1950s.

Faulkner first used this time-warping in *Requiem for a Nun,* his rethink of Temple Drake's life, published in 1951, twenty years after *Sanctuary.* Temple and Gowan surely haven't been married for twenty years: they are both still young, their children hardly more than infants. Yet the "Golden Dome" section declares itself set in "A.D. 1950," and the scorn Faulkner heaps on modern "bungalows" with modern conveniences and the plastic bibelots of modern life surely belong to the postwar boom. At any rate, Faulkner's first novel of the 1950s describes how the old, untamed nature of the South is being destroyed first by the order of the farm, then by urbanization. Jefferson grows,

> the four broad diverging avenues straight as plumb-lines in the four directions, beginning the network of roads and by-roads until the whole county would be covered with it: the hands, the prehensile fingers clawing dragging lightward out of the disappearing wilderness year by year as up from the bottom of the receding sea, the broad, rich, fecund burgeoning fields pushing thrusting each year further and further and further back the wilderness. (41)

Temple Drake, whose alleged "redemption" story is juxtaposed with the building and taming of Mississippi by white folks and their institutions, becomes a prisoner-victim to the same cult of respectability that kills Eula Varner. Nature, previously the unanswerable ally of women, has been suppressed. Sexuality, a force the community (especially the church-lady types like Narcissa Benbow) always tried to contain but couldn't, is now subjected to the rule of the nuclear family. In Eula's new home, her almighty body does not enjoy a feast of promiscuity; on the contrary, in *The Town,* everyone knows that she has been faithful to one man for eighteen years. Of course the man is not her impotent husband Flem but Manfred de Spain, the aristocratic war hero who sells the livery stable and substitutes the horses for horsepower, but still: Eula is hardly an orgy on two feet, despite the response she provokes in the men of the town. The way the community constructs her limits her, relegating her to an emblem of sexual possibility. We are told

> there was just too much of what she was for any one human female
> package to contain, and hold: too much of white, too much of female,
> too much of maybe just glory, I don't know: so that at first sight of her
> you felt a kind of shock of gratitude just for being alive and being male
> at the same instant with her in space and time.(6)

This is the Eula we tend to accept because we are offered so little challenge to the Aphrodite mask. But, as ever in Faulkner, who speaks is central. It's impossible to say anything meaningful about *Absalom, Absalom!* without being clear whether it's Quentin, his father, Shreve, or Miss Rosa remaking history through "impersonation and dream": there's almost nothing in the way of authorial omniscience. And we are used to resisting the portrait of Caddy Compson as drawn by her brothers, her mother, and her father (all that stuff about women having *"an affinity for evil"* (59).[10] Still, too many critics read Eula as the overbodied cipher in *The Hamlet* or the tragic "Helen" given us by Charles, Gavin, and Ratliff. While it's true that we have little else to go on, the goddess, so silenced by the excessive, mythic representations of her (it's hard to be heard with the white noise of Western sexual legend drowning out any individual voice), does begin to speak. In *The Town*, Eula has two conversations with Gavin, one to save his life, one to save hers. He fails to understand her either time, but then, you don't chat with the goddess as an equal, you fall down and worship her. When Eula fails either to seduce him or to get him to marry her daughter and so preserve the "good name" that she has been duped into believing is central to life in Jefferson, she kills herself—and continues to be misunderstood.

Though lamented as a relic of some Dionysian Golden Age, the like of whom will never be seen again, she is no longer embodied nature: removed from the land, the grapes and the honey and the milk of the Arcadian, she has become unnatural. For a fertility goddess, she is remarkably infertile. The triumphant parody of a corsage Manfred de Spain sends Gavin combines a rake head (which Gavin planted in the road to pop Manfred's tires) and two flowers, tied together with a used condom.

Gavin and Ratliff speculate that Eula kills herself because she "was bored." But perhaps her shooting herself (after visiting the hairdresser for the first time in her life—another admission that her "nature" has become artifice) was more an attempt to exercise power over her body—for the first and last time. While it's hard to see suicide as strength, by removing herself as a bone of contention, Eula ensures that her daughter can get away and a fiction of her "virtue" be preserved. It is also a choice she makes alone for herself—to defuse her powerful sexuality once and for all.[11] Of course, she is also silenced, eternally stuck with men who speak for her. Dawn Trouard reads it as a final refusal: "Eula's suicide presumably says no, and finally, through it, she is cured of 'the curse' of speech."[12] The last insult is a joint effort by Gavin Stevens and Flem Snopes, erecting that marker over her grave which reads "A Virtuous Wife Is a Crown to Her Husband/Her Children Rise and Call Her Blessed."

The pagan goddess is buried under a slab of Christian marble and labeled chaste: a comfortable fiction which seems to silence once and for all the vexed, powerful, and, to men, frightening collusion between the female and the natural. Later Flem concocts a deal to create a subdivision of tract houses of the sort Faulkner sneers at in *The Mansion*, as well as in *Requiem for a Nun* and *Intruder in the Dust*—houses "designed in Florida and California set with matching garages in their neat plots of clipped grass and tedious flower beds" presided over by "wives in sandals and pants and painted toenails puff[ing] lipstick-stained cigarettes over shopping bags in the chain groceries and drugstores" (*Intruder* 198). Flem's subdivision would be called Eula Acres, an attempt to control and contain the feminine in ownership: shackled land figuring silenced wife.

However, Eula's silence, and the silence in which her daughter Linda lives in her deafness, is not, as Gail Mortimer points out, "simply the absence of noise or even a quiet *place*. It has its own reality that can supersede other realities."[13] In other words, absence (or silence) is not "nonexistence" but another kind of *presence*. This is related, perhaps, to the often-expressed sentiment (by men in Faulkner and sometimes the authorial voice itself) that presence is only given shape and meaning by loss: that virginity must be lost in order to have existed at all, that the wilderness must be destroyed to have existed at all, large thematic concerns of earlier novels such as *The Sound and the Fury* and *Go Down, Moses*. Eula is more real in being dead and gone, just as the wilderness is now more poignant in being remembered: in Gavin's construction "doomed never to efface the anguish and the hunger from Motion even by her own act of quitting Motion and so fill with her own absence from it the aching void where once had glared that incandescent shape" (*Town* 133).[14]

In contrast, Linda Snopes Kohl is not a figure of loss, an emblem of nature or virginity unrecoverable in the modern world, much as Gavin Stevens wants her to be. She is wholly unlike any other woman in Faulkner's fiction. Distinct from her mother, whose being was equated with capital "N" Nature, Linda is not figured by the natural: her sexuality cannot be represented by swirling waters or bursting grapes or classical goddesses. As Hee Kang points out, Linda "changes the landscape of woman's space in [Faulkner's] fictional world, tracing a trajectory from the space of victimization, betrayal, and death to a newly configured feminine space of desire, autonomy, and freedom."[15] She is divorced from the wilderness, a child of the town, then of Greenwich Village. Ted Ownby calls her "Faulkner's only radical."[16] Certainly she is that rare thing in Faulkner: a *political* person.

In *The Town*, Linda lives mostly in the silence and stasis Southern "romance" insists surrounds young white girls. Flem and Eula try to impose ladyhood on her, sending her to Miss Melissa Hogganbeck's Female Academy (where time stopped at Appomattox), while Gavin tries to save her from Snopesism by trying to "form her mind" with books of poetry presented over the fanciest ice cream desserts in the drugstore.

Linda isn't free from the reductive representations of the men who tell her story—she speaks (and what a voice) in a way that her mother cannot, yet she still never gains her own narrative sections, unlike Ratliff, Chick, Gavin, and the third person "Faulkner." Chick and Gavin liken her at times to a hunting dog sighting prey, a "young pointer bitch, the maiden bitch of course, the virgin bitch, immune now in virginity, not scorning the earth, spurning the earth because she needed it to walk on in that immunity" (*Town* 132). But walk *on* the earth is all Linda does—she is not of it as her mother was. And though she is compared to an animal, with all that implies—instinctive sexuality, lack of language—she eludes such a categorization. She may not tell her story directly but she challenges others', especially Gavin's, constructions of her. Though she accepts Gavin's volume of Donne, and lets him talk to her about going to a Seven Sisters college, she is not such a promising pupil as Melisandre Backus, the truly speechless young girl who was Gavin's previous educational project, the woman who eventually becomes his wife, described by Chick as "defenseless and helpless," conferring "knighthood on any man who came within range" (*Town* 178). When Linda's Yankee boxer beau Matt Leavitt tries to mess with Gavin, she clocks him one and calls him "a clumsy ignorant stupid son of a bitch," causing Chick, if not Gavin, to reassess some white, Southern, male notions of young ladyhood (*Town* 190–91). She is just as blunt when she tells Gavin what he can do to her in *The Mansion*, saying "fuck" baldly and unashamedly. She speaks her own story, while Gavin tries to write her, literally as a character in a safe, containing fiction, as men have always done, on the fancy little pad he gives her to "feminize" and control her. In insisting on speaking, even with her "ugly" voice, she gains a power no other woman in Faulkner—no woman still attached to the social system of ladyhood or the mythic associations of nature—commands.

You could say *The Mansion* is about the return of the repressed: Mink, Linda, and the multifarious sins of the past come home to Jefferson to wreak all the havoc they can, taking revenge for what I am tempted to call crimes against Nature. As ever in Faulkner, there is a historical dimension to what people do. At the very beginning of the Linda section, Ratliff reports Chick (who has gotten to be a very tiresome young man) bugging his uncle, quite inaccurately calling Linda "the first female girl soldier we ever had" (*Mansion* 109). Chick should remember Drusilla Hawk who, while not "actually wounded by the enemy," was a soldier who went off to kill Yankees in *The Unvanquished*. Drusilla was a threatening new model of the feminine who had to be forced into skirts and respectable marriage by the church ladies of the town but then so fetishized honor that she let the lust for revenge destroy her. *The Mansion* raises her ghost and, rather more slyly, another Civil War lady who makes her one appearance in the slight, funny story "My Grandmother Millard, General Bedford Forrest, and the Battle of Harrykin Creek." She is the archetypal belle: fragile, beautiful, sensitive (of course the story makes much fun of this through young Bayard Sartoris's boy-voice) and her name, after she marries the gallant Confederate soldier who falls in love with her at first sight (surrounded by an exploding outhouse) is Melisandre Backhouse. It's spelled differently then, but surely Melisandre Backus is her direct descendant—and a contrast, perhaps even a rival, to Linda.

Melisandre, like her dainty great-grandmother, is the *princesse lointaine*, the white lady on her pedestal, gracious, sweet (even though she was, apparently unknowingly, married to a bootlegger-gangster), and silent. In *Knight's Gambit* we are told she was raised, like a prize tulip, in a "walled and windless garden."[17] Linda, like Drusilla, is disruptive, a cross-dresser, committed to honor (as a soldier should be), and justice: a politicized person; John Sartoris and Drusilla, in her wedding dress, killed the Bundrens for being Northern Reconstruction liberals and stopped blacks from voting in Jefferson's first postwar election. But Linda is what Drusilla and John Sartoris would have called a "nigger lover," and, unlike Drusilla, Linda seems to be a fully sexual woman, not an honorary boy. In the end, Drusilla is packed off back to Alabama, laughing insanely like Lady Macbeth, while Linda drives away in her Jaguar, less Lady Macbeth than the *femme fatale* in a *film noir*.

Still, the power of the past is considerable, even in a Jefferson which seems committed to Snopesian deracination or, at best, a reinvention of the past into travesty, like the *Gone with the Wind*-ish "improvements" made on the old Backus plantation or the "white colyums," as Ratliff calls them, on the de Spain house. Linda accomplishes revenge not only for her mother, but for all those silenced Southern women whose bodies were circumscribed, whose lives were directed by race, color, gender, and class, and whose voices were never heard.

To Jefferson, Linda is a freak, an anomaly. She does not fit. In some ways women never fit, preordained to be Other, inexplicable, forces in collusion with the mysterious boom-or-bust plays of the land. There's something uncomfortable about Linda, from her clothes to her politics to her name: a name that is barely hers. "Linda" means pretty; it was a fashionable prescriptive name of the forties and fifties. But she is not a "pretty girl" in the sexual economy any more than she is a sacred space to be defiled, like Temple, or a flower to be deflowered, like Narcissa. "Snopes" is a legal fiction, a state of disgrace from which Gavin seeks to rescue her and a name she herself will try to efface by engineering Flem's murder. Finally, "Kohl" just doesn't set well with Jefferson, belonging, as it does, to her dead New York Jewish husband, alien and difficult for Mississippi people (except the Harvard-and-Heidelberg-educated Gavin) to pronounce.

These "false" names further alienate Linda from the organic community. But her distance/difference from her mother's iconic sexuality does not mean she is asexual. She does, however, control her own sexuality; unlike Eula she owns her own body and expresses her desire directly, as Gavin discovers, when she uses that "unlovely" but quite plain word for sexual intercourse.

Which brings us back to Nature. Unlike *The Town*, which begins with many human interventions into and impositions upon the organic, *The Mansion* perversely (or perhaps appropriately) takes us back to the rural world of *The Hamlet*. The novel opens with Mink's dispute with Houston over a cow. Juxtaposed with this is a reiteration of Eula's story in animal terms, comparing her country swains to "rutting dogs" and Linda to "a woods colt in

[Will Varner's] back yard" (4). Following hard on this zoo of images, we have Mink's vision of religion and society in sexual anarchy. Here he muses on a preacher who gets "conveniently together the biggest possible number of women that he could tempt with the reward of the one in return for the job of the other—the job of filling his hole in payment for getting theirs plugged the first time the husband went to the field and she could slip off to the bushes where the preacher was waiting"(5–6).

In the Linda section, Chick starts off regarding her as sexual property even before she steps off the train from New York, making snide comments about rape (and managing to be anti-Semitic with it), speculating on "women like that . . . once you get their clothes off they surprise you," finally even asking Gavin, with sophomoric coarseness, if it's "all right with you if I try to lay her" (353).

I suppose this is the attitude we'd expect toward the daughter of the legendary Eula, and it's true that the world of The Mansion is highly sexualized. However, Linda is not part of this "natural" network of coupling and birthing: indeed, this culture of slipping off to the bushes is challenged by a new order of institutions. Instead of grand poetic and organic forces, we have the alphabet soup of officialdom and activism: the FBI, the KKK, the NRA, the WPA, the IWW, the NAACP, the CIO, the CP.[18] Eula is constantly described in The Mansion as a "natural phenomenon," compared to a "cyclone or a tidal wave," her "loins seeded" like land (127, 124). Ratliff says Eula just needed "to be like the ground of the field, until the right time come, the right wind, the right sun, the right rain; until in fact that-ere single unique big buck jumped that tame garden fence" (120). Eula here is the land (like Judith Sutpen) and the hortus conclusus, a passive figure waiting, like Danae, for the shower of gold that will impregnate her.

But that's the old order; Linda belongs to the new. She's not natural, she's social, thriving in that world of man-made institutional letters. Things are upside down: Linda, a woman, makes cool sexual choices, does a man's work, even has her own money (though so does Melisandre Backus—lucky Gavin has the choice of two rich widows). Moreover, Linda is not stuck with Southern conventions of Ladyhood: she won't let Chick open her car door for her and he fears she "had left the South too young too long ago" (358). While Gavin tries to feminize Linda with that little gold and ivory tablet with hardly room to write three words on it, she gives him a cigarette lighter with her magisterial initial muscling in between his—an inversion of the usual narrative of penetration.

Politics and sex have always gone together, especially in the South. The allegedly Christian Right points at the rumored peccadilloes of President Bill Clinton or the so-called homosexual agenda of the Left to discredit all progressivism, while the Left fingers the reported adulteries of Jimmy Swaggart and Newt Gingrich, crying "hypocrite." Before the Civil War, proslavery writers accused abolitionists of believing in "free love" while abolitionists reminded pro-Southern advocates that slavery was little better than institutionalized rape. *Uncle Tom's Cabin* scandalized the North and the South with its attack on slave masters' slave concubines (which, of course, Faulkner himself dealt with in *Absalom, Absalom!*, *Go Down, Moses*, and other works) and Harriet Beecher Stowe was stigmatized in proslavery circles as morally dubious, and "no lady."[19]

Linda doesn't quite fit here either: she's primarily attacked as a "Nigger Lover," a Jew, and a Communist, not a slut, though maybe her godless communism leads Chick to believe she's the sort of girl who'd be pretty undiscriminating when it comes to getting "laid." She is what was called, earlier in the century, a "New Woman," a creature that always interested (and attracted and repelled) Faulkner because she was sexually frank as well as sexually ambiguous, often rather masculine (think of Charlotte Rittenmeyer or Caddy Compson who, though mixed up with honeysuckle in Quentin's head, acted like a stereotypical elder son in her sexual sophistication and leadership). Linda goes beyond any New Woman in Faulkner in her actual political intervention. *The Mansion* is officially set in the thirties and forties but functions as a novel of the Cold War and the civil rights movement. Faulkner should have hauled off and had Linda lead a lunch counter sit-in like Northern liberal and SNCC kids were doing all over the South. It would have been entirely in character.

Faulkner in the fifties was politically aware and, at least in print and in speeches, involved. Noel Polk reminds us that his novels of the forties prepared his thinking: "at least part of his political engagement with racial problems in the fifties was a direct response to the racial morality of, say, *Go Down, Moses* and *Intruder in the Dust.*"[20] The most overt material is nonfiction, essays and speeches. "Mississippi," published in *Holiday* in 1954, uses Faulknerian characters to illustrate Northern economic colonization in the South.[21] "Letter to a Northern Editor" for *Life* in 1956 criticizes both the NAACP and the White Citizens' Council, as well as taking issue with the Supreme Court's "Brown" decision.[22] The 1955 "Address to the Southern Historical Association" is anticommunist, and his "Address to the Raven, Jefferson, and ODK Societies" at the University of Virginia in 1958, the year before *The Mansion* was published, tells the North to leave the South alone since "we" can handle "our Negroes" our "own way." Faulkner goes on to say "perhaps the Negro is not yet capable of more than second class citizenship. His tragedy may be that so far he is competent for equality only in the ratio of his white blood."[23] I cite all these not to accuse Faulkner of racism or red-baiting. These are the sentiments of the Southern "moderate" (who seems conservative only by late twentieth-century standards). Faulkner also incurred the wrath of many members of his own family for his prointegration stance, and he (rather quietly) used part of his Nobel Prize money to establish a scholarship for black students.

The point here is that Faulkner was very much involved in the burning issues of the day, and all these concerns—communism, states' rights, race—go into the creation of Linda. The narrators of *The Mansion* do their best to patronize Linda's reformist passion. We are told, smugly, that the Finnish communists who had been her allies became capitalists during the war. We are told of her "meddling with the Negroes": Chick reports the pained conversation between Gavin and the black school principal who begs that

Gavin control his protégée and make her leave them alone (there is much allusion to the conservative, no-social-equality philosophy of Booker T. Washington here). After the war, the third person narrative voice declares that Linda is without a hobby since "the new social revolution laws . . . had abolished not merely hunger and inequality and injustice, but work too by substituting for it a new self-compounding vocation or profession for which you would need no schooling at all: the simple production of children" (*Mansion* 350–51). It is even implied that racism is now "solved" since the blacks received "a newer and better high school building in Jefferson than the white folks had" (350). Obviously this is not a casual comment, coming from a writer who had plenty of things to say in public about the Emmett Till murder, Autherine Lucy's attempt to integrate the University of Alabama, and governmental measures taken to enforce equality.

If nothing else, it should be clear that Faulkner, like many angry white men (and other Southerners) today, was no fan of the federal government. In 1955 sociologist Rupert Vance said "the dominant psychology of the South is no longer agrarian, it is Chamber of Commerce." In 1956 Faulkner wrote, "Our economy is no longer agricultural, our economy is the federal government" (*Essays* 98). In fact, in 1959, 24 percent of the general revenues of state and local government in Mississippi came from Washington—the highest rate in the South.

So here is Linda, the would-be redistributor of wealth, the do-gooder to blacks, a woman who would seem, weirdly, to represent what Faulkner saw Big Government trying to do. Is she, then, the Enemy? She is a woman outside of the community decorum yet she does not succeed in overturning white, male hegemony. She does succeed, however, in destroying the Snopeses, representative of a force attacking the old, Bourbon order from the other side. So perhaps Gavin Stevens, the "liberal" who is nonetheless more invested in the Old South than the New, should be grateful to her.

Unnatural as she is, "monster" though she is called, there is something great about Linda. Her voice does, as Hee Kang says, break "the 'vault of silence' " that has reduced and bound women in this world.[24] That "ugly" quacking insists on being heard, even though she cannot hear what is said in reply, an inversion, maybe a parody, of the quiet woman whose real voice is ignored by the world of men as they make of her a fantasy figure, writing her story for her as Gavin tries to write words *for* Linda—words she usually rejects. Her quacking (Faulkner's description an attempt to link her, however grotesquely, to some residual animal quality?), her "mannishness," so unlike her ultrafeminine mother, and her intelligence overturn all the inscribed feminine of Faulkner's earlier works. Gavin sets out to educate her, but she finally educates him: he had never taken her intelligence as seriously as he should have. She ends up dignified, powerful, and unfathomable, not killed off by the object of her misguided philanthropy like Joanna Burden, not violated and silenced for challenging her place in the property system like Temple Drake, nor driven to efface her own troublesome body from the earth like her mother, the Earth Goddess Eula. Noel Polk observes that the Faulkner of the fifties "seems to understand that men cannot claim their own histories until women can claim theirs too, and tell it themselves, if they choose, in their own voices, in their own language, without yielding to the cultural narrative that binds us all to a singular narrative that is so frequently reducible to sexual pathology."[25]

Linda does flout her cultural narrative. She is associated not with fertile fields or vines or honey or flowers or cows but with a *car*, expensive and powerful. She leaves the South on her own terms, marking Gavin once again, this time not with her initial on his lighter but with red lipstick on his mouth (a signifier of female sexuality in Faulkner since at least *Sanctuary*), roaring off in a Jaguar. Not only is it a foreign car, but a final, bitterly ironic, underlining of her rejection of Nature—it may be named after a powerful jungle cat but it is a machine, a representative of the technology Faulkner felt uneasy about, close kin to Manfred de Spain's swaggeringly sexual roadster. Linda is more like the complex, expensive, efficient engine than any Yoknapatawpha flora or fauna. She has defied Nature, morality, capitalism, and the South itself, giving back the de Spain mansion with its sham Tara-fied front to the last broken-down de Spain heirs. The divorce from the "old Dionysic times" of the soil is complete. Linda gets away with murder.

NOTES

1. I have quoted from the following Faulkner works; page numbers are inserted parenthetically in the text: *As I Lay Dying* (New York: Vintage, 1964), *Essays, Speeches, and Public Letters of William Faulkner*, ed. James B. Meriwether (New York: Random House, 1966), *Flags in the Dust*, ed. Douglas Day (New York: Random House, 1973), *The Hamlet* (New York: Random House, 1940), *Intruder in the Dust* (New York: Random House, 1948), *Requiem for a Nun* (New York: Random House, 1951), *The Sound and the Fury*, ed. David Minter (New York: W. W. Norton Co., 1987), *The Mansion* (New York: Random House, 1959), *Sanctuary, The Corrected Text* (New York: Vintage, 1987), *The Town* (New York: Vintage, 1961).

2. See Cleanth Brooks, *The Yoknapatawpha Country* (New Haven: Yale University Press, 1963); Irving Howe, *William Faulkner: A Critical Study* (Chicago: University of Chicago Press, 1975); and Leslie Fiedler, *Love and Death in the American Novel* (New York: Criterion, 1960). I should like to acknowledge my debt to some more recent Faulkner scholars: Noel Polk offered very useful advice on this essay, and his book, *Children of the Dark House* (Jackson: University Press of Mississippi, 1996), was helpful throughout (Polk emphatically does not subscribe to the notion that the Faulkner of the fifties was a diminished talent). I have also used the ideas of Hee Kang, my former student, on Linda and Eula, as well as the work of Richard Gray, Gail Mortimer, Dawn Trouard, Theresa Towner, and Joseph Urgo.

3. See Polk, *Children of the Dark House*, 96–97, where he argues that the Old Frenchman Place had to be where Mink hid because it would be the only house big and fine enough to have a cellar.

4. Dawn Trouard, "Eula's Plot: An Irigarian Reading of Faulkner's Snopes Trilogy," *Mississippi Quarterly* 42:3 (Summer 1989): 281. Trouard examines the way Eula is "economically circulated" and silenced in her milieu. Hee Kang, in "A New Configuration of Faulkner's Feminine: Linda Snopes Kohl in *The Mansion*," *Faulkner Journal* 8:1 (1992): 21–41, basically concurs with Trouard. Evelyn Jaffe Schreiber, however, disagrees. In "What's Love Got to Do With It? Desire and Subjectivity in Faulkner's Snopes Trilogy," *Faulkner Journal* (Fall 1993/Spring 1994): 91, she insists that Eula "asserts herself as a subject" and demonstrates a certain amount of power over her own situation. I think Schreiber overstates the case. While Eula takes matters into her own hands at times (such as her affair with Manfred de Spain) her agency is, at best, confined within Yoknapatawpha expectations for the local sex goddess. Not until she commits suicide can she exercise real control though; like Caddy Compson, her voicelessness does not erase her.

5. See Diane Roberts, *Faulkner and Southern Womanhood* (Athens: University of Georgia Press, 1994), 198–202; Erskine Caldwell, *God's Little Acre* (1933) and *Tobacco Road* (1932).

6. Joseph R. Urgo, *Faulkner's Apocrypha: "A Fable," Snopes, and the Spirit of Human Rebellion* (Jackson: University Press of Mississippi, 1989), 1.

7. See Gail Mortimer, *Faulkner's Rhetoric of Loss* (Austin: University of Texas, 1983) on the feminine absence in the center of Faulkner's novels. See also John Matthews, *The Play of Faulkner's Language* (Ithaca: Cornell University Press, 1982) and Roberts, *Faulkner and Southern Womanhood*.

8. Urgo, 182.

9. Polk, 187.

10. For discussions of reading Faulkner's women against the grain of what Faulkner's men tell us, see Deborah Clarke, "Gender, Race, and Language in *Light in August*," *American Literature* 61: 3 (October 1989): 398–413; John N. Duvall, *Faulkner's Marginal Couple* (Austin: University of Texas, 1990); Minrose C. Gwin, *The Feminine and Faulkner* (Knoxville: University of Tennessee, 1990); John T. Matthews, "The Elliptical Nature of *Sanctuary*," *Novel* 17 (1984): 246–66; Mortimer, *The Rhetoric of Faulkner's Loss*; Roberts, *Faulkner and Southern Womanhood*.

11. One might argue that Edna Pontellier, in Chopin's *The Awakening*, kills herself as an act, perversely, of rebirth, taking ultimate and final charge over her body which she had been denied.

12. Trouard, 295.

13. Mortimer, 86.

14. Faulkner's own most pious act of remembering the loss of the wilderness comes in *Big Woods* (1955), his collection of hunting stories published between *A Fable* and the second and third volumes of the Snopes trilogy. In it, as James A. Snead says in *Figures of Division: William Faulkner's Major Novels* (New York: Methuen, 1986), blacks, women, and Indians mark "any otherness which white male settlers have despised yet desired as projections of an originality from which they are not forever separated" (184).

15. Kang, 129.

16. Ted Ownby, "The Snopes Trilogy and the Emergence of Consumer Culture," *Faulkner and Ideology*, ed. Donald Kartiganer and Ann J. Abadie (Jackson: University Press of Mississippi, 1995), 122.

17. Faulkner likes this description of a *hortus conclusus*: he uses it early on in *The Marionettes* where Marietta lives in a "high shut garden" and trots it out for Narcissa Benbow in *Flags in the Dust* (66), recycling his flower-maidens as well as the enclosed garden, one of the oldest images in western art for the female body.

18. The NRA refers not to the National Rifle Association but the National Recovery Agency, a Depression-era New Deal program. Faulkner was, as Noel Polk puts it, never "quite able to reconcile himself to many of the New Deal's welfare and assistance programs" (*Dark House*, 227). Faulkner seemed to have an almost hysterical "belief" in the individual, rather than the collective which came out more and more in the fifties as he became an occasional Cold Warrior for the U.S. State Department.

19. There is a vast quantity of anti-Stowe material: See Jane Gardiner, "The Assault on Uncle Tom: Attempts of Pro-Slavery Novelists to Answer *Uncle Tom's Cabin*," *Southern Humanities Review* 12:4 (Fall 1978): 313–23 and Roberts, *The Myth of Aunt Jemima* (London: Routledge, 1995), Ch. 2.

20. Polk, 164.

21. He writes of "long-leaf pines which Northern capital would convert into dollars in Ohio and Indiana and Illinois banks," *Essays, Speeches, and Public Letters*, ed. James B. Meriwether (New York: Random House, 1965), 32.

22. In this curious piece, Faulkner talks of getting a letter from a black woman on behalf of her pastor and church saying "the Till boy got exactly what he asked for coming down there with his Chicago ideas" (*Essays*, 90). As a number of scholars, most recently Richard Gray in his critical biography of Faulkner and Noel Polk in *Children of the Dark House*, have pointed out, Faulkner's racial politics were always all over the map. The infamous 1956 interview with Russell Howe, in which he managed to say "as long as there is a middle road, all right, I'll be on it" as well as "if it came to fighting, I'd fight for Mississippi against the United States, even if it meant going out into the street and shooting Negroes," was not the first time he contradicted himself. As Polk points out, on 15 February 1931, the Memphis *Commercial Appeal* published a letter from Faulkner answering a letter from W. H. James, a black Mississippian, thanking the Association of Southern Women for the Prevention of Lynching. Faulkner allows as how lynching is caused by black lawlessness and the rape of white women. Just two weeks before this letter, "Dry September," one of Faulkner's most powerful antilynching, antirape hysteria stories, was published. Polk suggests the death of Alabama Faulkner on 20 January (and Faulkner's grieved drinking) had

something to do with all this but that, more importantly, we must allow Faulkner his "complexity" on race (*Dark House*, 234–35). Writers do not have to be consistent.

23. *Essays*, 155–56.
24. Kang, 21.
25. Polk, 164.

Taking the Place of Nature: "The Bear" and the Incarnation of America

DAVID H. EVANS

If God is, and if he is holy and just and punishes the disobedi-ent while rewarding those who obey Him, what is there about America that offers us a special dispensation not given to the ancient Israelites, with whom He dealt harshly when they were disobedient?

CAL THOMAS, *Jackson (Mississippi) Clarion-Ledger*, August 1, 1996

The image of William Faulkner as a dedicated acolyte in the cult of Nature has proven to be remarkably enduring. In his "Introduction to *The Portable Faulkner*," Malcolm Cowley stresses Faulkner's "brooding love for the land" and his "fear lest what he loves should be destroyed by the ignorance of its native serfs and the greed of traders and absentee landlords."[1] Cleanth Brooks, though concerned to demonstrate the fundamentally Christian bases of Faulkner's attitudes, concedes a "powerful and deep-seated" love, which occasionally "rises up into great rhapsodic hymns" to nature's "power and continuity."[2] Most recently, Joel Williamson's widely read and justly admired study, *William Faulkner and Southern History*, rather bluntly reaffirms the consensus: for Faulkner, "humanity in the natural setting is good."[3]

I want to take some issue with these claims, not because I wish to deny that expressions of pleasure in various features of the land-scape are to be found in Faulkner's works, but for a more funda-mental reason. What all these arguments take for granted is that nature, in fact, exists, and it is this assumption that I wish to place in question. To make such an assertion without further qualifica-tion may, I realize, appear to be the symptom of an idealism verg-

179

ing on the pathological. What I mean can be clarified by reference to Simon Schama's remarkable recent book *Landscape and Memory*. Schama there argues that the notion of "nature" is ultimately as incoherent as Kant's noumenal world: there has never been a point when the lay of the land was not shaped by human interests and intentions, and the concept of the natural landscape is incomprehensible apart from the culture that defines it as its own opposite, which constitutes it by designating particular pieces of geography as noteworthy, investing them with symbolic significance, and enabling their social use or appreciation. Nature, that is to say, does not exist without culture, and does not exist otherwise than as a cultural category.

I am going to argue that Faulkner was no naive celebrant of the naturalness of nature, but that he was acutely conscious of the ways the concept had been defined, and the cultural symbolism that had been invested in the notion. I will do so by focusing on the work that has often seemed to be Faulkner's most "rhapsodic hymn" to nature's eternal redemptive force, "The Bear." Here, if anywhere, Faulkner stresses the opposition between nature and civilization. My claim, however, is that "The Bear" is really about the *invention* of nature or, more accurately, about the way in which the principal character, Ike McCaslin, defines a natural world in order to invest it with a special significance. Some critics have come to somewhat similar conclusions, suggesting that Ike's insistence on the moral purity of the forest wilderness has more to do with individual neurosis than it does with that wilderness itself. My claim is somewhat different and rather broader. First, what nature represents for Ike is not so much the place of the good as the place of the truth, the position from which it is possible to pierce illusion to the vision of the way things really are. And second, that conception of nature is not Ike's alone; rather it is part of a complex set of distinctly American ideas about nature, and it reflects the peculiar role of place in the American imagination.

"The Bear" is dominated by the question of place. Location, more than event, gives structure to the tale, and in particular the opposition between two places or spaces—the forest wilderness, "the big woods, bigger and older than any recorded document" (191),[4] and the "tamed land" (254), owned, ordered, and cultivated, whose "solar-plexus" is the commissary store, the "square, galleried, wooden building squatting like a portent above the fields" (255). "The disappearance of the Mississippi wilderness," says John T. Matthews, "stands at the center" of the story,[5] but it might be more accurate to say that it is the wilderness that stands around the tale. Sections 1, 2, 3, and 5, set in the forest, surround the long central scene in section 4, set in the commissary, like woods encircling a cultivated field, so that the form of the story itself reflects its own thematic concerns, and the frontier runs right through the structure of the narrative. For "The Bear" is, in effect, Faulkner's version of Frederick Jackson Turner's frontier thesis, his own reflection on the significance of the frontier in American history.

If there is anything that virtually all readers of "The Bear" agree on, then, it is that the opposition of places, and of the antagonistic values that they appear to represent, is key to the meaning of the story. In such a reading, the location of all that is naturally and truly valuable is invariably the forest wilderness, whose ceaseless violation by an encroaching civilization of plantations and logging companies takes on the overtones of a sexual assault. It is a reading that Ike above all promotes. Irving Howe's analysis is typical: "[the wilderness] forms an Eden co-existing with society but never mistaken for society by those who come to it for purification or refreshment. The whole development of Isaac McCaslin consists in his effort to reconcile wilderness and society, or failing that, to decide which will allow and which frustrate the growth of moral responsibility."[6] Whether or not Ike McCaslin succeeds in that effort—whether or not, that is, his decision to repudiate his inheritance after his discovery, in the commissary store, that his grandfather committed incest with his own slave daughter—and is to be seen as an effective agent of the values that are embodied by the wilderness, has long provided a rich vein for critical contention. But the conviction that Ike's experiences in the forest, his initiation into the mythic world of the wilderness, *should* have provided

the moral foundation for his response to his discovery, has remained the common ground of most interpretations.

I want to argue that the connection between the events in the
forest and the events in the commissary, between the scene of
hunting and the scene of reading, is indeed crucial; but the link is
not to be explained in terms of Ike's progress towards a morally
informed vision of truth. Instead, both in the woods and in the
commissary Ike moves in a world of myth—a specifically American myth of special epistemological privilege and redemptive mission. What renders Ike such a problematic protagonist is not, as is
often argued, the practical futility of his decision to renounce the
world to pursue a private salvation, but his prior claim to have
attained a position and perspective from which to read the true
meaning of history. Ike imagines that he has reached the point
from which he can comprehend and pass moral judgment on the
human, and specifically the American, past. But in passing judgment on that past, Ike is repeating the foundational gesture of the
myth of America, even as he imagines himself to be making a decisive break with that myth.

Ike's experiences in the forest have generally been read in terms
of mythic patterns and archetypes, a reading which Faulkner encourages.[7] The forest seems to be a sanctified world, infused with
the presence of the numinous, so that comparisons to Mircea Eli-
ade's notion of sacred space have been more than common.[8] It is
a place out of time, prior to a fall into history. The woods are
without beginning—"older than any recorded document"—or
end: "They did not change, and timeless, would not anymore than
would . . . summer, and fall, and snow, and wet and saprife spring
in their ordered immortal sequence, the deathless and immemorial
phases" (323–26). It is the realm of a local divinity, Old Ben, who
is no less timeless and immortal, "not even a mortal beast but an
anachronism indomitable and invincible out of an old dead time, a
phantom, epitome and apotheosis of the old wild life" (193). In
these holy precincts, the hunt takes on the form of a ritual: once a
year the hunters come together to celebrate "the yearly pageant-
rite of the old bear's furious immortality" (194), a rite in which the

prey itself appears to participate with equal solemnity, a ceremony "of the men . . . and the dogs and the bear and deer . . . ordered and compelled by the wilderness in the ancient and unremitting contest according to the ancient and immitigable rules" (191–92).

The hunt is not an uncertain and contingent activity that develops in time, but an *auto sacramental*, complete in itself and enacted on a plane out of time, whose shape is as predestined as the trajectory of any other drama, in which man and bear, like Eliot's boar-hound and boar, pursue their pattern as before, but are reconciled among the stars. Participating in his first hunt, Ike finds that already "even his motions were familiar to him, foreknown" (196). When the year arrives in which Old Ben is at last to be killed, this likewise seems predestined, "foreknown": "It seemed to him that there was a fatality in it. It seemed to him that something, he didn't know what, was beginning, had already begun. It was like the last act on a set stage" (226).

In this sacred world, so the usual reading goes, Ike's confrontation with Old Ben constitutes an essentially religious initiation into an immediate communication with the spirit of the natural land, which allows him to see the profane human realm in a true perspective. "He entered his novitiate to the true wilderness" so that it "seemed to him that at the age of ten he was witnessing his own birth" (197). Under the direction of his spiritual father, "Sam Fathers," Ike learns the ceremonies and lore of the forest. The climax of this process is reached when Ike comes to understand that the world of the wilderness and the world of civilization are essentially incompatible; only after relinquishing all the impedimenta of culture—gun, compass, and watch—is he granted the ecstatic vision of the bear-god, the moment of unmediated grace that establishes his election, and allows him access to the place of truth.

What this interpretation neglects, in its eagerness to assimilate Ike's progress to the patterns of universal myth, is that this conception of the purifying power of the wilderness and, more generally, the notion that spiritual redemption and moral wisdom are embodied in the land itself is a part of a distinctively American set of ideas. Roderick Nash's classic study *Wilderness and the American Mind* has analyzed how the Romantic sacralization of nature assumed particular importance in the context of American nationalism, since it offered a way of reversing the cultural inferiority that inevitably defined America's relation to the Old World. Perry Miller makes the same point, writing that "In various ways—not often agreeing among themselves—[Americans] identified the health, the very personality, of America with Nature, and therefore set it in opposition to the concepts of the city, the railroad, the steamboat. . . . [Thoreau, Melville, and Whitman] (along with the more superficial) present us with the problem of American self-recognition as being essentially an irreconcilable opposition between Nature and civilization—which is to say, between forest and town, spontaneity and calculation, heart and head, the unconscious and the self-conscious, the innocent and the debauched."[9] The benevolent, and ultimately religious, influence of Nature thus guaranteed a special destiny for the United States, a "truer" sense of things: "because America, beyond all nations, is in perpetual touch with Nature, it need not fear the debauchery of the artificial, the urban, the civilized. Nature somehow . . . had effectually taken the place of the Bible: by her unremitting influence, she . . . would guide aright the faltering steps of a young republic."[10]

The notion that the American wilderness was the privileged habitat of divinity found expression, in the nineteenth century, in the canvasses of the Hudson Valley school of painters and in the works of writers such as William Cullen Bryant and James Fenimore Cooper, who permits Natty Bumppo to declaim sententiously on the holiness of the unaxed woods with depressing regularity. Such literary effusions are the expression of a national consensus whose premises are even clearer in a writer like James Brooks, who declared in the pages of *The Knickerbocker* in 1835 that "God has promised us a renowned existence, if we will but deserve it. He speaks this promise in the sublimity of Nature. . . . The august TEMPLE in which we dwell was built for lofty purposes. Oh! that we may consecrate it to LIBERTY and CONCORD, and be found fit worshippers within its holy wall!"[11]

One particularly interesting manifestation of this national attitude towards nature is the sensation created by the discovery of the *Sequoia gigantea*, or the Big Trees of the Calaveras and Mariposa groves. For, as Schama observes, those forests, first discovered in 1852, rapidly took on a significance in the popular American imagination that was even greater than their extraordinary physical proportions. Not just another natural wonder of a region that had more than its share, the trees were almost immediately translated into symbolic terms, becoming embodiments of the meaning and destiny of the nation itself: "The Big Trees were . . . seen as the botanical correlate of America's heroic nationalism at a time when the Republic was suffering its most divisive crisis since the Revolution." Even more important than the extraordinary girth of the trees was the age that it indicated: "The phenomenal size of the sequoias proclaimed a manifest destiny that had been primordially planted; something which altogether dwarfed the timetables of conventional European and even classical history."[12] Almost from the beginning, the sequoia symbol took on religious associations. It became customary to speak of them in tones of religious veneration; not incidentally, one of their chief champions was the celebrated preacher Thomas Starr King, who eventually received his reward by having one named after him. Indirectly, the trees became arboreal imitations of Christ, since it became a common practice to measure their age with reference to the beginning of Christianity, sometimes with revealing literalness: [1869] "What lengths of days are here! His years are the years of the Christian era; perhaps in the hour when the angels saw the Star of Bethlehem standing in the East, this germ broke through the tender sod and came out into the air of the Upper World."[13] The sequoia thus transcended its earthy origins to become a kind of vegetable savior, the Word made wood, pointing towards heaven and holding forth the promise of eternal life.[14]

The discussions of Nash and Miller, however, should be supplemented by more recent studies that have argued that the geographic privileging of the American landscape as the sacred space of truth has an even longer genealogy. Sacvan Bercovitch, for example, has claimed that the crucial philosophical move in the foundation of the idea of America by the Puritans was the identification of the western continent as the foreordained site of revelation: "Explicitly and implicitly, [the second- and third-generation Puritans] adapted the European images of America . . . to fit the Protestant view of progress. . . . Reorienting their vision from a transatlantic to a transcontinental direction, they situated the Protestant apocalypse . . . in the New World."[15] It was precisely on this point that the American Puritans broke most clearly with the European Protestant tradition, which rejected the notion that places were invested with a special spiritual significance because it smelled suspiciously of Catholic superstition: "In effect, the New England Puritans delivered sacred space back to Protestantism with a vengeance, in the form of America."[16]

This distinctly American myth of "the meaning of *place*, the actual, terrestrial new continent,"[17] has been traced by Bercovitch and Myra Jehlen,[18] to whose study my title alludes, through a series of eighteenth- and nineteenth-century transformations. It is hard not to sense its influence in Emerson's declaration that "the land is the appointed remedy for whatever is false and fantastic in our culture. The continent we inhabit is to be physic and food for our mind, as well as our body. The land, with its tranquilizing, sanative influences is to repair the errors of a scholastic and traditional education, and bring us into just relations with men and things."[19]

Consideration of the geo-metaphysical foundations of America's self-definition suggests that the sacred significance invested in the wilderness in "The Bear" has less to do with universal patterns of myth than with the myth of America. Ike is only one more member of a tradition that runs from the Puritans through Emerson and beyond, seeing in American nature the "appointed remedy for whatever is false and fantastic in our culture." Like the Puritans, he and his fellow hunters attempt to flee a corrupt society and to undertake an errand into an innocent wilderness on the other side of culture. But as is inevitably the case, such a venture is fraught with contradictions. Nature must be culture's opposite, but at the same time it is invested with cultural forms and values that must appear to grow, as it were, directly out of the soil. The hunters, believing themselves to be escaping civilization and convention, only enter into even more conventionalized activity. Going "natural," they wind up abiding by an elaborate and rigid set of codes and rules—"the ancient and unremitting rules which voided all regrets and brooked no quarter" (192), "all the ancient rules and balances of hunter and hunted" (207)—so that the hunt is really a game, indeed "the best game of all" (192). The very ambiguity of the term "game" itself, as it were, gives away the game, since animals only become "game" when they are defined in terms of the "game" of hunting. And the game must also obey the rules of the game; when it appears that Old Ben has killed one of Major de Spain's colts, he declares, "He has broken the rules" (214). Needless to say, the only rules at issue here are those the hunters have brought with them.

It seems, therefore, rather difficult to accept at face value the hunters' claim to have left civilization behind, or for that matter the notion that the line between civilization and the wilderness is really much of a division, in spite of the fact that most readers tend to accept the opposition between the free world of the hunt and constricted and hierarchical regime of society.[20] In fact, the game of the hunt is not so much an alternative to the codes that prevail outside the forest as it is their symbolic extension, and its highly ceremonial and rule-governed form is closely related to the social conventions of the feudal world in which it originally developed. As Schama observes, "Outside of war itself, [the hunt] was the most important blood ritual through which the hierarchy of status and honor around the king was ordered. It may not be too much to characterize it as an alternative court. . . . But this was more than an exercise in physical prowess. Observing the initiation rites of the hunt required an elaborate display of learning. . . . From beginning to end, then, the hunt was not merely a kill that gave potency and authority to the aura of the royal warlord, it was also a ritual demonstration of the discipline and order of his court."[21]

And indeed, looked at closely, the hunting party resembles less

an example of the "communal anonymity of brotherhood" that Ike
so admires (257), the natural antithesis of the artificial society outside the forest, than it does a miniaturized version of it, an "alternative court." At the top are the titled aristocrats, Major de Spain
and General Compson; and the fact that the whole party of hunters
gathers in camp for two weeks each June to celebrate their birth-
days suggests that there is indeed a connection between the hunt
and "a ritual demonstration of the discipline and order of [the]
court." It is they who give the "orders" (222)[22] to a camp organized
loosely along military lines—at one point the party is compared to
the command that Major de Spain "had led in the last darkening
days of '64 and '65" (236). Next come the lower ranking members
of the party, Walter Ewell, McCaslin, Ike; and finally, there are
those at the bottom, Boon (who at least has the advantage of being
white), Uncle Ash, and Tennie's Jim. This lowest rank is where
Sam Fathers, with his combination of Negro and Indian blood,
would naturally go, except that his function as Master of the Hunt
gives him a status apart. Social position even determines what is
the appropriate game for each class: "Boon and the negroes (and
the boy too now) fished and shot squirrels and ran the coons and
cats" while their superiors, affecting a lordly disdain, "scorned
such other than shooting the wild gobblers with pistols for wagers
or to test their marksmanship" (204–5). The notion, then, as one
critic puts it, that in "the camaraderie of the hunting camp . . . the
strict hierarchy of classes in town is suspended for the fortnight in
the woods,"[23] seems difficult to sustain; on the contrary the natural
world is organized throughout by social orders.

The conventional reading that would argue that "The Bear" is
structured in terms of an opposition of natural and cultural is
therefore deeply questionable. If nature is always cultural, it does
not offer a place of truth *outside* of culture, or a privileged perspective by which to comprehend and judge the evils and injustices of
society. In fact the very privilege accorded to nature is itself a
cultural convention. This point is important for interpreting the
center of the tale, chapter 4. At age sixteen, Ike takes down the
old commissary ledgers, reconstructing through their faded entries

the sensational history of what he takes to be his grandfather's incest with his own slave daughter, a discovery which leads to Ike's own decision to renounce his heritage and adopt a life of penitential poverty. This scene of reading and its consequences have rightly been taken to be the core of the story, the part that turns a hunting yarn into a meditation on the meaning of American history, and the question of whether Ike makes the right decision has long provided material for critical debate. But what has attracted much less attention is whether or not Ike's interpretation of his grandfather's crime is right in the first place, whether it is actually a "discovery" of the truth or a projection of a reading that Ike desires, which he requires because it corresponds to a pattern of history that Ike wishes to be true, not least because it will accord him the central role of redeemer. According to the usual argument, it is because Ike has been cleansed of the conventions and prejudices of his culture by his experiences in the place of truth, the wilderness, that he is able to read the truth of his grandfather's sin.[24] My claim, on the contrary, is that Ike's interpretation of the history of his grandfather, and of the history of America of which it is a synecdoche, is thoroughly predetermined, and corresponds to patterns of historical interpretation with a long history in American thought.

The first point that needs to be made is that, despite the virtually universal assumption that Ike's grim conclusion about grandfather is true, nothing in the text ever demonstrates this to be more than Ike's invention, a fabrication of his own imagination on the basis of the slenderest of circumstantial evidence. A proposition that needs to be taken seriously is that Faulkner *does not intend* us to believe that Ike has made a real discovery; instead, he projects a past for reasons of his own. For Ike is of course claiming to be uncovering more than the awful truth about one individual in the past; he believes he has attained a perspective from which to read the truth of the past itself, and to be able to discern the grand pattern that informs the whole of the history of America. And as the secret truth of old Carothers's life reveals itself to Ike's prophetic soul to be a Gothic tale of unspeakable secrets, so that history is one of sin, guilt, and corruption. This is the story that Ike tells to his cousin Cass in the long conversation in which he explains why he has decided to repudiate his inheritance. But although Ike apparently believes, and has succeeded in convincing many critics, that he has finally succeeded in seeing the past as it really was, that he has transcended, in the words of one commentator, "the illusion of the past" and now "recognizes southern life on the land for what it is—a rigid hierarchy of pain and exploitation," his sermon in the commissary takes a very familiar and very conventional form. It is in fact a version of the original American literary genre, the American jeremiad that was developed among the first generations of immigrant Puritans.[25]

The American jeremiad followed a fairly regular pattern. Beginning with a reminder that the audience had been chosen by God to receive his special beneficence in the New World, set apart from the corruptions of the Old, on condition that his "peculiar people" fulfill their part of the covenant by dwelling in the ways of righteousness and serving as a model to the world, it proceeded rapidly to the heart of the matter, a lengthy denunciation of the people for failing to live up to their high mission, followed by an enthusiastically detailed account of the punishments that God had already inflicted upon them and of the many that he still had in store. What distinguished the American jeremiad from its European counterpart was that it invariably ended on an optimistic note, since the afflictions visited by God upon his chosen people served but to make more certain the high destiny for which they were intended: "Theirs was a peculiar mission, [the American Puritans] explained, for they were a 'peculiar people,' a company of Christians not only called but chosen, and chosen not only for heaven but as instruments of a sacred historical design. . . . To this end, they revised the message of the jeremiad. . . . In their case, they believed, God's punishments were *corrective*, not destructive. . . . In short, their punishments confirmed their promise."[26]

This is, in fact, the story of history as Ike presents it to his cousin. Ike's definition of the promised land has shifted from New England to the South, but the pattern remains identical to that of the Puritan jeremiad. Ike begins by expounding from the Bible God's plan: "He told in the Book how He created the earth, made it and looked at it and said it was all right, and then He made man. He made the earth first and peopled it with dumb creatures, and then He created man to be His overseer on the earth . . . [until for his sins he was] Dispossessed of Eden. Dispossessed of Canaan, and those who dispossessed him dispossessed him dispossessed" (257–58). Despairing of an old world lost in sin, God prepared a new Canaan across the ocean for his chosen few, a "whole hopeful continent dedicated as a refuge and sanctuary of liberty and freedom from what you called the old world's worthless evening" (283). But, as the form of the jeremiad demands, no sooner had the chosen people set out on their mission than they began to fail in it, to sink back in sin once more. Where the Puritan preachers detailed a long litany of sins, Ike reduces them all to one big one, the sin of ownership, a sin which reaches its most extreme form in the ownership of other human beings, so that the land was "already tainted even before any white man owned it by what Grandfather and his kind, his fathers, had brought into the new land which He had vouchsafed them" (259). As a consequence, Ike declares, the land is "cursed," or as he later clarifies, "not the land, but us" (298), and God has visited the fullness of his righteous wrath upon his people in the form of defeat and occupation, since *"apparently they can learn nothing save through suffering, remember nothing save when underlined in blood"* (286). This is not the end of the story, however, since for Ike, as for earlier American Jeremiahs, "God's punishments were *corrective*, not destructive": in the face of Cass's skepticism, he insists that God has inflicted pain and suffering upon Southerners precisely because they *are* his chosen, because they continue to the privileged agents of his providential plan. "So He turned once more to this land which He still intended to save because He had done so much for it . . . to these people He was still committed to because they were his creations" (285). Finally, then, the course of history leads, through sin and suffering, upwards towards redemption and a redeemer, a redeemer whom God has elected as surely as he had elected his

chosen people. "Maybe," Ike declares, "He chose Grandfather out
of all of them . . . maybe He had foreseen already the descendants
Grandfather would have, maybe He saw already in Grandfather
the seed progenitive of the three generations He saw it would take
to set at least some of His lowly people free—" (259).

It should come as no surprise at this point that the chosen redeemer, in Ike's interpretation, is none other than Ike himself—
"Chosen," as Cass says, with no protest from Ike, "out of all your
time by Him as you say Buck and Buddy were from theirs" (299).
Even as he renounces his heritage, Ike remains a "child of promise," as St. Paul describes his Biblical namesake Isaac.[27] Ike is by
no means embarrassed by the implications of his argument. He is
quite conscious of his emulation of the "Nazarene," and by his
reading, his repudiation of his inheritance is an act which termi-
nates the cycle of generations, and which makes him the climactic
end of the providential history of redemption.

Ike really stands at the end of history in two (mutually supporting) ways: he is the predestined point to which all history has
tended, the promised savior who will atone for and cancel a sinful
past, but he also occupies the transcendent position from which
history as a whole can be comprehended. Like the Puritan jeremiad, Ike's vision of history is dominated by the centrality of a
Providence that guarantees that every apparent setback is only a
stage in a trajectory that must ultimately lead in one predestined
direction. Everything in history is part of God's foreordained plan,
from the displacing of the original inhabitants of the New Canaan
by the elect (at one dark moment Ike proposes that "[m]aybe He
saw that only by voiding the land for a time of Ikkemotubbe's
blood and substituting for it another blood, could He accomplish
His purpose" [259]), through the infliction of suffering upon those
elect, to the ultimate salvation by the foreordained savior.

To perceive history as providential means to see it from a position outside of history, from which a transcendent synoptic vision
of its pattern as a simultaneous whole is possible. What makes Ike
the promised redeemer is precisely what makes him able to see
history's pattern; by the dialectical logic of transcendental truth,

his spiritual election implies an epistemological privilege, which in turn allows him to be certain of that election. When challenged by McCaslin as to the authority of his reading of history, Ike replies that it is not what is in the text but his prior certainty of his own perspicacity that guarantees his interpretation: "There are some things He said in the Book, and some things reported of Him that He did not say. And I know what you will say now: That if truth is one thing to me and another thing to you, how will we choose which is truth? You dont need to choose. The heart already knows" (260). It is because Ike already occupies the transcendental place that he can read the "one truth" that can decipher the truth of his own transcendental place.

Ike thus claims, or better, "takes" the place of truth from which he can read the whole moral pattern of history; it does not require a large jump to see this act as a precise parallel to his reading of the landscape. Just as he detects a whole pattern of moral meaning inherent in that landscape, structured by an opposition of the sacred wilderness and the corrupt space of civilization, so he claims to discern the moral values inherent in the events of history. In effect, Ike reads the landscape as though it expressed a moral history, because he reads history as if it were a moral landscape. What Ike fails to recognize is that the events of history are no more moral in themselves than the landscape; "the communal anonymity of brotherhood" is no more inherently just than a system of private ownership, nor is the forest inherently better than the cultivated field. In both cases, the moral distinction is Ike's projection, a projection that is ultimately determined by his own desire to assign himself a central and privileged role in the drama of the world, to be at once redeemer and judge.

Like the Puritan Jeremiahs, Ike does not simply discover the truth of human sin and guilt all about him; he *needs* to read the history of the South in terms of sin in order for it to correspond to the pattern required by the jeremiad. In both cases it is the reading of history that produces the sin, not the moral acuity of the Jeremiah that discovers it. Ironically enough then, in passing a negative judgment on history, and more particularly on American history, Ike is repeating the essential American gesture: his denunciation of the crimes of American history in his jeremiad is ultimately a reinforcement of the essential providential assumptions of epistemological privilege and special election that have subtended that history from the beginning. Ike is extending the myth of America with the very gesture with which he believes he is terminating it; he places himself at the end of American history, but the end of history is precisely the place where America begins.

The long argument among critics over whether or not Ike's withdrawal from the world represents the right response to his "discovery" of the corruption of his world may therefore be somewhat beside the point, to the extent that Ike's real problem is his inability to recognize that his discovery is ultimately his own invention. In fact, in passing judgment on Ike, readers replicate his own gesture, to the extent that they also imagine themselves to have the moral "high ground," from which to discover the inherent value of Ike's decision and to fit it into a moral historical pattern. What is required, instead, is to resist the desire to occupy a place from which the "one truth" can be told. It is my argument that Ike's claim to occupy that place is ultimately another version of the aspiration to transcendental truth that has always been the myth-guided mission of America. Faulkner recognized in that aspiration both a philosophical and a national temptation to take the place of truth, to take the place of nature, which could just as accurately be described as a temptation to take the place of Christ—to stand, like Ike, where X marks the spot on the map of providential history, at the intersection of truth and place, God and Nature—to be in every sense the Incarnation of America.

NOTES

1. Malcolm Cowley, "Introduction to The Portable Faulkner," rpd. in Faulkner: A Collection of Critical Essays, ed. Robert Penn Warren (Englewood Cliffs, N.J.: Prentice-Hall, 1966), 42–43.

2. Cleanth Brooks, William Faulkner: The Yoknapatawpha Country (New Haven: Yale University Press, 1963), 32.

3. Joel Williamson, William Faulkner and Southern History (New York: Oxford University Press, 1993), 358.

4. This and subsequent references are to William Faulkner, *Go Down, Moses* (New York: Random House, 1942).

5. John T. Matthews, *The Play of Faulkner's Language* (Ithaca: Cornell University Press, 1982), 213.

6. Irving Howe, *William Faulkner: A Critical Study*, 3rd ed. (Chicago: University of Chicago Press, 1975), 92. See also R. W. B. Lewis, "The Hero in the New World: William Faulkner's 'The Bear,' " *Kenyon Review* 13 (1951): 643: "It is the honorable that permeates the wilderness, scene of the main action and home of the main actors of the story"; William Van O'Connor, "The Wilderness Theme in William Faulkner's 'The Bear,' " *Accent* 13 (1953): 15: "This in general is the meaning of the story—Old Ben is the wilderness, the mystery of man's nature and origins beneath the forms of civilization; and man's proper relationship with the wilderness teaches him liberty, courage, pride and humility"; Olga Vickery, *The Novels of William Faulkner: A Critical Interpretation*, rev. ed. (Baton Rouge: Louisiana University Press, 1964), 132: "Sam Fathers has provided [Ike] with the wilderness and the code of the hunter as an alternative to the plantation world"; Viola Sachs, *The Myth of America: Essays in the Structure of Literary Imagination* (The Hague: Mouton, 1974), 125–27: "Right from the outset of the story, the wilderness is opposed to another existent order ruled by laws of property, bondage and social hierarchy. . . . [The values of the wilderness] are the only life-giving immortal ones"; Susan V. Donaldson, "Isaac McCaslin and the Possibilities of Vision," *The Southern Review* 22 (1986): "In the pristine wilderness Faulkner's dedicated woodsman is awarded fleeting moments of epiphany, and so marked is he by them that his very presence in the novel rebukes the privileged aura of the past and tradition"; Williamson, 414: "[In 'The Bear'] Faulkner seemed to argue that man's best chance for earthly salvation, of again finding and embracing the primal human virtues, was a return to nature."

7. For readings that stress the mythic aspects of "The Bear," see John Lydenberg, "Nature Myth in Faulkner's 'The Bear,' " *American Literature* 24 (1952): 62–72; Alexander Kern, "Myth and Symbol in Criticism of Faulkner's 'The Bear,' " in *Myth and Symbol: Critical Approaches and Applications*, ed. Bernice Slote (Lincoln: University of Nebraska Press, 1963), 152–61; Walter Brylowski, *Faulkner's Olympian Laugh: Myth in the Novels* (Detroit: Wayne State University Press, 1968), 150–67; Francis Lee Utley, "Pride and Humility: The Cultural Roots of 'The Bear,' " in Francis Lee Utley, Lynn Z. Bloom, Arthur F. Kinney, eds., *Bear, Man, and God: Eight Approaches to William Faulkner's "The Bear,"* 2nd ed. (New York: Random House, 1971), 167–87; Gorman Beauchamp, "The Rite of Initiation in Faulkner's 'The Bear,' " *Arizona Quarterly* 28 (1972): 319–25; Lynn Gartrell Levins, *Faulkner's Heroic Design: The Yoknapatawpha Novels* (Athens: University of Georgia Press, 1976), 78–94; Donald M. Kartiganer, *The Fragile Thread: The Meaning of Form in Faulkner's Novels* (Amherst: University of Massachusetts Press, 1979), 131–36; Donaldson; Daniel Hoffman, *Faulkner's Country Matters: Folklore and Fable in Yoknapatawpha* (Baton Rouge: Louisiana State University Press, 1989), 145ff.

8. For example, Utley; Beauchamp; Elizabeth Kerr, *William Faulkner's Gothic Domain* (Port Washington, N.Y.: Kennikat Press, 1979), 147, 155, 156; and Donaldson.

9. Perry Miller, *Errand into the Wilderness* (Cambridge: Harvard University Press, 1956), 207–8.

10. Miller, 211.

11. Quoted in Miller, 210.

12. Simon Schama, *Landscape and Memory* (New York: Alfred A. Knopf, 1995), 187, 188.

13. *Boston Daily Advertiser*, 3 November 1869. For other examples, see Schama, 190.

14. Anyone who thinks this tradition is long dead need only look at the section entitled "The Tree of Life" in Michel Serres's recent book, *Detachment*, which describes a visit to a sequoia in terms that ingenuously recycle, in thoroughly modern style, all the most conventional nineteenth-century associations:

"Upright and praying for four millennia, with its elbow-like branches raised to the light, it has been here, massive and terrifying, in vigil, a unique founder.

I am afraid with that kind of fear my Latin tongue calls a religious fear. I know because of my terror that this giant tree is a sacred tree. All the sequoia trees in the vicinity, some just as tall seem to me to belong to this forest, this one partakes of a temple. One should perhaps be kneeling. My body is looking for a posture. The uprightness of this god induces in me a bowing pose, nearly a prostration. I know that the space enclosed by its trunk and prominent roots, on which nobody should walk, delineates indeed a sylvan protection, but mostly it defines profanation. In front of its epiphanic presence, the entire forest, myself included, becomes profane. Someone is here, established in a formidable silence. Already here two thousand years ago, when our God was born from a virgin, young, unchangeable, twenty centuries old, when our God broke the laws of living." (Michel Serres, *Detachment*, trans. Genevieve James and Raymond Federman [Athens: University of Ohio Press, 1989], 54).

15. Sacvan Bercovitch, *Rites of Assent: Transformations in the Symbolic Construction of America* (New York: Routledge, 1993), 75–76

16. Ibid., 77–78.

17. Ibid., 77.

18. "For the rhetoric survived, finally, not by chance but by merit, because it was compelling enough in content and flexible in form to invite adaptation . . . since the source of meaning lay in the American landscape, the terms of signification could change with changing national needs. What for Mather had been the purifying wilderness, and for Edwards the theocratic garden of God, became for Emerson's generation the redemptive West, as frontier or agrarian settlement or virgin land." (Bercovitch, *The Puritan Origins of the American Self* [New Haven: Yale University Press, 1975], 186). I do not mean to suggest that the arguments of Bercovitch and Jehlen are not quite distinct, but only that both would agree that "the decisive factor shaping the founding conceptions of 'America' and of 'the American' was . . . the physical fact of the continent" (Jehlen, 3).

19. Ralph Waldo Emerson, "The Young American," in *Essays and Lectures* (New York: Library of America, 1983), 214.

20. Umphlett describes the hunting camp as "an idealized community . . . as opposed to the false standards of a man-made society," and contrasts "the noble actions of men governed by nature" with "the petty ones of men restricted by the laws of society" (62). Larry Marshall Sams, in "Isaac McCaslin and Keats's 'Ode on a Grecian Urn,' " *Southern Review* 12 (1976): 632–39, describes the hunters as "primitive, free, self-reliant, proper, ceremonious, and exact" (634). See also Hoffman, 155.

21. Schama, 145. Matt Cartmill, *A View to a Death in the Morning: Hunting and Nature through History* (Cambridge: Harvard University Press, 1993), 61–67, provides a fascinating description of the elaborate rituals and ceremonies that the aspiring huntsman had to master, down to the proper way of presenting deer turds to one's social superior: "hunting became associated with upper-class status, and hunting practices became encrusted with courtly ceremony that served to demonstrate the genteel manners (or expose the pretensions) of the participants in the chase" (61). See also Barbara A. Hanawalt, "Men's Games, King's Deer: Poaching in Medieval England," *Journal of Medieval and Renaissance Studies* 18 (1988): 175–93.

22. Strikingly, in spite of the fact that Boon Hogganbeck has devoted himself to the care and training of Lion, Ike reflects that it would take only a word from one of the social superiors to transfer the dog to Sam: "*I wonder what Sam thinks. He could have Lion with him, even if Boon is a white man. He could ask Major or McCaslin either.*" His mind is only put at ease when he comes to a clearer sense of the social order of the hunting camp: "It had been all right. That was the way it should have been. Sam was the chief, the prince; Boon, the plebeian, was his huntsman" (222).

23. Hoffman, 155.

24. E.g., Umphlett, 59–60: "Ike's [life in the woods] is an experience in self-discovery that enables him to transcend the illusion of the past and to examine himself in the light of what really happened, thus compelling him to look squarely at the issues and make a moral decision. . . . Each confrontation with Old Ben during Ike's youth becomes another crucial step toward his 'essential encounter,' culminating as it does with the renunciation of his

heritage at the age of twenty-one for a simpler life unencumbered by the evils of a social order"; Donaldson: "Having known vision and true brotherhood in the Edenic wilderness presided over by Sam Fathers, Ike recognizes southern life on the land for what it is—a rigid hierarchy of pain and exploitation."

25. The classic discussions of the American jeremiad and its tradition are Miller, 1–15, and Sacvan Bercovitch, *The American Jeremiad* (Madison: University of Wisconsin Press, 1978).

26. Bercovitch, *American Jeremiad*, 7–8. See also 58–61. Compare for example Increase Mather's argument in *The Day of Trouble Is Near*: "Christ himself was exposed to sufferings, [and] David speaking as a Type of Christ saith, Thou has showed great and sore troubles. [Thus] God hath Covenanted with his people that sanctified afflictions shall be their portion, that they shall have Physick as well as Food, [both] ordered according to the Covenant of Grace. . . . He dwells in this place: therefore we may conclude that he will scourge us for our backslidings. . . . So [with other places] it may be he'll reckon with them once for all at last; but if New-England shall forsake the Lord, Judgment shall quickly overtake us, because God is not willing to destroy us." Quoted in *American Jeremiad*, 60.

27. Gal. 4.28. It seems likely that in naming his hero "Ike," Faulkner had in mind the function of Isaac in the New Testament more than in the Old, or more accurately, St. Paul's use of him. For Paul, Isaac becomes the privileged symbol of the endurance of God's exclusive promise to his chosen people: "But it is not that the word of God has taken no effect. For they are not all Israel who are of Israel,/nor are they all children because they are the seed of Abraham; but, 'In Isaac your seed shall be called.'/That is, those who are the children of the flesh, these are not the children of God; but the children of the promise are counted as the seed" (Rom. 9.6–8). In fact, Paul uses Isaac as his example to explain the very principle of God's fulfillment of his promise, in the fourth chapter of Galatians. As promised antitype stands to type, so Isaac stands to Ishmael. Since this is the ur-text for the concept of Biblical hermeneutics, Isaac could be said to represent fulfillment as such.

Return of the Big Woods: Hunting and
Habitat in Yoknapatawpha

WILEY C. PREWITT JR.

As an activity that brings humanity into contact with the natural world, hunting has become a vital issue in contemporary ecological debate. Some environmentally orientated writers believe that hunting can lead to a positive relationship between humans and the land. Such writing echoes the work of philosophers like Ortega Y. Gassett and Aldo Leopold who saw hunting as a positive and abiding factor in the cultural evolution of humanity and the thought of Paul Shepard who argued that hunting and gathering societies maintained the highest expression of human physical, social, and mental health. In contrast, some thinkers describe hunting as a dark anachronism that humans must strive to overcome. One of the best of these scholars, Matt Cartmill, offers the idea that hunters justify their killing in part by a perverse and false philosophical boundary between the values of human and animal lives. Thoughtful, ecologically concerned people remain divided with regard to the hunt wherever it occurs.[1]

And few places contain a more abundant and diverse hunting legacy than the South. Scholars have often acknowledged the importance of hunting in the South. Social and cultural historians have characterized the Southern fascination with hunting as manifestations of innate violence, regional ideals of manhood, the need for indulgent recreation, or simply the subsistence needs of an often impoverished populace. Environmental historians interested in the South have only begun to use hunting as a point of inquiry for describing human interaction with the natural world. In one of

the few environmental histories devoted to the chase, Stuart
Marks created an intimate portrait of hunters in a North Carolina
county by relying heavily on the oral traditions and hunting literature of the region. Hunting and its literature have been largely
ignored as sources, as two critics recently complained: "our writers
and poets have paid more attention to American hunting than have
our academic environmental historians." Of writers who have used
hunting in their work, William Faulkner has portrayed the chase
with the most striking combination of realism and spirituality. His
rich descriptions of the separate worlds of farm and wilderness in
turn-of-the-century Mississippi invite a specific examination of the
ways people lived with the land. At the same time, his hunting
stories imply a mystical cycle of regeneration in which such large
game as deer and bear are not only flesh and blood but spiritual
representations of the natural world.[2]

Faulkner wrote his hunting stories during a time of widespread
environmental upheaval within Mississippi and the South. During
his lifetime, habitat types and their accompanying game species
prospered and declined in relation to the agricultural systems and
socioeconomic interworkings of humans. As a hunter he encountered the effects of environmental change in habitats and game
populations. As a hunter who was also a writer, the local environmental background must have influenced his fiction as much as
did his region's history, culture, and society. My paper places
Faulkner's hunting stories within the changing environmental context of his locale and his lifetime. It also shows that the idea of a
natural cycle in his hunting fiction makes Faulkner's work peculiarly appropriate for an inquiry into long-term environmental
change.

The land of North Mississippi in the late nineteenth century
was a place of distinct dichotomy between the wild and the domes-
ticated. Until the 1880s, land clearing and the establishment of
farms proceeded in the upland areas and a in few well-drained
bottomlands. The overwhelming majority of people engaged in
agriculture to some degree, and that farming population was
broadly distributed over the arable land. Large expanses of bot-

tomland hardwoods stretched along the alluvial plains of rivers throughout the state where frequent floods and the costs of land clearing discouraged farms. Bottomlands were the wilderness counterpoint to settled areas all over Mississippi, located along rivers and streams both large and small like the Big Black in the central counties, the Pascagoula in the south and the Tombigbee in the east, in addition to Faulkner's Tallahatchie. Faulkner's imagery of a "tall and endless wall of dense November woods" juxtaposed with "skeleton stalks of cotton and corn in the last of open country" offer excellent illustrations that typified much of the land in Mississippi.[3]

By the 1880s, however, Northern timber speculators began purchasing the timberlands of the South, sometimes for as little as one dollar per acre. Attracted first by the vast longleaf pine forests of the coastal plain, timber buyers soon moved to acquire the bottomland hardwoods. The timberland of the upper Yazoo and its tributaries, including the Tallahatchie, changed hands in their turns. Lumbering interests from the exhausted cutovers of the Great Lakes region bought the lands or timber rights from speculators as railroads subsequently crept into the bottoms, making it feasible to remove the timber in quantity. Timber cutting pushed back the Big Woods along rivers all over the state. The dynamic of clearing land, with the moving boundary of the virgin timber and the approach of the cotton farm, runs throughout Faulkner's hunting stories. Ike McCaslin remembered that in just some twenty years the logging train grew from an ineffectual example of human technology to an ominous portent of inevitable changes in the land. Across Mississippi the felling of the virgin forests took only about fifty years. From 1880 to 1930 sawmills reduced the vast stands of timber to only scattered remnants surrounded by farmland.[4]

Wildlife populations responded to the land clearing and to what one scholar called "live at home semisubsistence farming." Until the years of intensive logging, the dichotomy between wilderness and farmland was reflected in the distribution of game in Mississippi. Large game like deer, turkeys, and bear occurred in wild unsettled areas while such small game as quail, rabbits, and foxes

Premechanized
agriculture involved most
people in Mississippi
before the 1940s.
Courtesy of Mississippi
Cooperative Extensive
Service Photograph
Collection, University
Archives, Mississippi
State University.

This plantation scene typifies much of the Mississippi landscape around the turn of the century. Several levels of grassy growth in the foreground give way to cultivated fields that extend to uncut timber in the background. The brushy margins of fields provided ideal habitat for small game, while the uncut forest harbored larger animals. Courtesy of Mississippi Department of Archives and History.

lived in the brushy margin habitats created by premechanized agriculture. Farming itself did not repel large game; the raiding of cornfields and the killing of shoats by Old Ben has some basis in fact. Rather, large game could not withstand the intensive hunting pressure from the hungry and well-armed rural population. The agricultural cycle allowed ample time for hunting and trapping both large and small animals by a farm population almost uniformly interested in taking a share of the game. Farm life encouraged a very direct and often subsistence-oriented relationship between people and local wildlife. Hunting and trapping were both recreation and important sources of protein for the farm family. Small game adapted to this constant pressure with high reproductive rates and by benefiting from the ideal habitat that small-field agriculture provided. Settled areas sustained frequent and

A crew using oxen and mules hauls logs out of a hardwood forest in Mississippi around the turn of the century. Courtesy of James Craig Papers, Special Collections, Mississippi State University Library.

long-term hunting of species like quail and rabbits that thrived in close communion with humans while larger, less prolific species like deer and bear simply could not make up their losses and were confined to nonfarm habitats.[5]

As timber cutting advanced, the cotton culture followed, bringing with it the habitat that favored small game and exposing the last refuges of larger animals. In 1928, more than a decade before Faulkner's hunting stories appeared, Aldo Leopold, one of the pioneers of modern wildlife biology and environmental ethics, conducted a historic survey of game in Mississippi and estimated that only a few thousand deer and turkeys survived statewide. Bears were so scarce that he ignored them as a viable game specie in the very state where Teddy Roosevelt's bear hunting exploit had led to the creation of that most familiar of toy animals. Compared with the near total devastation of large game he found adequate numbers of small creatures, particularly quail, that helped make possible what Leopold called a "widespread and intense popular interest in game and hunting."[6]

Camp on Low Copperas Bayo
Tallahatchie Co. Miss.

It was in this environmental mix of diminished wilderness, disappearing large game, and the pursuit of predominantly small
game that Faulkner developed his ideas about hunting and the
human connection with nature. Scholars offer a multitude of interpretations that deal with "The Bear" and to a lesser extent Faulkner's other hunting stories. A common theme in interpretations is
that the activity of hunting provides humans with a connection to
the natural world that critics have seen variously as positive, negative, or both. However, not just any hunting will do. For Faulkner's hunters, only the pursuit of large game reaffirmed a bond
between humans and the natural world. In his fiction, Faulkner
made much of the distinction between hunting small game in the
farmland and hunting large game in the Big Woods. Animals that
coexisted with humans were somehow less worthy as game and
Faulkner's hunters pursued them only as training or when nothing
else was available.[7]

Large game hunting, and particularly deer hunting, was in Ike
McCaslin's eyes the hunter's reason for being. Deer hunting took

A hunter begins skinning a whitetail, and a square stretched raccoon skin dries in this image of a bottom land hunting camp. Courtesy of Mississippi Department of Archives and History.

Men and women pose before the deer on the game pole of a bottom land hunting camp in 1897. Note the man with drawn knife and bear in the center right of the photo. Courtesy of Mississippi Department of Archives and History.

place in the Big Bottom, away from the farm and the human dominated landscape. The chase for large game outside the boundary
of the settled land gave a balance to the life of the young deer
hunter in "Race at Morning" so that he could say, "the hunting
and the farming wasn't two different things at all—they was jest
the other side of each other." Deer were rare enough for a kill to
be an event, and a proper first kill could become a rite that would
initiate a novice into a group of hunters. Conversely, hunting the
farmland became to young Ike McCaslin "the child's pursuit of
rabbits and 'possums." And one can sense the disdain in Sam
Father's voice when during a fox hunt he tells young Isaac, "I done
taught you all there is of this settled country . . . you can hunt it
good as I can now. You are ready for the Big Bottom now, for
bear and deer. Hunter's meat." Years later, the elderly McCaslin
surveyed the changes in the land he had known and mused that
"now a man has to drive a hundred miles to find enough woods to
harbor game worth hunting." The settled land was too understand-
able, its mysteries too easily found out. Sam Fathers taught Isaac
before he reached ten years of age all there was to know about
hunting the animals of the settled country while the boy dedicated
his entire life to hunting the Big Woods. In Faulkner's work, small
game assumed part of the less-than-noble character of civilization.
Just as Isaac attempted to repudiate his family's land because of
his perception of its taint of slavery, miscegenation, and incest, he
also disavowed small game hunting because of its symbiotic relation to agriculture.[8]

Faulkner rejected small game hunting in his fiction when rabbits, raccoons, 'possums, squirrels, birds, and especially quail constituted the most available game for Southern hunters, including
himself. J. M. Faulkner remembered that Mr. Bill himself was an
avid quail hunter and had a great appreciation for a fine dog and a
good shotgun. Also, Faulkner's endorsement of wilderness and the
pursuit of large game was significant because it emerged during a
time when hunting writers were creating a vast body of literature
surrounding that most typical of Southern small game creatures,
the bobwhite quail. If, as some scholars suggest, Faulkner de-

scribed hunting as a quasi-religious activity of mythic and spiritual meaning connected to the wilderness, then other Southern writers recorded the parameters of a parallel cult of quail hunting in the settled country. Stuart Marks in *Southern Hunting in Black and White* found that as quail became more common after the 1880s hunting writers began explaining the practice of upper-class quail hunting and praising its virtues in a voluminous body of work that involved much of the South. The association of quail hunting with the upper class is due largely to the enthusiasm of wealthy Northerners who bought large estates in the South where quail hunting became a highly ritualized winter pastime. The editor of an 1980 anthology of quail hunting literature lists works by over fifteen different authors that cover over one hundred years. In the mid-South few writers were more closely associated with the rituals of quail hunting than was Nash Buckingham. A native of Memphis, born in 1880, educated at Harvard, Buckingham came of age during the same era of environmental change as Faulkner. The child of a wealthy banker, Buckingham hunted at some of the finest duck clubs in the Arkansas and Mississippi Deltas and could afford considerable quail hunting time in the uplands of north Mississippi. In books and articles from the '20s through the '50s Buckingham reinforced some of the connections between the pursuit of quail and the upper class that Stuart Marks found.[9]

In his 1936 collection of stories called *Mark Right!*, Buckingham portrays quail hunting as an extension of upper-class views and expectations for society. For Buckingham, one's social position translates into one's position in the hunt. In the story "Buried Treasure Hill" he reminisces over the quail hunts he and three friends took over the years on a large plantation. Only the upper-class whites hunt in the story, assisted by fawning black servants. They pass over a landscape radically different from the Big Woods, following well-trained bird dogs through "meadows," "old orchards," "ragweed flats," and the ruins of an antebellum plantation house. Their access to the game is associated with their agricultural dominion over nature and their social position, as opposed to any spiritual connection to the earth.[10]

Nash Buckingham's quail hunts reflected the order the upper class wanted in society. In other stories Buckingham elaborated on the themes of good breeding in dogs, fairness to the birds, and an understood system of courtesy and respect between hunters. Poor whites appear in Buckingham's work, and they sometimes hunt, but generally only for food; the complexities of ritual are lost on them, like the rural blacksmith Mr. Fenley in the story "Carry Me Back." Buckingham and his friend accepted a challenge from Fenley that his pointer bitch Belle was a bird dog comparable to one of their animals. The hunt proceeded, Belle proved exceptional, and several days later as if to affirm that a dog of her caliber was out of place with a blacksmith, Buckingham purchased her and two of her pups, giving them what he termed a "Cinderella start in life." Fenley kept one pup, saying he could "kill over her all the birds he needed to eat."[11]

Even though hunting literature associated the bird with the upper class, there were a great many Mississippi quail hunters and they more closely resembled Mr. Fenley than Nash Buckingham. Bobwhite quail, which Southern hunters invariably called simply "birds," were immensely popular as game and were generally available to people in farming areas. Almost every rural family had a shotgun and a dog with some level of ability for quail hunting. For those without guns or the money for shells, the birds could be trapped easily. Rural folk frequently sold or bartered quail in local communities, and wild birds were occasionally on the menu of Mississippi restaurants until game law enforcement discouraged the practice in the '30s and '40s.[12]

A fascination with quail did not quell all regrets for the passing of the bottomland forests among hunting writers in Mississippi and the region. Even Buckingham himself, a devoted wingshooter, mourned the loss of the "unlogged wilderness" where he and his companions might happen upon a deer or turkey to add to their game bag. Hunting writers frequently depict specific places or times that give their stories meaning simply through inaccessibility and distance associated with the hunts they describe. Stories about the "Good Old Days" abound in hunting literature. Mississippi

By the late 1930s deer
hunters like these men
near Hollandale faced a
dwindling deer popula-
tion in the shrinking
Delta forests. Courtesy of
Mississippi Museum of
Natural Science.

By the 1940s most hunters
pursued such small game
as quail that adapted well
to the agriculture of the
time. Courtesy of
Mississippi Museum of
Natural Science.

writer Reuben Davis left a poignant memory of the bottomland in his novel *Shim*. The novel turns on the hunting and early life of young Shim Govan, heir to a remote Delta plantation around the turn of the century against a backdrop of timber cutting and the expansion of cotton culture. Davis began writing *Shim* in the late '40s and his story lines parallel some of those in Faulkner's hunting fiction, particularly the role of Sam Fathers as a hunting mentor and the use of Old Ben as a symbol of the wilderness. Young Shim received his instruction in hunting and woods lore from Henry, his father's black plantation foreman. During a hunt at the end of the story, Shim's brother Dave kills a black wolf that symbolizes the old indomitable Delta wilderness before the arrival of the logging crews. With the death of the wolf, the spell of the free hunting life in the wilderness is broken. The next day Henry departes for a refuge deeper in the woods and Shim is left alone to ponder the enormous sawmill equipment that slowly approaches the forest he knew.[13]

Nash Buckingham and Reuben Davis crafted a lament for the passing of the wilderness that combined a sense of regret and nostalgia with a belief in the positive progress of civilization. In their stories, hunters have the most to lose from the destruction of the wilderness, but they are unable and probably unwilling to save it. Ike McCaslin accepts a sad and inevitable end to the wilderness but simply continues hunting in the ever dwindling remnant of the Delta forest. Indeed there seemed little reason for optimism about the Big Woods of Mississippi and its complement of large game. Yet, within Faulkner's fiction, scholars have noticed a cycle of destruction and renewal among humans and the natural world. That cycle implies a chance for a future hunt absent in the work of most other hunting writers.[14]

The idea of a cycle owes much to the reflection of Native American belief systems in Faulkner's work. Francis Lee Utley and other scholars have compared some of the rituals in the hunting of Old Ben to the ceremonial bear hunts of certain eastern Native American tribes. Further similarities exist in the commitment to the spirit of the deer that elderly Ike McCaslin finally articulates in the reminiscence of his first kill. In his memory he comes close to apologizing to the deer and dedicates himself to hunt thoughtfully thereafter in such a way as to honor the life the deer had given. Many Native American tribes believed that animals gave themselves to hunters who had shown the proper respect and had fulfilled various rituals in the preparation and the carrying out of the hunt. After the hunt, more ceremony followed in the butchery, division, and consumption of the animal, often concluding with a symbolic return of some part of the body to the earth. With the fulfillment of the rituals a hunter appeased the spirit of the animal, which then assumed another body. Sam Fathers had "taught the boy the woods, to hunt, when to shoot and when not to shoot, when to kill and when not to kill and better, what to do with it afterward." Thus, the deer that revealed itself to Sam Fathers and young Ike after the boy had made his first kill was both flesh and spirit, able to leave physical tracks, yet it was also the spirit of a deer that emerged from Walter Ewell's kill.[15]

The system of reincarnation among game and the appearance of animals like old Ben, the large deer, and even the large rattlesnake as creatures of symbolic significance owe more to Native American belief systems than to a Judeo-Christian oriented interpretation of wilderness in Faulkner's hunting stories. While critics caution against attributing too much anthropological background to Faulkner's work, the idea of a cycle of renewal that is reminiscent of Native American ideology exists within the stories. Many critics interpret the snake that Ike encountered at the end of "The Bear" as a symbol of fundamental evil in the wilderness garden of Eden. Some connect the snake to the entrance of human evil into the forest, and certainly Ike McCaslin's comparison of the logging train to "a small dingy snake" reinforces that idea. In the light of Native American ideology, however, the snake suggests power, and certainly danger, but not pure evil in the Judeo-Christian sense of Lucifer in the garden. For many tribes in the Southeast, snakes represented an underworld, a terrifying place inhabited by strange monsters, but also according to one anthropologist, "the source of water, fertility, and a means of coping with evil." Since

Ike's experience occurred in North Mississippi, we can assume that this serpent is Crotalus horridus whose local name of timber or canebrake rattlesnake closely links it to the forested bottomland. The rattlesnake was a particularly potent creature in Southern and Southwestern Native American belief systems. Rattlesnake motifs were common enough among the artifacts of the Southeastern Native Americans that in 1906 an anthropologist described the artwork on a sandstone disk from a mound in Issaquena county as "the conventional, mythical, feathered rattlesnakes of the South." Thus Ike's reverential meeting with the rattlesnake immediately after he comes from the graves on the knoll may be an affirmation of the ultimate cycle of renewal that signified, in his words, "There was no death, not Lion and not Sam: not held fast in earth but free in earth."[16]

The visions that young Ike experiences expose him to a mythical world in which he maintains a faith until the end of his life. After the spirit/deer reveals itself to young Ike, his cousin suggests that they participate in an economy of souls and bodies; as he tells Ike of living and hunting, he says "and all that must be somewhere; all that could not have been invented and created just to be thrown away. And the earth is shallow; there is not a great deal of it before you come to the rock. And the earth dont want to just to keep things, horde them; it wants to use them again." It was in that hope that Ike buries Sam, Ben, and Lion and it is in that hope that he approaches death and another dimension when toward the end of his life he dreams "the wild strong immortal game ran forever before the tireless belling immortal hounds, falling and rising phoenix-like to the soundless guns." If Faulkner's use of reincarnation imagery reflected some elements of Native American ideology, then that spiritual dimension must have a physical component that was possibly suspended with the death of Sam, Ben, and Lion but was not destroyed. If the deer that young Ike saw was both flesh and spirit, then we can expect that the spirits of the dead game have not utterly vanished and may some day assume bodies.[17]

Even if one only accepts the implication of a natural cycle of renewal in Faulkner's work, it makes his view of the hunt vastly different from standard hunting literature and from straightforward laments for lost wilderness. The hint that the mysteries of nature might still be alive urges us to look beyond the decline of the traditional wilderness, and the high point of the premechanized small farm way of life. During the forties, forces emerged that would alter the habitat of Mississippi as drastically as had the lumbering boom and the cotton culture of the earlier decades. While a deepening agricultural depression began displacing the rural poor after the turn of the century, and rural exodus occurred between 1900 and 1940, the decades stand out more for the increasing density of the rural population in Mississippi. Farm acreage increased and the average acreage in farms decreased as the number of people actually living on the land grew. As agricultural historians have shown in their studies of the fragmentation of cotton production in the postbellum South, cotton culture and its share and tenant systems resisted change until government subsidy programs made it profitable to limit cotton acreage and technology allowed planters to produce with less labor. During the forties, agricultural herbicides, pesticides, tractors, and (by the end of WWII) a few cotton pickers appeared on Mississippi farmland. As farmers mechanized their operations, the need for tenant labor disappeared and agricultural employment began a sharp decline. From around 420,000 directly involved in farming in 1940, farmers numbered only 41,000 in 1980. In Mississippi, as across the South, the number of farms decreased and the size of individual farms increased.[18]

Faulkner personally experienced the last gasp of small-scale farming during what Joel Williamson called his "Greenfield years." After Faulkner purchased the 320 acres he called Greenfield, he brought in several tenant families and in testimony to the times lost a good deal of money, subsidizing the operation with his writing income. Williamson sets the dates for Faulkner's interest in his farm from 1938 to the early 1950s, coinciding with the time of transformation in Mississippi agriculture. The fact that Faulkner was a writer and not a farmer certainly contributed to the failure of Greenfield as a viable operation; however, his experience followed the pattern of most small farms throughout the state. As the position of the small farmer grew more untenable, many families joined the migration from the state or simply commuted to work in the towns. Mechanized agriculture concentrated in the flat expanses of blackland prairie and in the Delta, while the long-farmed upland began losing its rural population. And more importantly for the habitat of the uplands, the decline of premechanized farming took people out of a direct relationship with the land. With agriculture in the hands of a small cadre of professional farmers, what rural life there was became simply living outside the city rather than a personal struggle with nature on a day to day basis.[19]

Abandoned farmland in north Mississippi returned to various forest types, sometimes regenerating on its own to a mix of oak, hickory, and shortleaf pine and sometimes through the planting of loblolly pine seedlings. Lafayette County followed a pattern of reforestation typical of north Mississippi with the addition that Oxford was the headquarters of the forestry division of the Yazoo-Little Tallahatchie Flood Control Project. The Y-L T, as it is known in Forest Service literature, grew out of the 1928 Flood Control Act. Its environmental impact on the upland areas included dams on the tributaries of the Yazoo constructed by the Corps of Engineers, including the Tallahatchie in 1940 and the Yocona in 1953. The Forest Service planted over 600,000 acres to trees, primarily loblolly pine, in parts of nineteen counties after 1948. From 1949 to 1959 Forest Service personnel helped plant some 39,000,000 young pines in Lafayette County alone. Joel Williamson argued that Faulkner recognized the end of the small farm and the move to town in his Snopes trilogy and that he had abandoned his own plain farmer persona by 1959. Significantly, in September of that same year the *Oxford Eagle* published an eight-page section praising the "growth and advancement made in the field of forestry in this county" and Oxford's mayor Pete McElreath issued a proclamation anointing the town the "Reforestation Capital of the World."[20]

The abandoned farms of the uplands and the general depopula-

This image with its original Forest Service caption illustrates the way much hill land reverted (or was planted) to forest. While some agriculture survived in the bottoms, some type of forest cover reclaimed the slopes. Notice the hardwoods in the left background and the planted pine seedlings in the foreground. Courtesy of the United States Forest Service.

tion of the countryside brought back a wealth of opportunities for the large game that Faulkner's hunters had found so important. The Mississippi Game and Fish Commission had created refuges, purchased deer from other states, and attempted deer restocking on a small scale since its inception in 1932. After WWII, with Federal money and more manpower, the Commission began an aggressive restocking program with deer trapped on Mississippi refuges that targeted suitably depopulated areas. Deer responded well to the releases, and the population showed steady growth to an estimate of around 20,000 in 1947. That year the Commission estimated the deer kill at around 1500 statewide with most still concentrated in the last of the Delta bottoms that had escaped the saw and the plow in the counties of Warren, Sharkey, Issaquena, and Yazoo, those lowest parts of the Delta that Faulkner called "the notch where the hills and the Big River met." Hunters in Lafayette, Marshall, and Benton counties killed around ninety deer in 1947 primarily out of the Holly Springs National Forest areas. Sixteen years later, whitetails numbered about 160,000 statewide and the Lafayettte County kill was over 300. Turkey restocking also proved successful after biologists perfected capture techniques for the wild birds, and by 1960 the population stood close to 35,000. The Bottomlands of the Delta, once the richest environment of the state, had become in biological terms, a howling wasteland of monocultural agribusiness. Nonmigratory game species in the Delta retreated to the batture forest between the Mississippi river levees and the isolated patches of forest on either public land or hunting clubs. And in a further exercise in irony, much of the small game regime of the state began collapsing as the upland forest returned. Today, the memories of the quail hunting tradition can generate as much nostalgia among north Mississippi hunters as the vestiges of deer hunting fostered in 1940. Across Mississippi, counties that had not held deer and turkey for generations now supported hunting seasons. Through a cycle of wilderness destruction, a wrenching dislocation of the rural poor, and the rise of agribusiness, large game found refuge in a new forest on the Mississippi upland where the hunt continues; sometimes in that familiar "gray and constant light of the late November dawn."[21]

The new upland forest is not as majestic as the virgin bottomland timber, and modern forestry's emphasis on loblolly pine monoculture sometimes inhibits its potential biological diversity. Yet the withdrawal of a large human population from an intimate daily contact with the countryside and its wildlife has renewed the possibility of if not wilderness, then at least an alternative to the city and the cotton field that Faulkner would have appreciated. As people have withdrawn further from the daily facts of sustaining life, the counterpoint to a human dominated environment can be just beyond the air conditioning and the mowed lawn. And in parts of

After World War II agriculture became increasingly mechanized and concentrated in the Delta areas. Abandoned hill farmland like this on the Ed Eggerson place near Taylor was often planted to loblolly pine. In these two classic Forest Service "before and after" photographs, a nine years' growth of pines transformed the hillside from a primarily small game habitat to a type more suited to large game. Courtesy of the United States Forest Service.

As the rural population diminished and forest cover returned, the Game and Fish Commission intensified large game restocking efforts like this well-attended deer release in the 1950s. Courtesy of Mississippi Department of Archives and History.

Large game and automobiles hint at some of the changes in the land-scape of Mississippi. Large game, like deer, directly benefitted from the concentration of humans in urban centers and the exodus from small farms after World War II. Hunting large game involved a drive back to the growing forest in the uplands. Courtesy of Mississippi Museum of Natural Science.

the forest where deer and turkey returned some biologists believe the bear can follow. Possibly fifty black bear inhabit the timberland of extreme southwestern Mississippi in addition to an undetermined number in the batture lands between the levees of the Mississippi River. The Mississippi survivors along with larger numbers of bears in the Tensas and Atchafalaya basins of Louisiana are slowly increasing and, though anything like a restoration of the bear to its historic range may be impossible, the fact of a small growing population is a miraculous testimony to the regeneration of wild places in Mississippi.[22]

The regeneration of game populations can astound us even today. Not due to any one factor or group of people and not without its own set of environmental problems, the recovery of large game must be seen as a part of ongoing changes in the land. Through his hunting stories, Faulkner left us a faith in the resilience of the natural world and the chance to see ourselves as only parts of a broad cycle of life and death. If we can truly recognize our place in the land with the creatures we hunt, we will have gone a long way toward the humility young Ike McCaslin sought.[23]

NOTES

1. Ted Kerasote, *Bloodties: Nature Culture and the Hunt* (New York: Random House, 1993). Jose Ortega y Gasset, *Meditations on Hunting* (New York: Charles Scribner's Sons, 1972). Aldo Leopold, *A Sand County Almanac with Essays on Conservation from Round River* (New York: Ballantine Books, 1990). Paul Shephard, *The Tender Carnivore and the Sacred Game* (New York: Charles Scribner's Sons, 1973). Matt Cartmill, *A View to a Death in the Morning: Hunting and Nature through History* (Cambridge: Harvard University Press, 1993).

2. Stuart A. Marks, *Southern Hunting in Black and White: Nature History and Ritual in a Carolina Community* (Princeton: Princeton University Press, 1991). Thomas Altherr and John F. Reiger, "Academic Historians and Hunting: A Call For More and Better Scholarship," *Environmental History Review* 19:3 (Fall 1995): 39–56; quote on 47. Most of the information on land use and animal populations in this paper comes from my unpublished M.A. thesis, Wiley Prewitt, "The Best of All Breathing: Hunting and Environmental Change in Mississippi 1890–1980" (University of Mississippi, 1991).

3. Prewitt, "The Best of All Breathing," 34–130. William Faulkner, *Big Woods* (New York: Random House, 1955), 14,15.

4. Prewitt, "The Best of All Breathing," 34–96. William Faulkner, *Go Down, Moses* (1942; New York: Random House, 1990), 304–6. Michael Williams, *Americans and Their Forests: A Historical Geography* (Cambridge: Cambridge University Press, 1989), 238–88.

5. Jack Temple Kirby, *Rural Worlds Lost: The American South, 1920–1960* (Baton Rouge: Louisiana State University Press, 1987), 369, 370. Prewitt, "The Best of All Breath-

ing," 34–96. For a further note on intense hunting and fishing, see Frank E. Smith, *The Yazoo River* (Jackson: University Press of Mississippi Press, 1988), 192–94.

6. Aldo Leopold, "Report on a Game Survey of Mississippi" submitted to the Game Restoration Committee, Sporting Arms and Ammunition Manufacturers Institute, 1 February 1929, unpublished typescript in Mississippi Museum of Natural Science Library, 1–80; quote on 10.

7. Francis Lee Utley, Lynn Z. Bloom, Arthur F. Kinney, eds., *Bear, Man, and God: Eight Approaches to William Faulkner's "The Bear,"* 2nd ed. (New York: Random House, 1971), particularly 127–87. Mary Jim Josephs, *The Hunting Metaphor in Hemingway and Faulkner* (Ph.D. diss., Michigan State University, 1973), 124–249. Thomas Altherr, "The Best of All Breathing: Hunting as a Mode of Environmental Perception in American Literature and Thought from James Fenimoore Cooper to Norman Mailer" (Ph.D. diss., Ohio State University, 1976), 240–65. Faulkner, *Big Woods,* 14,15.

8. Faulkner, *Big Woods,* 195; 125,124; 201; *Go Down, Moses,* 243–301.

9. Marks, *Southern Hunting in Black and White,* 170–99. Nash Buckingham, *"Mr. Buck": The Autobiography of Nash Buckingham,* ed. Dyrk Halstead and Steve Smith (Traverse City, Michigan: Countrysport Press, 1990), 70–132; *Mark Right!* (New York: Derrydale Press, 1936); and *Hallowed Years* (Harrisburg, Pennsylvania: The Stackpole Company 1953).

10. Buckingham, *Mark Right!,* 121–40.

11. Buckingham, *Hallowed Years,* 69–81; quotes 79 and 81. For more on attitudes toward hunting, see Prewitt, "The Best of All Breathing," 161–211.

12. Prewitt, "The Best of All Breathing," 97–130.

13. Buckingham, *Mark Right!;* quote on 144, 141–53 incidental deer kill; *Hallowed Years,* 8–20. Reuben Davis, *Shim* (Jackson: University Press of Mississippi, 1995), review by Wiley Prewitt, *Mississippi Folklife* (Summer/Fall 1995), 48, 49.

14. Destruction and at least some renewal is evident in Joseph's *The Hunting Metaphor in Hemingway and Faulkner,* 124–208.

15. Utley, Bloom, Kinney, *Bear, Man, and God* 127–87. Faulkner, *Big Woods,* 121. Works on Native American belief systems and how they related to wildlife: Calvin Martin, *Keepers of the Game: Indian Animal Relationships and the Fur Trade* (Berkeley: University of California Press, 1978). Shephard Krech III, ed., *Indians, Animals, and the Fur Trade: A Critique of Keepers of the Game* (Athens: University of Georgia Press, 1981). Neal Salisbury, *Manitou and Providence: Indians, Europeans, and the Making of New England, 1500–1643* (New York: Oxford University Press, 1982). Richard K. Nelson, *Make Prayers to the Raven: A Koyukon View of the Northern Forest* (Chicago: University of Chicago Press, 1983). J. Donald Hughes, *American Indian Ecology* (El Paso: Texas Western Press, 1983).

16. Utley, Bloom, Kinney, *Bear, Man, and God,* 127–87, 202–8. Charles Hudson, *The Southeastern Indians* (Knoxville: University of Tennessee Press, 1976), 165–69; quote on 166. Fannye A. Cook, *Snakes of Mississippi: Survey Bulletin* (Jackson: Mississippi Game and Fish Commission, 1954) 34, 35. Calvin S. Brown, *Archeology of Mississippi* (Jackson: University Press of Mississippi, 1992), 227–30. The quote is on 230 where Brown quotes one Dr. Holmes whose work on the stone disk or "Mississippi Tablet" appeared in the *American Anthropologist,* January/March 1906. Calvin Brown's book first appeared in 1926, published by the Mississippi Geological Survey as a popular work for the "lay reader of the 1920s" according to Janet Ford's introduction to the 1992 edition. It is not too much of a stretch to guess that Faulkner knew of the book or perhaps Brown himself whose tenure at the University of Mississippi lasted from 1905 until 1945. Faulkner, *Big Woods,* 94.

17. Faulkner, *Big Woods,* 137, 209.

18. Prewitt, "The Best of All Breathing," 34–50.

19. Joel Williamson, *William Faulkner and Southern History* (New York: Oxford University Press, 1993), 272, 273, 326–34. Prewitt, "The Best of All Breathing," 34–50.

20. Hamlin L. Williston, "The Yazoo–Little Tallahatchie Flood Prevention Project: A History of the Forest Service's Role," United States Department of Agriculture, Forest Service, Forestry Report R8–FR8 (February 1988), 1–7, 36–55. Williamson, *William Faulkner and Southern History,* 332. *Oxford Eagle,* 24 September 1959, quote on front page;

Pete McElreath's proclamation on page 1, section 2; number of pines in Lafayette county from front page.

21. Prewitt, "The Best of All Breathing," 51–96. Faulkner, *Big Woods*, 171, 113. *Mississippi Game and Fish*, 11.7 (January 1948), 5, 6. *Mississippi Game and Fish*, 24.15 (January-February 1963), 14.

22. Steve Walton, "Project head helping bears reclaim home," *Clarion-Ledger*, 12 August 1994, 1B, 3B. Bruce Reid, "Group aims to save hives while protecting animals," *Clarion-Ledger*, 21 January 1996, 1A, 12A.

23. Environmental historians, ecologists, and the like often advocate placing humans within the study of nature. Humans are not simply destroyers or saviors in the natural world; rather, like Ike McCaslin, they are both participants and victims. For more on the broad view, see William Cronon, *Changes in the Land: Indians, Colonists, and the Ecology of New England* (New York: Hill and Wang, 1983), 159–70. Timothy Silver, *A New Face on the Countryside: Indians Colonists and Slaves in South Atlantic Forests, 1500–1800* (Cambridge: Cambridge University Press, 1990), 35–66, 186–98. Mart A. Stewart, *What Nature Suffers to Groe: Life, Labor, and Landscape on the Georgia Coast, 1680–1920* (Athens: University of Georgia Press, 1996), 21–52, 243–52.

Learning from Faulkner: The Obituary of Fear

WILLIAM KENNEDY

When William Faulkner died I wrote his obituary for my newspaper, the *San Juan Star*, in Puerto Rico. I had been a founder of that paper but, after two years as managing editor, I quit to become weekend editor only; for I'd begun a novel and discovered I could do justice to neither the editing nor the novel while trying to do both; and I knew, with certainty, that I must become a novelist.

My novel was about a family, the Phelans. I was also giving prolonged attention to another family novel, *The Sound and the Fury*. I'd been reading Faulkner for a dozen years and was mesmerized in assorted ways. Not surprisingly, Faulknerian syntax had crept into some of my sentences, and I even found myself cheering when I wrote a sentence that went on for a page and a half with only two commas. I knew this was a mistake and eventually I got rid of all such baggage, just as I had earlier banished my imitations of eight-word Hemingway sentences. But I was a young writer in search of a voice, and Faulkner and Hemingway were the most distinctive and unwitting literary ventriloquists in this country.

There was another aspect of Faulkner from which I felt no need to distance myself: the way his characters moved from one story to another, one novel to another; and Malcolm Cowley's explanation of the Yoknapatawpha saga made this intertwining of lives in a single place the most ambitious fictional device I could imagine. I was just beginning to discover Albany, my home town, through the writing of that Phelan family novel, but I knew so little about Albany back then that I'm sure I never consciously thought of creating my own fictional cosmos. Writing just one novel was an immensity; never mind a saga.

And yet my fascination with recurring characters continued, fueled not only by Faulkner's work but by the prismatic lives of Nick Adams in the stories of Hemingway, of J. D. Salinger's Glass family, of Stephen Dedalus in Joyce's books. The creation of interlocking works is as old as Aeschuylus and Sophocles, and probably reaches the height of human possibility in the novels of Balzac. Faulkner, said his biographer Frederick Karl, was "the closest figure to a Balzac that America has produced."

Faulkner made the unlikely comparison of Balzac with Sherwood Anderson, who was Faulkner's early mentor; but the comparison was mainly on the basis of the difficulties each man experienced by being a writer in a culture hostile to artists. Faulkner recognized that Anderson "probably didn't have a concept of a cosmos in miniature which Balzac . . . had," but he acknowledged that Anderson had taught him how to enter that cosmos:

"I learned," Faulkner wrote, "that to be a writer, one has first got to be what he is, what he was born; that to be an American and a writer, one does not necessarily have to pay lip-service to any conventional American image such as [Anderson's] and Dreiser's own aching Indiana or Ohio or Iowa corn or Sandburg's stockyards or Mark Twain's frog." And Faulkner then quoted what Anderson said to him on this subject: " 'You *have* to have somewhere to start from: then you begin to learn. . . . It don't matter where it was, just so you remember it and aint ashamed of it. Because one place to start from is just as important as any other.' "

I started using Albany in Puerto Rico, although I didn't know I had started until maybe a dozen years had passed. I finished that Phelan novel, which went nowhere; and I then wrote a dozen short stories that went to the same place. But in time I published a novel, then published another one, and by 1975 was beginning my third novel, about a young pool hustler. I went back to that old Phelan novel and took it out of its nowhere box and imposed the Phelan family on my pool hustler, whose book I called *Billy Phelan's Greatest Game*. I made the wino character, Francis Phelan,

Billy's absentee father, and next I gave Francis his own book, *Iron-weed*. In time I turned that whole dead Phelan book into a living story, *Very Old Bones*. And now I have seven novels and a play, *Grand View*, and more works to come—a new novel just begun, a second play in its fourth draft—and all—and maybe more if I continue drawing breath—will be intertwined with recurring events and characters in what I call the Albany Cycle.

Some critics called Faulkner the Balzac of Mississippi; some book reviewers now call me the William Faulkner of Albany; and a Philadelphia book critic recently told me of two young writers who have been called the William Kennedy of Glasgow and the William Kennedy of Miami.

Any comparison of my work with Faulkner's on the basis of writing styles, or subject matter, or execution of the books, is presumptuous. My turf, my people, my language, and my limitations are my own, and Faulkner should not have to bear any onerous linkage; and neither should I. Like unhappy families, writers are also unhappy in their own way.

I noted in a history of Albany that I published in 1983, called *O Albany!*, that my city has been associated with any number of writers in its long life: "Bret Harte was born [there] and left almost immediately, came back as a mature celebrity but was snubbed by the press, left in a terminal huff and died in England trying to forget the place. Harold Frederic worked [there] as an editor of the Albany Evening Journal, Dickens read from *A Christmas Carol* at Tweddle Hall, Mark Twain defended osteopathy at the Capitol, Robert Louis Stevenson passed through on his way to the Adirondacks, Edith Wharton's great friend Walter Van Rensselaer Berry grew up [there], Joyce may have referred to the place secretly in *Finnegans Wake*, Hemingway married Martha Gellhorn, who used to work on the [Albany] Times-Union, and William Faulkner died unaware that Albany existed."

Faulkner's birthplace *was* New Albany, Mississippi, but I had in mind the *old* Albany of New York, the oldest chartered city in the nation, where I was born. And yet now Faulkner does have a posthumous link to old Albany through what I learned from him about literary geography: my creation of Albany in the abstract image of Yoknapatawpha County; which is to say that I have tried to make my city real in ways that it actually was, and fictional in ways it never was; that I've imagined generations of the several families and assorted characters who inhabit the place, and that I control their destinies absolutely. My world, my people.

Because I work this way there have been indictments of me as a regional writer, an ethnic writer obsessed with social history; plus an odd begrudgery at my staying in one place, and writing exclusively about the past. It's true that the closest I've come to time-present in any novel in the Cycle has been *Very Old Bones*, set in 1958, which I consider yesterday afternoon. I've gone as far back as the 1840s in *Quinn's Book*. My new novel, *The Flaming Corsage*, makes time leaps from 1884 to 1912. The other three novels are set in the 1920s and '30s, and my novel-in-progress in 1945.

Faulkner often talked of time in his work, and once said that, "There isn't any time . . . only the present moment, in which I include both the past and the future, and that is eternity."

Everything I've written is about today, about the moment that I write it, no matter how far back in time the story is set. The past becomes the vehicle simply because it seems—though it never is—complete; and I can at least begin to cope with it.

The social forces, the political, religious, and ethnic heritages that influence the lives of the people of my fictional city, are vastly different from those of, say, San Juan or Mississippi. I began discovering this singularity of place as a young newspaperman covering Albany crime and politics, and, more deeply in later years, when I wrote a series of articles on the origins of Albany's neighborhoods. I almost drowned myself then in the riches of history: an endless uncovering of events and social groupings and the peculiar lives of individuals who made the American nation, and often made it first in Albany.

Albany's history is fabulous—its life is as long before the Revolutionary War as it has been since then. I began exploring it by marking out the turf, then digging like the archeologist I once wanted to be; and I have been unearthing what I consider treasure ever since.

It would take me decades to understand anyplace else in an equivalent way. I knew this, decisively, forty-five years ago when I first started writing about Albany; for I found in that work a strength I'd never had in any writing I'd done about Puerto Rico. Even in those early writing days I knew infinitely more about the city than I thought I did.

It is very easy to become a victim of your own love of place, and of research. History is addictive, and can overload and cripple the imagination. But history never was the reason I wrote fiction and never will be. I distort history whenever it's necessary for the story. My ethnic heritage is Irish-American but my characters are ethnic mongrels, no matter what their names are. Fellini, Bunuel, and Bergman, Camus, Kafka, and Nathanael West have had more influence on me creatively than any Irish-American writer or historian ever did. I am, and always have been, just a writer; a writer whose subject is not Albany or its locals; a writer whose overarching concern in fiction has been the repetitive asking of two questions: What does it mean to be alive? and How is this meaning made manifest?

Faulkner responded to regional pigeonholing in a letter to Cowley: "I'm inclined to think that my material, the South, is not very important to me." And, to a group of law school wives at the University of Virginia, he elaborated: "People are the same . . . the milieu, the background, the environment will change the *terms* of their behavior, not the act itself, and so the writer simply uses the background he knows."

To some critics the most flawed of Faulkner's ambitious novels is *A Fable*, and this is seen as the consequence of his leaving the background he knew in Yoknapatawpha. Robert Penn Warren saw *A Fable* as "abstractly conceived; it is an idea deductively worked out—and at critical moments, blurred out. . . . Faulkner, like Antaeus, could fight only with his feet on the ground—on home ground; . . . only in that world could he find the seminal images that would focus his deepest feelings into vision."

I'm inclined to think that if I left Albany and undertook a novel set in Madrid or Havana, I might bring off a contemporary tale of romance, intrigue, double-dealing, mortal error, and so on. But I fear it might be romance and mortal error in a vacuum, that I'd probably recidivize into journalistic fiction; that my novel would lack what should be most profoundly explored in any romance or tale of mortal error. It would lack the enduring influence of place and time, the vital connection of history with the antic flash of the contemporary moment. It would lack what I believe essential to any story: the palpable life that *was* at the moment it becomes *is*.

The mother of a good friend of mine, in her early eighties, had outlived all her close friends and family; and near the end she said she was glad of her long life because, "I got to see how everybody turned out."

That attitude is central to my attention to the past and to a single place. The primary motive is to follow the ongoing lives of my characters, who rarely die a permanent death. They recur in antecedent story, or in the subsequent memory of other characters. They are with me forever, whenever I need them, whenever they demand to be heard: the inhabitants of my own eternal city, six hundred characters in search of their author.

In *The Flaming Corsage*, for example, I focused on a woman and man I've been tracking for twenty years: Katrina Taylor and her husband, Edward Daugherty. I invented them and their tragic marriage in *Billy Phelan's Greatest Game*, a novel set in 1938. Later I put Katrina into *Ironweed* in the year 1897, but only part of her. In *The Flaming Corsage* I went back to her youth in the 1880s and gave her life as much of its due as my story could tolerate. But I'm still not sure I'm done with her. I also have unfinished business with Daniel Quinn, protagonist of *Quinn's Book*, and likewise with Patsy McCall, Albany's Irish-American political boss who's been in two novels and a play; but about Patsy I have only just begun to write. And the Phelan family, having gone through three novels, emerged into their unpredictable present tense only at the end of their last novel, *Very Old Bones*, when the hidden past transformed them utterly from all that I, and they, thought they had been. And so it continues.

*   *   *

That obituary of Faulkner—I wrote it because I felt the wire stories about his career were insufficient. The next day I wrote an essay on him for the newspaper because my obituary was insufficient. The essay was weak and I never published it; but one line of it is still valid: "He gave us something heroic to try to be equal to."

I was then so new as a writer that I was only intuiting what was heroic in Faulkner: the scope of his literary ambition, very visible of course; his language, like nothing else in literature; and maybe his combative attitude toward fear. I remember being impressed by that.

The writer, Faulkner said, "must teach himself that the basest of all things is to be afraid." And he said elsewhere that you combatted fear through work: "if you have something to get up to tomorrow morning, you're too busy to pay much attention to fear."

I don't know what, if anything, I was fearful of in those old days. The world seemed to be opening up before me; I had no serious enemies, no malaise of spirit, plenty of ambition, and a fair amount of faith that if I didn't own any talent I'd soon figure out how to get some. I was impressed by Faulkner's advice, but I didn't think fear was my problem. And then the curtain rose on the real world.

I had a wife and two children and almost no money. I had an agent who could sell nothing I'd written. Foreclosure was relentlessly imminent, and I was writing in a critical void. I'd had some, but very little, valuing of my work. I had my own faith in what I was doing, but that faith was being eroded by a shapeless fear: "You are the problem," wrote Kafka. "No scholar to be found far and wide." What did it mean, I was the problem? How could I shape an answer to a question of such immense dimension?

Time passed and I somehow kept writing and published three novels. They made some money, but not much, and so in desperation, as Faulkner had when he was financially desperate, I turned to the movies and paid the mortgage writing film scripts for a few years.

By the time I finished my fourth novel, *Ironweed*, which I judged my best work to that point, more Faulknerian darkness had descended: all my books were out of print, as were his in the years just before Cowley's *Portable Faulkner* effected his renaissance. Also *Ironweed*, like *The Sound and the Fury*, was about to be rejected thirteen times. My kinship with Faulkner seemed akin to a death wish. Yet if it *was* that, it proved also to be a prescription for how you elude all assassins: you refuse to die from trouble.

I am struck by how many people tell me they are buoyed, even inspired that, in spite of rejection, and no money, I continued to write novels. I did not think it so unusual. What I possessed was a simple truth: that I wanted to write more than I wanted to pay the mortgage. Time and again I put the work aside to do temporary hack work; I borrowed and begged; my wife became remarkable in her ability to find money through assorted ventures and her natural acuity for business. And always I got back to work. I suppose I was tougher and more ruthless than I knew, for I would've done anything to finish that novel, and get on to the next one.

I also discovered that I not only wanted to write, I loved to write; that creation was everything, and if its consequences were impoverishing, they were also sublime. Platoons of dunning creditors could not diminish the exaltation I felt at one o'clock one morning, having written a seventeen-page scene in *Ironweed* during the previous seventeen hours, this exaltation followed by the giddy contemplation that I was probably mad to think this was a serious way to live, and concluding, as the night waned and I waited in euphoria for the sun to come up, that no other way would do.

Faulkner wrote of such a feeling, which he had when he knew he was ready to write *The Sound and the Fury*. "One day I seemed to shut a door between me and all publishers' addresses and book lists. I said to myself, Now I can write. Now I can make myself a vase like that which the old Roman kept at his bedside and wore the rim slowly away with kissing it."

Without knowing the first word of Faulkner's plan, or his desire, or his creative ecstasy, I confronted *The Sound and the Fury* as a young writer and loved its mystifying structure, its characters, its language. And for years to come I would offer my gratitude to whatever it was that created William Faulkner, the man whom adversity could not prevent from writing a great book.

I'm sorry I never met him. I'm sorry he never came to Albany. But I'm very glad I've been able to come to Yoknapatawpha County.

Contributors

Lawrence Buell is professor of English at Harvard University. He is the author of *Literary Transcendentalism: Style and Vision in the American Renaissance, New England Literary Culture: From Revolution Through Renaissance,* and *The Environmental Imagination: Thoreau, Nature Writing, and the Formation of American Culture.* He has been awarded fellowships and grants from the Woodrow Wilson Foundation, the National Endowment for the Humanities, and the John Simon Guggenheim Foundation.

Mary Joanne Dondlinger completed her M.A. at Arizona State University and is the author of essays on Emily Dickinson and Faulkner.

David Evans completed his Ph.D. degree at Rutgers University, with a dissertation titled "Communities of Confidence: William Faulkner, William James, and the American Pragmatic Tradition." He is a Postdoctoral Fellow at the University of Calgary.

Myra Jehlen is the Board of Governors Professor at Rutgers University. She is the author of *Class and Character in Faulkner's South, American Incarnation: The Individual, the Nation, and the Continent, The Literature of Colonization: 1590–1800* in the *Cambridge Literary History of the United States,* and *The Literature of Colonization in English.* She has received fellowships and grants from the Woodrow Wilson Foundation, the National Endowment for the Humanities, and the John Simon Guggenheim Foundation.

William Kennedy is the author of the critically acclaimed "Albany Cycle" of novels, including *Legs, Billy Phelan's Greatest Game, Ironweed* (winner of the Pulitzer Prize and the National Book Critics Circle Award), *Quinn's Book, Very Old Bones,* and, most recently, *The Flaming Corsage.* A playwright and screenwriter, he wrote the motion picture adaptation of *Ironweed*. He is a member of the American Academy of Arts and Letters and a Commander of the Order of Arts and Letters in France, and is the founder and director of the New York State Writers Institute.

Thomas L. McHaney is Kenneth M. England Professor of Southern Literature at Georgia State University. He is the author of *William Faulkner's "The Wild Palms": A Study* and numerous essays on Faulkner and other Southern writers, and is coeditor of the 44-volume edition of facsimiles of Faulkner's literary manuscripts. He has also published several short stories and has had four plays produced by Atlanta theater companies.

Wiley Charles Prewitt Jr. received an M.A. in history from the University of Mississippi in 1991. He recently completed *For the Sake of Future Generation: A History of Organized Wildlife Conservation in Mississippi, 1890–1995*, an exhibition at the Museum of Natural Science in Jackson, Mississippi, and is currently at work on an environmental history of hunting in Mississippi.

Diane Roberts is associate professor of English at the University of Alabama. She is the author of *Faulkner and Southern Womanhood* and *The Myth of Aunt Jemima: Representations of Race and Region*. She is a frequent commentator for National Public Radio's *Weekend Edition*, and has recently made a documentary on Faulkner for the BBC.

Theresa M. Towner is Lecturer in English at the University of Texas at Dallas. She is the author of essays on Faulkner, Toni Morrison, and T. S. Eliot, and is secretary-treasurer of the Faulkner Society.

Jay Watson is associate professor of English at the University of Mississippi. He is the author of *Forensic Fictions: The Lawyer Figure in Faulkner* and essays in Southern literature, psychoanalytic theory, and law in the humanities. He is coeditor of *Journal x: A Journal in Culture and Criticism*.

Louise Westling is professor and department head of English at the University of Oregon. She is the author of *The Evolution of Michael Drayton's "Idea," Eudora Welty, Carson McCullers, and*

Flannery O'Connor, and *The Green Breast of the New World: Landscape, Gender, and American Fiction.* She has been a visiting professor at the Universities of Tubingen and Stuttgart, and a Fulbright lecturer at the University of Heidelberg.

Index